Flatiron Classics

The west side of the Third Flatiron

Flatiron Classics

Easy Rock Climbs Above Boulder

SECOND EDITION

Gerry Roach

The Colorado Mountain Club Press
Golden, Colorado

WARNING: Mountain Climbing and hiking are high-risk activities. This guidebook is not a substitute for your experience or common sense. The users of this guidebook assume full responsibility for their own safety. Weather, terrain conditions, and individual technical abilities must be considered before undertaking any of the climbs and hikes in this guide. The Colorado Mountain Club and the author do not assume any liability for injury, damage to property or violation of the law that may result from the use of this book.

Flatiron Classics: Easy Rock Climbs Above Boulder, Second Edition
© 2008 Gerry Roach
Photos © 2008 Gerry Roach   .

PUBLISHED BY

The Colorado Mountain Club Press
710 Tenth Street, Suite 200, Golden, Colorado 80401
303-996-2743   e-mail: cmcpress@cmc.org

Founded in 1912, The Colorado Mountain Club is the largest outdoor recreation, education, and conservation organization in the Rocky Mountains. Look for our books at your local bookstore or outdoor retailer or online at www.cmc.org/books.

DISTRIBUTED TO THE BOOK TRADE BY
Mountaineers Books, 1001 SW Klickitat Way, Suite 201, Seattle, WA 98134, 800-553-4453,
www.mountaineerbooks.org

COVER IMAGE: The Third by Gerry Roach

We gratefully acknowledge the financial support of the people of Colorado through the Scientific and Cultural Facilities District of greater metropolitan Denver for our publishing activities.

Second Edition

ISBN 978-0-9799663-2-3

Printed in Canada

In the mountains there is a strange market where you can barter the vortex of life for boundless bliss.

MILAREPA

DEDICATED TO GABE LEE

The Third Flatiron

CONTENTS

Introduction

THIS BOOK IS A CELEBRATION OF THE JOYS that come from moving over easy rock. The Flatirons above Boulder, Colorado offer one of the finest arrays of easy rock climbs anywhere in the world. The fact that they are located close to a major population center makes them even more precious. This guide reports on more than 20 miles of routes—not 20 miles along the base of the range, but 20 miles as measured with a rope!

The Flatirons are a startling array of sandstone slabs tilted at 45 degrees on the east faces of Green and Boulder Mountains southwest of Boulder. The area covered in this guide is in the Boulder Mountain Park, and you can easily reach the Flatirons on a network of trails. Chapter One covers trailheads, hiking trails and a few off-trail hiking routes. The remainder of the book is devoted to climbing routes on the rocks. This guide does not cover Boulder Canyon, Flagstaff Mountain or Eldorado Canyon.

No climb in this book is harder than 5.8. I have watched the sport of rock climbing develop for the last 50 years and feel that it is now two activities. There is what I call rock gymnastics, where elite athletes train like Olympians and do very difficult climbing, but these climbs are far beyond most of us. The original sport of rock climbing puts more emphasis on the movement and the experience than on the difficulty, and almost anyone who has the desire to try can enjoy easier climbs. Easy rock climbing is the basis for rock gymnastics, and I believe that easier rock climbs provide better training for general mountaineering than do very difficult short climbs. Most Flatiron climbs are rewarding mountaineering experiences, since they involve approaches, route finding, weather considerations and honest summits. Rock gymnasts training for big mountains should consider putting in some time on the Flatirons.

I grew up climbing with the following definition of difficulty: 5.7 is hard climbing, 5.8 is where you are really worried about falling off, and 5.9 is where you are falling off. If that definition rings a bell, then this book is for you. Only two references to the rating 5.9 are in this book, and you have just read the last one. This guide takes a clean look at more than 250 Flatiron routes and most of them are 5.6 or easier. I have rated 51 routes *Classic*, and denote my choice of the ten best Flatiron climbs with *Classic – Top Ten*. I don't describe any aid climbs.

This book describes where to climb but not how to climb. Climbing by its very nature is dangerous and each individual should approach these great rocks with caution. Climbing and route finding on the Flatirons can be very deceptive, since hard moves can lurk near trivial scrambling, and the easiest line up a face can be difficult to find. Sometimes the presence or absence of a single small hold can make all the difference. The ability to read the rock and spot holds and combinations from below is a big asset in Flatiron climbing. Flatiron rock is often hard to protect, especially where the climbing becomes difficult. You can often climb almost anywhere on a Flatiron face, but I describe natural lines on the rocks. My routes follow the easiest line in an area, not the hardest, so my rating assumes that you follow the easiest route. Where they are significant, I describe more difficult alternatives as variations. My route lengths are not vertical heights but the length of the climb as measured with a rope. I describe the rocks and the routes on them from north to south.

I pay particular attention to descents. When several routes to a summit share a common set of descents, I list the descents before all of those routes. When a particular route has a unique descent, I describe that descent with that route. I give the warning, "This is a dangerous rock to be on top of without a rope" when a downclimb is 5.5 or harder.

I do not pass judgment on whether or not you should use a rope on a particular route. Many individuals could solo up and down every route in this guide and many more could not do any of the routes at all, with or without a rope. Most of us are somewhere in between these extremes, which means that many people will want a rope on many these routes. The decision of when to rope up must always be the individual's. If climbing is dangerous, then soloing is surely more so. Its only technical advantages are speed and the ability to move past long unprotectable sections without having to stop and set up a belay. I give information for both the roped and unroped climber.

This guide is not a history book, since the early history of rock climbing in the Boulder area has been nicely captured in Pat Ament and Cleve McCarty's *High over Boulder*. I do not record the names of those who did the first ascent of a route, since the climbs in this book are easy enough that the first ascent cannot be known with any certainty. Somehow, this information does not seem relevant on the Flatirons, since these routes belong to everybody. Many times I have found evidence on obscure routes indicating that these routes were more popular decades ago then they are now. Many of these once popular routes are rarely climbed today. You can spend days climbing on the Flatirons and never see another climber, since most of the Flatirons climbing activity is centered on a handful of routes. If you are tired of standing in line to climb, then try the Fatiron, the Stairway to Heaven, the Primal Rib, Rehatch or Fi.

Unlike most guidebooks, which are a compilation of many people's route descriptions, this book is my solo labor of love, which gives consistency to the descriptions. I started climbing on the Flatirons in 1955 and have spent more than half a century climbing these routes. I have climbed all of the routes in this guide, most of them many times, climbed most of the routes specifically for the preparation of this book and wrote my descriptions immediately after my climbs. Of course, errors and inconsistencies may exist, and I post corrections and additions on my website at *www.climb.mountains.com/ Book_Land_files/Flatiron_Classics_files/Flatiron_Classics_Fixes.htm.*

My photo annotations use larger numbers for rocks and smaller numbers for routes. Dashed lines are Variations and and dotted lines are Extra Credits. White and black lines and numbers are used interchangeably depending on the background.

I have tried to remain objective, but my bias occasionally creeps in. I have not been comprehensive in my coverage, and have not revealed all the secrets of this special place. Never lose the spirit of discovery, and finish each work-out, climb and book wanting more.

Leave No Trace

IF YOU HIKE OR CLIMB IN THE FLATIRONS, it is your responsibility to help protect the rocks and the area around them from recreation-related damage. The old adage "Take nothing but pictures; leave nothing but footprints" is no longer good enough. The footprints of thousands of visitors can cause extensive damage to fragile plants. It may take a hundred years for some plants to recover. In some cases, they may never recover.

Tread lightly. Stay on available trails and where trails do not exist travel on durable surfaces like rock. Let your eyes do the walking sometimes. You do not have to explore every inch on foot. Respect the environment you are entering. If you don't show respect, you are an intruder, not a visitor.

The Leave No Trace Center for Outdoor Ethics, an international nonprofit organization dedicated to educating people about responsible enjoyment of the outdoors, recommends a few simple techniques for minimum-impact travel through fragile environments. Learn them. Abide by them. For more information about Leave No Trace and minimum-impact outdoor ethics, call (800) 332-4100 or visit their website at *www.LNT.org*. Tailored for the Flatirons, the principles of Leave No Trace are:

1. Plan Ahead and Prepare
- Know the regulations and special concerns of the Flatirons.
- Prepare for extreme weather, hazards and emergencies.
- Avoid popular climbs during times of high use.
- Visit in small groups when possible. Consider splitting larger groups into smaller groups.
- Choose equipment and clothing in subdued colors.
- Repackage food into reusable containers.

2. Travel on Durable Surfaces
- Stay on designated trails. Walk in single file in the middle of the path.
- Do not shortcut switchbacks.
- Where multiple trails exist, choose the one that is most worn.
- Where no trails exist, spread out across the terrain.
- When traveling cross-country, choose the most durable surfaces available: rock, gravel, dry grasses or snow.

- Rest on rock or in designated sites.
- Avoid wetlands and riparian areas.
- Do not build rock cairns, scar trees, or leave ribbons.

3. Dispose of Waste Properly

- Pack it in, pack it out. Carry out all litter, trash and spilled foods—even tidbits.
- Deposit human waste in catholes dug 6 to 8 inches deep at least 200 feet from water or trails. Cover and disguise the cathole when finished.
- Use toilet paper or wipes sparingly. Pack them out.

4. Leave What You Find

- Treat our national heritage with respect. Leave plants, rocks, other natural objects and historical artifacts as you find them for others to discover and enjoy.
- Do not build structures or furniture or disturb vegetation.

5. Minimize Use and Impact of Fires

- Do not camp or build any fires in the Flatirons.

6. Respect Wildlife

- Observe wildlife quietly from a distance. Do not follow or approach them.
- Never feed wild animals.
- Protect wildlife and your food by storing rations securely.
- Control pets at all times. Remove dog feces.
- Avoid wildlife during sensitive times: mating, nesting, raising young or winter

7. Be considerate of other visitors

- Respect other visitors and protect the quality of their experience.
- Be courteous. Yield to other users on the trail.
- Step to the downhill side of the trail and talk softly when encountering horses.
- Take breaks away from trails and other visitors.
- Let nature's sounds prevail. Keep loud voices and noises to a minimum.

Closures

WHEN I WROTE *FLATIRON CLASSICS* IN 1987 there were no restrictions to climbing in the Flatirons. You could hike and climb when and where you wanted, and many aficionados developed a deep love for the Flatirons during this golden age. In the years since, the modern world has intervened and multiple user groups, interests and opinions have intertwined over the Flatirons. The City of Boulder has added its weight to the cacophony, and the end result is that much of the Flatiron habitat is now closed half of the time. The city closures are intended to protect birds, bats, bugs, bears, snails, grasses and a few rare plants. Most of the closures are seasonal, and the usual closure period is from February 1st to July 31st each year. For the whys and wherefores of these closures please see the City of Boulder Open Space and Mountain Parks website at *www.osmp.org* and select the closures page. You can also call 303-441-3440, check postings on the signboards at the major trailheads and read signs on the boundaries of the closed areas. Climbers have been quite good about observing these closures, and I urge readers of this guide to abide by them. There are significant penalties for disregarding the rules.

For additional information contact the Access Fund, a national non-profit advocacy organization that works to keep climbing areas open and to conserve the climbing environment. Their website is *www.accessfund.org*. Another great source for information and community involvement is the Flatiron Climbing Council; their website is *www.flatironsclimbing.com*.

The closures can and have changed significantly over time, so please check with the city for the latest information. In the text, I include the 2007 closure dates for every affected rock and route. Here is a summary of the 2007 closures.

— The Amphitheater has some closures.

— The First and Second Flatirons are unrestricted.

— The Third Flatiron and the rocks around it are closed from 2/1 – 7/31.

— The Royal Arch Trail is open.

— The Fourth and Fifth Flatirons are unrestricted.

— The entire Skunk Canyon area is closed from 2/1 – 7/31. The Skunk Canyon route is included in this closure.

— The east face of Der Zerkle is closed from 4/1 – 9/1.

— Mallory Cave and the area around it is closed from 4/1 – 10/1.

— Bear Creek Spire is often closed.

— Harmon Cave and the area around it is closed from 4/1 – 10/1.

— The entire area north of Fern Canyon is closed from 2/1 – 7/31.

— The Fern Canyon Trail is open.

— The entire area on both sides of Shadow Canyon including the Matron is closed from 2/1 – 7/31.

— The Shadow Canyon Trail is open.

— The Maiden is open with access from the east only.

— The city will sometimes close trails if bears or lions are in the area—check for these closures.

— The city will sometimes open areas early if no nests are in the area.

The Rating System

I USE A SIMPLIFIED YOSEMITE DECIMAL SYSTEM to rate each route's difficulty. I do not use the YDS Grade for these short routes, only the Class rating that rates the route's most difficult free climbing pitch. A route's class is denoted by the word Class, followed by a number from 1 to 5.8, in ascending order of difficulty. A Class rating refers to a single pitch or move. I describe difficulties from Class 1 to Class 4 with a single digit preceded with the word Class. When the difficulty reaches Class 5, the description includes decimal places, and I do not use the word Class. When I do not distinguish between 5.0, 5.1 and 5.2, I indicate difficulty in this range with 5.0–5.2. Similarly, I sometimes group 5.3–5.4 and 5.5–5.6. Many times the difficulty rating for a long climb is determined by the difficulty of a few crux moves with the rest of the climb being much easier. I point out climbs where there is a large discrepancy between the hardest moves and the average difficulty.

My Class rating makes no statement about how exposed a move or pitch is. Exposure triggers a subjective fear that varies widely from person to person. Exposure usually increases with difficulty, but there are many exceptions to this correlation. Some Class 2 passages are very exposed. If exposure bothers you to the point where it impairs your movement, then increase my ratings accordingly.

I do not define difficulty in terms of equipment that you might or might not use. Historically, Class 3 meant unroped climbing and Class 4 was roped climbing, and unfortunately, a lot of historical momentum is behind those old definitions. Under the old definition, when people say that they "Third Classed" a pitch, all I know is that they climbed it unroped; I do not know how hard it was. After all, the Casual Route (5.10) on the Diamond of Longs Peak has been "Third Classed." Everyone knows how hard a pitch they are willing to do unroped, but they do not know how hard a pitch someone else is willing to do unroped. Many people can climb every route in this guide unroped, and many more cannot do any of the routes, with or without a rope. You must always decide when to rope up.

I do not use a lot of confusing adjectives to describe difficulty; I define difficulty by example. The answer to the question, "Just how hard is 5.7 anyway?" is, "Climb Friday's Folly, then you will know." A list of example routes follows with the routes ordered from easiest to hardest within each range.

Class 1   Mesa Trail, Fern Canyon Trail

Class 2   Upper Mallory Cave Trail

Class 3   Mallory Cave to Dinosaur Mountain Route
            Porch Alley
            Der Freischutz–Free Shot

Class 4   Tangen Tunnel Route
            Second Flatiron–Freeway
            Second Flatiron–Dodge Block
            The Regency–El Camino Royale
            Der Freischutz–South Ridge
            The Hammerhead–Yodeling Moves (east ridge)

5.0–5.2   Third Flatiron–East Face
            Third Flatiron–Southwest Chimney
            Two Move Rock
            Angel's Way
            Frontporch–Tiptoe Slab
            Fi Fun
            The Spy–East Ridge
            The Slab–Diagonal

5.3–5.4   First Flatiron–North Arête
            First Flatiron–Atalanta
            Sunset Flatironette–Chase the Sun
            Third Flatiron–1911 Gully
            Third Flatiron–South Chimney
            Third Flatiron–Winky Woo
            Queen Anne's Head–East Face
            Fourth Flatiron–East Face
            Upper Tangen Tower
            Stairway to Heaven–Love

5.5–5.6   Lower Tangen Tower
            Dinosaur Eggs–Hatch
            Dinosaur Eggs–Rehatch
            Second Flatiron–Free For All
            First Flatiron–Fandango
            First Flatiron–East Face Center

Green Mountain Pinnacle–West Chimney
Backporch–East Face
Satan's Slab–East Face
Overhang Rock–Junior Achievement

5.7   Morning After–East Face
         Der Zerkle–East Face North Side
         Willy B–Swing Time
         Third Flatiron–Friday's Folly

5.8   W. C. Fields Pinnacle–A Very Ament Slab
         Finger Flatiron–Mere Wall
         The Maiden–South Face
         Green Thumb–Green Corner Right

These difficulty ratings are for dry conditions. Remember that Flatiron faces rapidly become harder as they become wet and that they become very difficult when covered with snow. For example, the difficulty of the East Face of the Third Flatiron can jump from 5.0–5.2 to 5.8 when covered with snow. The letter S after the difficulty rating indicates that this climb is serious, dangerous and difficult to protect.

Any climber who climbs all the classic routes in this guide deserves the title Dr. Flatiron. Anyone who does that plus climbs a total of 100 routes has clearly graduated Summit Cum Laude! Climb safely and remember to have fun.

Vaya con Dios!

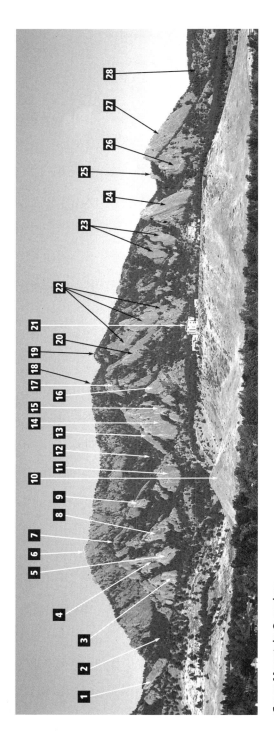

Green Mountain Overview

1 Overhang Rock
2 Bear Canyon
3 Dinosaur Rock
4 Mallory Cave
5 Der Zerkle
6 South Green Mountain
7 Dinosaur Mountain
8 Red Devil
9 Backporch
10 Yuri Point

11 Frontporch
12 Skunk Canyon
13 Mohling Arête
14 Satan's Slab
15 Stairway to Heaven
16 Hillbilly Rock
17 The Fist
18 Green Mountain
19 East Green Mountain
20 Fifth Flatiron

21 NCAR
22 Fourth Flatiron
23 Ironing Boards
24 Third Flatiron
25 Sunset Flatironette
26 Second Flatiron
27 First Flatiron
28 Gregory Canyon

ONE

Peaks, Trailheads and Trails

PEAKS

Green Mountain

A stranger at a party once asked me, "What is your favorite mountain in the world?" After a short deliberation, I stared out the window and said "Green Mountain!" The questioner was disappointed in my answer and didn't seem to understand my choice. Hopefully this book will foster a better understanding.

Green Mountain is the peak southwest of central Boulder, and it supports the most treasured Flatirons. Green Mountain has four summits. In addition to the 8,144-foot main summit, a small false summit is east of the main summit, to the south is the dramatic 8,073-foot rock summit of South Green Mountain, and the 7,380-foot summit of Dinosaur Mountain is 0.75 mile southeast of the main summit. In addition to a multitude of rocks, the trails on Green Mountain offer hikers a wonderful variety of adventures. The trail system on Green Mountain is one of the best in the country, and the million people that live within 40 miles of this mountain are privileged to have such an unspoiled playground in their backyard. The major trails are well-marked, easy to follow and are a nice introduction to the mountain. Green Mountain's finer aspects are more fully revealed by following some of its less traveled routes, since they lead to parts of the mountain that are secluded and primal in their beauty.

Dinosaur Mountain

Getting to Dinosaur Mountain is easy and that is part of its charm. Dinosaur Mountain is the 7,380-foot summit 0.7 mile southeast of Green Mountain. It is bounded on the north by Skunk Canyon and on the south by Bear Canyon. The Mesa Trail runs north–south on the east side of Dinosaur Mountain. By far the most popular approach to Dinosaur Mountain is the NCAR Trail, but there are also approach trails up lower Skunk Canyon and lower Bear Canyon.

Hiking and exploring on the slopes of Dinosaur Mountain can be a lot of fun. Because of the wonderful array of rocks that reside here, even a simple hike will likely turn into a game of dodge rock. It is usually possible to go where you want between the rocks, but there are a few notable dead ends.

Figuring out the secrets of this area requires just a little patience and the willingness to back track when confronted with difficulty that was not planned on.

In addition to the Bear Canyon and Skunk Canyon Trails that skirt the edges of Dinosaur Mountain, one designated trail penetrates this overgrown rock garden. This is the Mallory Cave Trail. In recent years this trail has become one of the most popular hikes above Boulder and for good reason. The distance to Mallory Cave is short, but the adventure quotient is high. It has been reported that Mallory Cave was lost for several years, and before the trail became so well worn, its rediscovery was a bit of a challenge. The now popular rediscovery of Mallory Cave still retains a lot of the original charm. It must also still retain a bit of the old challenge, since I have encountered hikers fumbling along, miles off course, looking for the darn cave. In a new turning of the history wheel, the cave is now closed.

You can approach many of the finest climbs on Dinosaur Mountain by using at least some of the Mallory Cave Trail, and no matter where you wander on Dinosaur Mountain it is good to know how to get to the Mallory Cave Trail. If, when hiking toward Mallory Cave you are seized by some primal urge to climb up a rock, I understand completely. I have spent the last 50 years trying to satisfy these urges, and can now report that this is a lifelong addiction. If you do veer off the Mallory Cave Trail and head up a rock, remember that Mallory himself once cautioned that a momentary negligence can destroy the happiness of a lifetime. Your long life can be reduced to a few terrifying seconds tumbling down the object of your primal urge. Carefully consider where your urges are leading you.

Boulder Mountain

Boulder Mountain is a large massif southwest of Boulder that is composed of four named peaks. The most visible from Boulder is the pointed 8,461-foot summit of Bear Peak. The Nebel Horn is the 7,580-foot summit a half-mile northeast of Bear Peak. South Boulder Peak is hidden from view from most Boulder locations. It is a half-mile southwest of Bear Peak, and at 8,549 feet is the highest peak above Boulder. The hikes on Boulder Mountain are longer and less traveled than the popular trails on Green Mountain so it is easier to get away from people up here.

Shirttail Peak

Shirttail Peak is the small 7,340-foot summit at the southern end of the long southeast ridge of South Boulder Peak. Small but mighty, Shirttail Peak soars 1,300 vertical feet above Eldorado Canyon. The easiest route to the summit of

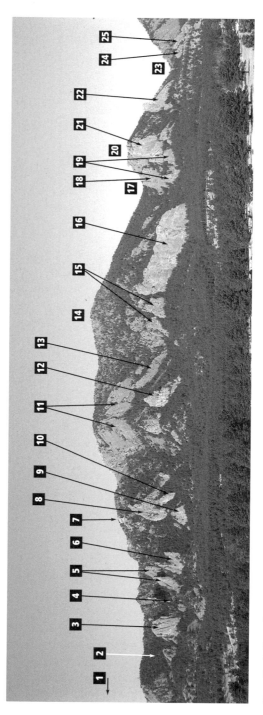

Bear Peak Overview

1 The Matron (out of picture)
2 Shadow Canyon
3 The Crackiron
4 The Maiden
5 The Fatiron
6 Icarus
7 Devil's Thumb
8 Flying Flatiron
9 The Apostle
10 Devil's Advocate

11 The Wings
12 The Sphinx
13 The Keel
14 Bear Peak
15 Shanahan Crags
16 The Slab
17 Fern Canyon
18 Fern Canyon Slabs
19 Goose Eggs
20 Nebel Horn

21 The Goose
22 Seal Rock
23 Bear Canyon
24 Harmon's Flatironette
25 Overhang Rock

Shirttail Peak

Shirttail Peak is on its northeast face. Start at the South Mesa Trailhead and follow the Mesa Trail northwest for a mile, hike south over a grassy saddle, and hike
west up steepening slopes. The slope becomes quite steep, and several small
Flatiron faces are near the top. The easiest line can be difficult to find, and once
off route the small faces can give you fits. Aim for a point south of the summit,
climb up a steep, narrow gully, and reach a tiny saddle a few feet southeast of the
highest point. The exposed summit is a short Class 3 scramble from this saddle.
From the top there is a great view down into Eldorado Canyon.

TRAILHEADS

Gregory Canyon Trailhead

This trailhead is at 5,800 feet and provides access to the Gregory Canyon Trail, Saddle Rock Trail, Amphitheater Trail and Bluebell–Baird Trail. To reach it, go 1.4 miles west on Baseline Road from the intersection of Baseline Road and South Broadway. Where Baseline Road turns sharply north (right) and starts climbing Flagstaff Mountain, turn west (left) onto a dirt road and go 0.15 mile to a small parking lot at the trailhead. This is a fee parking area.

Realization Point Trailhead

This trailhead is at 6,750 feet and provides access to the Ranger Trail, the Greenman Trail, the Long Canyon Trail and the upper end of the Gregory Canyon Trail. To reach it, go 1.4 miles west on Baseline Road from the intersection of Baseline Road and South Broadway and continue on the paved road for another 2.9 miles up Flagstaff Mountain. There is a junction at this point where the Flagstaff Road turns north and the Kossler Lake Road continues west. Two small parking areas are near this junction, and the dirt road that is the beginning of the trail is south of the junction.

Kinnikinic Trailhead

This trailhead is at 5,660 feet and provides access to the Chautauqua Trail, Mesa Trail, Royal Arch Trail and the southern end of the Bluebell–Baird Trail. To reach it, either go 0.95 mile west on Baseline Road from the intersection of Baseline Road and South Broadway, or go 1.0 mile south on 9th Street from the intersection of 9th and Canyon Boulevard to reach the intersection of 9th and Baseline. From this intersection, go one block west on Baseline, and turn south onto Kinnikinic Road. There is a parking lot and also a bike rack here.

Auditorium Trailhead

This trailhead is at 5,730 feet and is at the start of the McClintock Nature Trail and both of the Enchanted Mesa Trails. To reach it, go 0.7 mile west on Baseline Road from the intersection of Baseline and South Broadway. Turn south (left) onto 12th Street, go one block, turn west (right) on Columbine, and go 0.25 mile up the steep hill to the Chautauqua Auditorium. A small parking lot is south of the Auditorium. You can also reach the Chautauqua Auditorium by winding up through Chautauqua from Baseline and Kinnikinic.

Mariposa Street

This trail access is at 5,650 feet and serves the McClintock Nature Trail and both of the Enchanted Mesa Trails. To reach it, go 0.55 mile west on Baseline Road from the intersection of Baseline Road and South Broadway. Turn south (left) onto 15th Street and go two blocks to Mariposa Street. Turn west (right) on Mariposa and go 0.2 mile up the steep hill to a circle at the top of the street. The trail starts on the west side of the street.

King Street

This trail access is at 5,500 feet and serves both of the Kohler Mesa Trails and the upper part of the main Enchanted Mesa Trail. To reach it, go 0.4 mile west on Baseline Road from the intersection of Baseline Road and South Broadway. Turn south (left) onto 17th Street and go four blocks to King Street. The trail access is south of this intersection.

Sierra Drive

This trail access is at 5,640 feet and serves both of the Kohler Mesa Trails and the upper part of the main Enchanted Mesa Trail. To reach it, go 0.55 mile west on Baseline Road from the intersection of Baseline Road and South Broadway. Turn south (left) onto 15th Street and go four and one half blocks to Bellevue Drive. Follow Bellevue Drive for 0.1 mile to Sierra Drive, turn east onto Sierra and follow it for 0.1 mile to its end. The trail starts east of the circle. A trail contours 100 yards east to join the northern Kohler Mesa Trail. This is a higher and shorter start for this trail than from King Street.

Hollyberry Lane

This trail access is at 5,700 feet and serves the lower Skunk Canyon Trail and the southern Kohler Mesa Trail. To reach it, go 0.15 mile west on Table Mesa Drive from the intersection of Table Mesa Drive and South Broadway. Turn north (right) on Stanford Avenue and follow it as it winds north and west for 0.5 mile to Kohler Drive. Continue 0.55 mile west on Kohler Drive to Deer Valley Road. Go west on Deer Valley Road for one block to the trail access, which is at the corner of Hollyberry Lane and Deer Valley Road.

NCAR Trailhead

This trailhead is at 6,300 feet and is at the start of the NCAR Trail that provides access to the Mesa Trail, the Mallory Cave Trail, the Bear Canyon Trail and the Skunk Canyon Trail. To reach the National Center for Atmospheric Research (NCAR), go 2.5 miles west on Table Mesa Drive from the intersection of Table Mesa Drive and South Broadway. The last 1.3 miles of this road is open to the public from 6 A.M. to 10 P.M.

Wildwood Road

This trail access is at 5,660 feet and serves the Mesa Trail, the Bear Canyon Trail, the Bear Peak West Ridge Trail, the Fern Canyon Trail and the Yuri Pass Trail. To reach it, go 0.7 mile west on Table Mesa Drive from the intersection of South Broadway and Table Mesa Drive to Lehigh Street, which is at the end of the divided parkway. Turn south (left) onto Lehigh, go 0.15 mile, turn west (right) onto Bear Mountain Drive, and follow it for 0.4 mile to Wildwood Road. Turn north (right) onto Wildwood and follow it for 0.1 mile to the trail access. The beginning of the dirt service road into Bear Canyon is west of Wildwood Road and east of a power substation.

Stony Hill Road

This trail access is at 5,700 feet and serves the Mesa Trail, the Bear Canyon Trail, the Bear Peak West Ridge Trail, the Fern Canyon Trail and the Yuri Pass Trail. To reach it, go 0.7 mile west on Table Mesa Drive from the intersection of South Broadway and Table Mesa Drive to Lehigh Street, which is at the end of the divided parkway. Turn south (left) onto Lehigh, go 0.15 mile, turn west (right) onto Bear Mountain Drive and follow it for 0.6 mile as it curves south to Stony Hill Road. Turn west (right) onto Stony Hill Road and follow it for 0.25 mile to its end. A short trail crosses to the north side of Bear Creek and joins the dirt service road in lower Bear Canyon. This access is on private property. Please respect it.

Cragmoor Road

This trail access is at 5,750 feet and serves the Shanahan Trails, the Mesa Trail and the Fern Canyon Trail. It is the closest trail access to Bear Peak for an ascent via Fern Canyon. To reach it, go 0.7 mile west on Table Mesa Drive from the intersection of South Broadway and Table Mesa Drive to Lehigh Street, which is at the end of the divided parkway. Turn south (left) onto Lehigh, go 0.85 mile, turn west (right) onto Cragmoor Road, and follow it 0.15 mile west to its end in Cragmoor Place. An unmarked trail climbs 0.2 mile west to join the main Shanahan Trail.

Lehigh Drive

This trail access is at 5,780 feet and serves the Shanahan Trails, the Mesa Trail and the Fern Canyon Trail. To reach it, go 0.7 mile west on Table Mesa Drive from the intersection of South Broadway and Table Mesa Drive to Lehigh Street, which is at the end of the divided parkway. Turn south (left) onto Lehigh and follow it for 1.1 miles as it curves east to an open area south of the road. You can also reach this point by driving 1.5 miles southwest on Greenbriar Drive from South Broadway. Greenbriar turns into Lehigh after 1.1 miles. The Shanahan Trail starts from Lehigh, 100 feet west of Hardscrabble Drive, and heads southwest to join the Shanahan service road.

Southern Mesa Trail Trailhead

This trailhead is at 5,600 feet and provides access to the southern end of the Mesa Trail and the Shadow Canyon Trail. To reach the Southern Mesa Trail Trailhead, go 2.5 miles south from the intersection of South Broadway and Table Mesa Drive to the intersection of Colorado Highways 93 and 170. Turn west (right) onto Colorado 170 toward Eldorado Springs and go 1.7 miles to the signed trailhead, which has a large parking lot on the north side of the highway.

TRAILS

Saddle Rock Trail

The Saddle Rock Trail begins on the southwest side of the Gregory Canyon Trailhead parking lot and climbs steeply for 1.0 mile to the Greenman Trail. The elevation gain to Saddle Rock is 1,250 feet and the gain to the junction with the Greenman Trail is 1,400 feet. The total elevation gain to the summit of Green Mountain is 2,350 feet.

The Saddle Rock Trail and the Gregory Canyon Trail start together. After 100 feet, the Saddle Rock Trail follows the south (left) branch of a V-junction with the Gregory Canyon Trail. It continues west, crosses a bridge, and after another 300 feet, turns sharply south and climbs steeply up the hill on the south side of Gregory Canyon. It then winds upward into Contact Canyon where the sandstone rock to the east meets the granite rock to the west. The trail climbs for some distance past its junction with the Amphitheater Trail, crosses the contact point between sandstone and granite, and eventually angles back northwest to reach a ridge south of and above Saddle Rock. From there, it climbs south, then traverses southwest to connect with the Greenman Trail.

Amphitheater Trail

The Amphitheater Trail starts from the southeast side of the Gregory Canyon Trailhead parking lot, climbs steeply around the south side of the Amphitheater for 0.5 mile, and connects with the Saddle Rock Trail after a gain of 550 feet. The Amphitheater Trail is a nice alternative to the first section of the Saddle Rock Trail and has the added attraction of passing the Amphitheater where you can often see rock climbers. From the south side of the parking lot cross a bridge, then stay west (right) at a V-junction with the Bluebell–Baird Trail. The Amphitheater Trail initially climbs south, then turns southwest, passes south of the Amphitheater and climbs to its junction with the Saddle Rock Trail.

Amphitheater Express Trail

This short useful trail leaves the Amphitheater Trail 150 yards south of the eastern bridge at the Gregory Canyon Trailhead, and reaches the north side of the First Pinnacle outside the Amphitheater. It then climbs to the top of the Amphitheater's West Bench. The Express also climbs along the west side of the Amphitheater to reach the West Bench.

Northeast Ridge Trail

This is an unmarked but often-used shortcut trail that ascends directly up the northeast ridge of Green Mountain. It connects the Saddle Rock and Greenman Trails. The trail leaves the Saddle Rock Trail 200 yards south of the point where the Saddle Rock Trail first arrives on the ridge south of Saddle Rock. This unmarked junction is near the point where the Saddle Rock Trail begins to contour southwest into the south fork of Gregory Canyon.

The Northeast Ridge Trail climbs steeply south up the hill, and after a climb of 300 vertical feet, reaches the crest of the ridge at a pleasant spot overlooking the Third Flatiron. The trail climbs south along the rocky ridge for 0.25 mile, then swings west below a rock buttress. It descends west over some rocks for 30 vertical feet, then contours south for 100 feet to join the Greenman Trail. First timers on this trail often lose it, but once you know its secrets, it is the fastest way to reach the summit of Green Mountain from the Gregory Canyon Trailhead.

Gregory Canyon Trail

The Gregory Canyon Trail is 1.0 mile long and gains 850 feet in elevation. The trail starts on the southwest side of the Gregory Canyon Trailhead parking lot. After 100 feet, the Gregory Canyon Trail follows the northern (right) branch at a V-junction with the Saddle Rock Trail and continues west on the north side of the canyon. The trail passes the contact point between sandstone and granite after 0.25 mile and becomes rougher. After 0.6 mile, the trail crosses to the south side of the creek and continues winding upwards into a meadow south of Realization Point. In the springtime a waterfall on Green Mountain offers impressive views.

Ranger Trail

The Ranger Trail starts at the Realization Point Trailhead and joins the Green Mountain West Ridge Trail after 1.5 miles. Elevation gain is 1,150 feet to this junction, and the summit of Green Mountain is close to this junction. The total elevation gain from the low point of the trail to the summit of Green Mountain is 1,480 feet.

From the Realization Point Trailhead, the trail switchbacks down to the south on a dirt road for 400 feet to the junction with the western end of the Gregory Canyon Trail. This is the low point of the trail. Continue gently up to the south in a pleasant valley for 0.2 mile to the locked Green Mountain Shelter. Continue 0.3 mile southeast from the shelter to a junction with the Greenman Trail. At this point, the Ranger Trail turns west and climbs steeply until it reaches a ridge. It then turns south, climbs gently up along the ridge and finally switchbacks up to the intersection with the Green Mountain West Ridge Trail. From here, you can go 300 yards east up the West Ridge Trail to the summit of Green Mountain.

Greenman Trail

The Greenman Trail is one of the two trails that reach the summit of Green Mountain. You access it by following the Ranger Trail for 0.6 mile from the Realization Point Trailhead to the junction that is 0.3 mile southeast of the Green Mountain Shelter. From this junction, the Greenman Trail is 1.3 miles long and gains 1,200 feet to the summit of Green Mountain.

From the junction with the Ranger Trail, the Greenman Trail climbs 100 yards east to a ridge, crosses to the east side of the ridge and contours gently south and east into the south fork of Gregory Canyon. This is one of the nicest stretches of trail on Green Mountain. The trail then crosses an intermittent stream and soon joins the Saddle Rock Trail.

From its junction with the Saddle Rock Trail, the Greenman Trail continues up to the south, passes Greenman Springs, climbs steeply south on the west side of the ridge above Saddle Rock and finally reaches the Green Mountain Saddle. This saddle is between the false summit of Green Mountain to the east and the main summit to the west. From the saddle, the trail switch-backs west on the north side of the main summit to reach the summit from the north. A permanent rock tower contains the summit register. On top of the tower, a brass mountain finder identifies the many Front Range peaks that you can see in the beautiful panorama to the west.

A variation to the lower part of the Greenman Trail follows an old road that crosses the Gregory Canyon Trail 200 yards east of the junction between the Gregory Canyon Trail and the Ranger Trail. This road climbs along a ridge to the south for 0.5 mile and 325 vertical feet to join the Greenman Trail 100 yards east of its junction with the Ranger Trail. This road does not go by the Green Mountain Shelter.

Green Mountain West Ridge Trail

The Green Mountain West Ridge Trail is one of the two trails that reach the summit of Green Mountain. It is the easiest and shortest route to the summit of Green Mountain. To reach the beginning of the trail, go steeply up to the west from the Realization Point Trailhead for 1.7 miles on the Kossler Lake Road to the western boundary of the Boulder Mountain Park. The Green Mountain West Ridge Trail begins at the park boundary on the south side of the road and follows the west ridge of Green Mountain for 1.5 miles to the summit. The elevation gain is 500 feet.

Long Canyon Trail

The Long Canyon Trail is a beautiful and secluded trail along the upper portion of Gregory Creek. It is 1.5 miles long and rises 800 feet. To get to the eastern end of the Long Canyon Trail, follow the Ranger Trail to the Green Mountain Shelter. The Long Canyon Trail begins west of the shelter and immediately crosses Gregory Creek. It then turns south and follows the west side of the creek for 0.7 mile. Here the trail turns west again and climbs along the north side of Long Canyon to the Kossler Lake Road. The trail reaches the road 0.2 mile above Cathedral Park and 1.3 miles west of the Realization Point Trailhead.

Chautauqua Trail

This short but useful trail starts west of the small parking lot at Baseline and Kinnikinic. It climbs southwest across the large Chautauqua Meadow and provides wonderful views as it heads toward the First Flatiron. The trail enters the trees and joins the Bluebell–Baird Trail after 0.6 mile and an elevation gain of

460 feet. There are some variations to this trail. After a short distance another trail angles up to the west-southwest and reaches the Bluebell–Baird Trail farther north. Another trail near the trailhead heads directly west and parallels Baseline Road. This trail eventually reaches the Amphitheater Trail.

Bluebell Shelter

To reach Bluebell Shelter, start at the Kinnikinic Trailhead and walk south up the old road for 0.75 mile to the shelter. The two sided, open shelter is equipped with picnic tables and a barbecue, but no drinking water is available.

Bluebell Baird Trail

This gentle trail connects the Gregory Canyon Trailhead with the Bluebell Shelter. The trail is 0.7 mile long and gains 300 feet from the Gregory Canyon Trailhead. It starts together with the Amphitheater Trail at the southeast corner of the Gregory Canyon Trailhead parking lot. The trail soon branches east from the Amphitheater Trail and climbs through a meadow to reach a wooded mesa. It contours south across this gentle mesa and finally drops down to reach the west side of the Bluebell Shelter.

Royal Arch Trail

The Royal Arch Trail is 1.1 miles long and gains 950 feet between Bluebell Shelter and Royal Arch. The trail begins southwest of Bluebell Shelter, starts west, then climbs gently southeast along the northwest side of Bluebell Canyon. There is a classic boulder problem on this stretch of the trail where a 6-foot roof is right above the trail. The moves over this overhang are 5.8.

As Bluebell Canyon turns west, the trail contours into the canyon and crosses to its south side. The Third Flatiron and Queen Anne's Head tower above the trail to the northwest as the trail climbs steeply up to the west on the south side of Bluebell Canyon. This part of the trail is often icy in winter. The trail then climbs steeply up the hillside to the south, and after 13 switchbacks, reaches Sentinel Pass, which is a gateway between several large overgrown boulders on a ridge. From Sentinel Pass, the trail descends south for 150 yards, losing 80 vertical feet. The low point of this part of the trail is at the bottom of the Fourth Flatironette. The trail climbs again along the south side of the Fourth Flatironette, which has an alluring cave in its south side. One hundred feet up to the southwest from the cave, the trail passes within kicking distance of the bottom of the first piece of the Fourth Flatiron, a large east-facing slab with a curious cave high on its south side.

Less than 100 feet past the first piece of the Fourth Flatiron is Tangen Spring which is nestled in the base of the lower Tangen Tower, a 60-foot high rock with steep north, east, and south faces. This is a verdant and pleasant place to rest. The trail continues up to the south from the spring and after several switchbacks reaches Royal Arch, which is on a ridge. Trees hide the 20-foot natural sandstone arch until you get close to it. It is easy to walk through the arch to some sunny slabs on its south side.

Cavernous Sinus

Those willing to look for it have enjoyed this delightful cave for many years. Its existence has been reported in other guidebooks, but exact directions to it have never been published. Many decades ago the rediscovery of Mallory Cave provided a wonderful route finding challenge and today's search for Cavernous Sinus preserves that challenge. The cave is worth the hunt. It is different in character from Mallory Cave but rivals it in size. A detailed description of the cave follows, but I give only hints for its location.

The cave is located some distance above the Royal Arch Trail between Bluebell Canyon and Sentinel Pass. It is between two Flatiron formations, one named and one unnamed that are 30 feet apart. Hike up the distinct gully between the formations into an improbable cul-de-sac. The entrance to the hidden cave is on the north side of this cul-de-sac.

Crawl up into the entrance and find a tight passage up to the south (left). Worm up through this hole into a large room (5.0–5.2). On the north side of this room, climb another 5.0–5.2 move to reach the upper part of the room. There is a window in the cave near here, but escape from the cave is not feasible at this point. Continue up for 30 feet under a huge chockstone and scramble up into an attic. Two escape holes are east of the attic and the lower of the two is the easiest. The escape from the cave is in hiking territory near the top of the gully. The route up through the cave is the only easy way to ascend this gully.

Mesa Trail

The Mesa Trail is the backbone trail of Boulder Mountain Park and one of the most enjoyable trails anywhere. It goes north-south between Chautauqua and South Boulder Creek along the eastern base of Green and Boulder Mountains. It provides a wonderful tour underneath the Flatirons as it descends into canyons, rises to cross meadows and winds through forested areas. In addition to the main trailheads at each end, it has many access points along the way.

From the Kinnikinic Trailhead on its north end to the Southern Mesa Trail Trailhead is 6.9 miles. Many runners set the goal of running this distance in one hour. Some intermediate distances from the Kinnikinic Trailhead are: 1.0 mile to the Enchanted Mesa Trail, 1.7 miles to the NCAR Trail, 2.2 miles to Bear Canyon, 3.7 miles to the southern Shanahan Trail and 5.0 miles to the upper Shadow Canyon Trail.

Much of the trail is relatively flat, which makes it very popular, but there are many small climbs and descents along the way, and the total elevation gain is 1,400 feet when going from north to south. The gain from south to north is 1,460 feet. I describe the trail from north to south.

From the Kinnikinic Trailhead, hike 0.6 mile up the Bluebell Shelter road to the start of the trail, which is 200 yards below Bluebell Shelter. From the road, the Mesa Trail contours southwest into Bluebell Canyon, crosses the intermittent creek, and starts to climb southeast. It comes to the junction with the McClintock Nature Trail 200 yards past Bluebell Canyon. Beyond this junction, the trail turns south and climbs gently across Enchanted Mesa to meet the Enchanted Mesa and Woods Quarry Trails. This sanguine section is in the trees.

The Mesa Trail continues climbing south across the upper end of the Kohler Mesa, passes the junction with the southern Kohler Mesa Trail and contours into the canyon below the Fourth and Fifth Flatirons. Often a cool breeze comes down this canyon. The trail climbs gently southeast, crosses a mesa with expansive views in all directions, then contours southwest to the entrance to upper Skunk Canyon. Near here you can get a fractured echo from Echo Rock to the east across Skunk Canyon. From the entrance to upper Skunk Canyon, the trail descends east and crosses the canyon.

From Skunk Canyon, the trail climbs 0.1 mile east, turns south and passes the junctions with the two branches of the NCAR Trail. From the NCAR Trail, the Mesa Trail contours south across another mesa, passes the junction with the Mallory Cave Trail, descends to the dirt service road in lower Bear Canyon and follows the road 0.1 mile west to Bear Creek.

The trail crosses Bear Creek and winds 0.33 mile up the road to the junction with the Bear Canyon Trail. This stretch can be icy in winter. The Mesa Trail continues south up the road for another 0.15 mile to the junction with the Fern Canyon Trail. One hundred yards east of this junction, the Mesa Trail leaves the road, climbs south to a broad saddle and continues south before descending southwest into Fern Canyon.

From Fern Canyon, the Mesa Trail climbs southeast and crosses the northern branch of the Shanahan Trail. It then turns southwest and descends into Slab Canyon. From there the trail climbs steeply south, crosses a beautiful meadow with a clear view of the Maiden, crosses Shanahan Canyon, then Shanahan Draw. The junction with the southern branch of the Shanahan Trail is between Shanahan Canyon and Shanahan Draw.

From Shanahan Draw, the Mesa Trail rolls 0.4 mile gently across another mesa before descending to the junction with the Big Bluestem Trail that descends southeast. This trail is a shortcut to the southern end of the Mesa Trail. From this junction, the Mesa Trail climbs 0.2 mile south to a water trough. The junction with the northern spur of the Shadow Canyon Trail is at the water trough. You can easily see the Maiden and Devil's Thumb west of here. The Mesa Trail then turns southeast and climbs over a meadow with wonderful views.

The trail descends south and forks. A spur goes southwest and connects with the Shadow Canyon Trail. The main trail descends 0.2 mile south on a dirt road to rejoin the spur trail, which is now a road, then turns east. It continues descending 0.8 mile east on a road, turns south and winds 0.9 mile down to the Southern Mesa Trail Trailhead. Shortly before the end of the trail is a bridge over South Boulder Creek.

McClintock Nature Trail

The McClintock Nature Trail starts at either the Auditorium Trailhead or Mariposa Street and soon crosses the Enchanted Mesa Trail, which is a road at this point. It then climbs 0.7 mile on the southeast side of Bluebell Canyon and reaches the Mesa Trail. Its junction with the Mesa Trail is 250 yards south of the start of the Mesa Trail on the Bluebell Shelter Road. Twenty nature stations are along the way and each gives a description of a different aspect of the surroundings. The elevation gain is 400 feet. This trail provides excellent views of the Flatirons.

Enchanted Mesa Trails

Enchanted Mesa is southeast of Bluebell Canyon and northwest of Mesa Canyon that separates Enchanted Mesa from Kohler Mesa. A large covered city reservoir is on the eastern end of Enchanted Mesa. Two trails climb gently across Enchanted Mesa to reach the Mesa Trail.

The main Enchanted Mesa Trail starts at both the Auditorium Trailhead and Mariposa Street and follows a dirt road 1.2 miles up the mesa to reach the Mesa Trail. The elevation gain is 450 feet. From the Chautauqua Auditorium, follow the dirt road leading south, then east to a large covered reservoir. From Mariposa Street, follow the McClintock Nature Trail southwest to reach the road. Turn east onto the road and hike up to a covered reservoir. From the reservoir, the road winds gently up to the south and west through the woods to reach the Mesa Trail. Its junction with the Mesa Trail is also at the beginning of the Woods Quarry Trail.

The northern Enchanted Mesa Trail provides a secluded alternative to the main Enchanted Mesa Trail. It climbs along the northwest edge of Enchanted Mesa and provides spectacular views of the Flatirons. This unmarked trail leaves the main Enchanted Mesa Trail 100 yards east of Bluebell Canyon where the McClintock Nature Trail crosses the Enchanted Mesa Trail. The hidden junction is 30 feet east of a power pole. The trail climbs steeply to the mesa and after a short distance meets two spur trails that connect to the McClintock Nature Trail and the main Enchanted Mesa Trail. The northern Enchanted Mesa Trail continues gently southwest through the woods and rejoins the main Enchanted Mesa Trail 100 feet east of the Mesa Trail.

Woods Quarry Trail

This short trail starts at the junction of the main Enchanted Mesa Trail and the Mesa Trail. It climbs steeply west, then 0.25 mile south along an old road to reach a flat platform at the base of Woods Quarry. The elevation gain from the Mesa Trail to the quarry is 200 feet. A useful extension to this trail starts at the south side of the quarry. It climbs steeply to the west for another 0.2 mile and 250 vertical feet to join the Royal Arch Trail south of Sentinel Pass.

Tomato Rock Trail

This is an unmarked trail that provides a seldom-used alternate route to Woods Quarry. The trail follows an old road and is a bit faint in places. A short distance south of the Mesa Trail–McClintock Nature Trail junction, the Mesa Trail heads 100 yards east. The Tomato Rock Trail starts where the Mesa Trail turns back south. The Tomato Rock Trail heads 100 yards up to the west to Tomato Rock, which is a well-named 12-foot high boulder.

From the south side of Tomato Rock there are two old roads. The more visible road heads south and reaches the Woods Quarry Trail a few feet west of the Mesa Trail. The more interesting route climbs west, then southwest near the southeast rim of Bluebell Canyon. There is another old quarry here and some terrific views of the Third Flatiron. The trail then climbs southwest to another little quarry and finally drops slightly south to reach the Woods Quarry Trail 50 feet south of Woods Quarry.

Kohler Mesa Trails

Kohler Mesa is the mesa south of Enchanted Mesa. The eastern end is on US Government land and Boulder Mountain Park land begins part way up the mesa. The public is allowed on the government land on the eastern end of the mesa. Two pleasant trails climb southwest across Kohler Mesa.

The northern Kohler Mesa Trail starts at King Street and joins the main Enchanted Mesa Trail after 1.0 mile and a vertical gain of 520 feet. From King Street, the trail climbs steeply southwest on Boulder park land to reach the eastern end of the mesa at the government property boundary. The trail then climbs gently along the northern side of the mesa for a half-mile into Boulder Mountain Park, then contours north a short distance to reach the main Enchanted Mesa Trail 300 yards east of the Mesa Trail. One hundred yards east of the point where the northern Kohler Mesa Trail turns north, two short side trails head south and east to join the southern Kohler Mesa Trail.

The southern Kohler Mesa Trail starts at Hollyberry Lane, climbs to the Kohler Mesa from the south on a dirt road and reaches the Mesa Trail after 1.3 miles and a vertical gain of 550 feet. From the trailhead, descend slightly north, cross lower Skunk Canyon, climb to the large dirt road that switchbacks on the south side of Kohler Mesa, and follow it up to the eastern end of the mesa. There are excellent views of the Flatirons from here. Follow the dirt road southwest to reach the Boulder Mountain Park boundary, continue 0.55 mile up on a trail and reach the Mesa Trail near a cabin below Woods Quarry. You can also reach the southern Kohler Mesa Trail by following the lower Skunk Canyon Trail for 0.4 mile, then following a side trail up to the north.

Tangen Tunnel Route

This is a rough unmarked hiking route to the summit of Green Mountain. It climbs between the Fourth and Fifth Flatirons to reach the southeast ridge south of the eastern false summit of Green Mountain. This route is overgrown, rough, and poison ivy lurks in the gullies, but is a rewarding one for adventurous hikers.

Follow the Royal Arch Trail to Tangen Spring. Leave the trail here, and hike directly west into the narrow gully between the first piece of the Fourth Flatiron to the north and the lower Tangen Tower to the south. Some huge chockstones appear to block this gully, but the Tangen Tunnel winds up through them. One exposed Class 4 move is required to reach the top of the chockstones. Above the chockstones, the saddle between the lower and upper Tangen Towers will be to the south.

Continue west above the Tangen Tunnel into the gully between the upper Tangen Tower and the second piece of the Fourth Flatiron. Some water-polished slabs in this gully are Class 4 when dry, but much harder when wet. Above the upper Tangen Tower, angle southwest on the north side of the Fifth Flatiron. Stay south of Schmoe's Nose, north of the Fist, and reach the southeast ridge of Green Mountain. Hike north to Green's eastern false summit, then head west to the Green Mountain Saddle and follow the Greenman Trail to the summit.

Variations

1. You can easily reach the saddle between the lower and upper Tangen Towers and the upper part of the Tangen Tunnel Route by continuing 100 feet on the Royal Arch Trail past Tangen Spring, then hiking west on the south side of the lower Tangen Tower. This easy alternative avoids the Tangen Tunnel.

2. Climb up the gully between the upper Tangen Tower and the Fifth Flatiron. Near the top of this narrow gully are some large chockstones that block the way. Hike up into a slot on the south side of the chockstones and find a narrow hole. It is possible for small people to wiggle up through this hole (5.5–5.6) but I know someone over six feet tall that failed to get through the hole. Tall people can avoid the hole by stemming up the slot and doing an elegant 5.5–5.6 move to the top of the chockstone.

3. Above the upper Tangen Tower, hike up the gully between the third piece of the Fourth Flatiron to the north and Schmoe's Nose to the south. Some huge chockstones with a dark hole under them also block this gully. To reach the dark hole, do a 5.0–5.2 move over a short step, and a little higher, a 5.5–5.6 move over another step. From the dark hole, hike and scramble south around the chockstones. Continue up to the west along the south side of the third piece of the Fourth Flatiron to reach the southeast ridge of Green Mountain.

Skunk Canyon Trail   *Closed 2/1 – 7/31*

Skunk Canyon is between Dinosaur Mountain and the southeast ridge of Green Mountain. The wilderness of Skunk Canyon provides a wonderful escape from civilization. A rough, unmarked trail climbs up the canyon to reach the Green Mountain Saddle and the Greenman Trail. There is also a nice trail in lower Skunk Canyon east of the Mesa Trail.

The lower Skunk Canyon Trail starts from Hollyberry Lane, climbs west and reaches the Mesa Trail after 0.9 mile and a vertical gain of 600 feet. You can also reach the lower Skunk Canyon Trail from the bottom of the NCAR road where there is a bike rack. A sidewalk/bike path heads northwest and joins the eastern end of Deer Valley Road. A dirt service road goes 0.4 mile straight west from this junction to a power station. The lower Skunk Canyon Trail is just north of this power station. The trail stays on the canyon's north side for 0.5 mile beyond the power station. The trail splits and a side-trail heads steeply west up the hillside and soon joins the Mesa Trail while the main trail angles more sedately up to the south to join the Mesa Trail farther to the south.

To continue up into upper Skunk Canyon west of the Mesa Trail, follow the Mesa Trail south. Stay west (right) at a junction and the Mesa Trail will contour west as it curves into Skunk Canyon. As the Mesa Trail begins to switchback down to cross the canyon, leave the trail and head west past a small quarry to the entrance of Skunk Canyon.

When approaching upper Skunk Canyon from NCAR, take the NCAR Trail and follow its northern spur to join the Mesa Trail. Follow the Mesa Trail north then west as it descends into Skunk Canyon. Cross the creek (usually dry), climb 100 yards up switchbacks, leave the Mesa Trail at the west end of either of two switchbacks and hike west past the small quarry to the entrance of Skunk Canyon.

Beyond this point, the true nature of Skunk Canyon becomes apparent. The trail is rough and often hard to follow, but the cool recess of this verdant place is your reward. Soon, the great rocks begin passing in review. The first rock encountered is the Stairway to Heaven on the north side of the canyon. Shortly beyond is a tight portal formed by the Achean Pronouncement to the south and Satan's Slab to the north. The easiest route past this portal is Class 3 and can be hard to find. Immediately west of Satan's Slab on the canyon's north side is a smaller rib called the Angel's Way. The final rib on the canyon's north side is the Mohling Arête. The final two ribs on the canyon's south side are the Rainbow and the North Ridge of Dinosaur Mountain.

Beyond the rocks, Skunk Canyon curves up to the north, and the hiking becomes easier. Eventually, reach the Green Mountain Saddle east of Green's summit, and follow the Greenman Trail to the summit. While Skunk Canyon is often used as an approach to climbs on Dinosaur Mountain, I do not recommend it as a hiking route to the summit of Dinosaur Mountain. The gullies between the rocks on the south side of the canyon are all hikeable, but they are steep and unpleasant.

NCAR Trail

The NCAR Trail goes 0.5 mile west from the NCAR Trailhead to join the Mesa Trail. The trail begins north of the buildings and climbs gently west. After 250 yards, near the end of the mesa, drop down across a grassy saddle which is not far from the NCAR road. A trail contours southwest from this grassy saddle but this is not the main NCAR Trail and it will lead you into some rough hiking in the rocks beyond. The main NCAR Trail continues steeply uphill to the west and passes a large green water tank on a ridge. The trail descends west of the water tank, then contours close to a view point 150 feet east of and above the Mesa Trail. The view of Dinosaur Mountain is excellent from here.

From this viewpoint, two trails go down and join the Mesa Trail. The main trail angles down to the south, and a spur angles down to the north. The southern trail is the shortest route to Mallory Cave and the northern spur is the shortest route to Skunk Canyon.

Mallory Cave Trail and Dinosaur Mountain Route

The Mallory Cave Trail leaves the Mesa Trail where the southern branch of the NCAR Trail reaches the Mesa Trail. A large sign marks the start of the Mallory Cave Trail. The Mallory Cave Trail leaves the Mesa Trail and climbs steeply southwest. After 200 yards, some good views develop, and you will pass two large well-named boulders known as the Square and the Babyhorn. At this point you are approaching the first tier of rocks on Dinosaur Mountain. Der Zerkle looms directly ahead and Dinosaur Rock is prominent to the southwest. The trail crosses a meadow west of the Square and the Babyhorn, enters the trees and goes very close to the low point of Der Zerkle.

The trail ascends the large gully between Der Zerkle to the north and Dinosaur Rock to the south. You have now penetrated the first tier of rocks and your adventure unfolds. The trail swings up to the north, close under the west face of Der Zerkle, then dodges west a few feet to the base of the Hand, which is the second tier Flatiron that is south of Mallory Cave. The trail continues up to the north along the base of the Hand and the Mallory Flatironette, which is a smaller rock directly below the cave.

The trail soon swings into a small alcove formed by the north side of Mallory Flatironette and a new rock, the Finger Flatiron, which is north of the cave. Continue hiking north along the base of the Finger Flatiron and soon you will emerge into the bottom of the broad alleyway between the Finger Flatiron and the Box, which is the rock uphill to the northwest. Follow a small trail west up this broad alley and hike to a small saddle on the west side of the Box. You have now breached the second tier of rocks on Dinosaur Mountain.

The third tier of rocks is a more serious obstacle. The third tier, including the small Flatirons Fee, Fi, Fo, Fum, Dum and the Rainbow, forms a very nearly continuous barrier of rock that runs all the way from Bear Canyon to Skunk Canyon. In this entire distance there are only four east-west hiking routes across the third tier. They are: south of Fee, the Fee–Fi col, the Fum–Dum col and the Dum–Rainbow col.

Fortunately, the Fum–Dum col is directly west of the Box. From your perch on the small saddle west of the Box, move west until you bump into the third tier. Find and climb 20 feet of easy Class 3 rock up an obvious weakness. This spot is one of the keys to this route. Continue ascending west to the Fum–Dum col. If you find the proper spot, it is easy to move west into a long north-south gully called the Bowling Alley. The Bowling Alley separates the third and fourth tiers.

Hike 100 yards north up the Bowling Alley to a pleasant saddle at its top. The summit of Dinosaur Mountain is only 100 feet west of this point. Scramble up a 15-foot Class 3 crack south and west of the saddle that takes you past the small east face of the fourth tier. The exposed summit of

Dinosaur Mountain is just beyond on top of a 20-foot Class 3 slab. To make a nice loop hike, descend from here into Bear Canyon using the Southwest Slopes Route on Dinosaur Mountain.

Porch Alley

This is an adventurous hiking route up Dinosaur Mountain that has much of the charm of the Mallory Cave Trail but none of the crowds. It ascends the small valley north of the Mallory Cave area, passes several little glens and tests your route finding skills.

A few feet south of where the southernmost NCAR Trail joins the Mesa Trail, follow the Mallory Cave Trail 100 feet southwest up the hill until it crosses a small gully. This is Porch Alley. One hundred fifty feet south of Porch Alley, leave the Mallory Cave Trail, hike west up the hill and climb along the south side of Porch Alley. After a few hundred yards the trail bumps into the Frontporch. During spring and early summer, part of the NCAR deer herd likes to graze in this pleasant area.

Continue west, staying south of the Frontporch and the Lost Porch, a small Flatironette west of the Frontporch that you may not notice it unless you are looking for it. A nice glen is west of the Lost Porch. Continue west, staying south of the Backporch, a fierce looking rock with steep north, west and south faces, and a V-shaped overhang on its east face. The Rainbow is southwest of the Backporch. Stay south of the Rainbow, and while you are still below the level of the notch on the west side of the Backporch, you will bump into some scruffy overgrown boulders. Continue uphill to the west, staying south of the Rainbow. Climb a 20-foot, Class 3 pitch and scramble onward to a more coherent Flatiron called Dum. Angle southwest in a small gully along the base of Dum (some Class 3), continue south through a broken boulder-strewn area, and find the Fum–Dum col, which is on the Mallory Cave to Dinosaur Mountain Route. This col is one of the few places where it is easy to hike through the third tier of rocks on Dinosaur Mountain, and it is the only hiking route high on Dinosaur Mountain. Continue on the Mallory Cave to Dinosaur Mountain Route, descend west into the Bowling Alley and hike north to the top of Dinosaur Mountain.

Variations

1. There is another route to the Frontporch on the hillside north of Porch Alley. North of the NCAR–Mesa–Mallory Cave Trail junction, hike west up the steep hill to some rocks east of the Frontporch and north of Porch Alley. To join the Porch Alley Route, descend south to the low point of the Frontporch.

2. From the scruffy overgrown boulders southwest of the Backporch, angle southwest, stay below the scruffy boulders and join the Mallory Cave to Dinosaur Mountain Route in the little saddle west of the Box.

3. From the base of Dum, continue straight up on the north side of Dum to a small col. Contour southwest into Uncle Grumpies gully, which is the northern extension of the Bowling Alley, and climb south up Uncle Grumpies to the col at the top of the Bowling Alley.

Southwest Slopes of Dinosaur Mountain

This route is the easiest route to the summit of Dinosaur Mountain. It does not have the charm of the east side routes, but is important because of its ease and the fact that it is often used as a descent route. In the afternoon, long after the sun has left the rocks on the east side, it is still beaming on this route. After a pleasant morning spent climbing or hiking on the east side of Dinosaur Mountain, you can descend the Southwest Slopes Route in the afternoon sun.

Follow the main Bear Canyon Trail as it climbs west on the south side of the canyon. As you hike on this trail, the rocks of Dinosaur Mountain will pass silently in review to the north. Pass them all. Near the last rib of rock, the trail joins the level of the canyon floor, and soon after that, crosses to the north side of Bear Creek. The dominant feature on the west side of Dinosaur Mountain is a large grassy meadow several hundred yards wide. This meadow is continuous from the floor of Bear Canyon to the broad saddle between Dinosaur Mountain and South Green Mountain.

Ascend this meadow, gradually moving east toward the rocks of Dinosaur Mountain. Don't ascend all the way to the saddle. One hundred yards below the saddle is a break in the nearly continuous rock rib that is the westernmost tier of rock on Dinosaur Mountain. Scramble east through this break into a north-south gully known as the Bowling Alley.

Hike 100 yards north up the Bowling Alley to a pleasant saddle at its top. The summit of Dinosaur Mountain is 100 feet west of this saddle. Scramble up a 15-foot Class 3 crack south and west of the saddle that takes you past the small east face of the fourth tier. The exposed summit of Dinosaur Mountain is just beyond on top of a 20-foot Class 3 slab.

Bowling Alley

This 100-foot wide gully separates the third and fourth tiers of rock on the south side of Dinosaur Mountain. The third and fourth tiers of rock are quite continuous and there are only a few places to get into and out of the Bowling Alley. Both the Mallory Cave to Dinosaur Mountain and the Southwest Slopes

Route use the uppermost 100 yards of the Bowling Alley to reach the top of Dinosaur Mountain. The gaps that these two routes use to get into and out of the Bowling Alley are across the alley from each other, 100 yards below the small saddle at its top.

Most of the Bowling Alley is filled with loose rocks, and it is an easy, but unpleasant hiking route. It is often used by people who miss the gap 100 yards below the top of the Bowling Alley while attempting to descend the Southwest Slopes route. This is not a fatal error as it is possible to descend the Bowling Alley all the way into Bear Canyon, but if you try to escape lower down, you may end up feeling like a gutter ball.

To use the Bowling Alley as an ascent route, hike west up Bear Canyon to the point where the trail joins the level of Bear Creek. The Bowling Alley is the westernmost alleyway between the rocks on the south side of Dinosaur Mountain. To the west of the Bowling Alley is the broad meadow that separates Dinosaur Mountain from South Green Mountain. Once you determine which lane to use, simply drop down, cross Bear Creek and roll on up the hill.

Bear Cave

Although smaller and less well known than Mallory Cave, Bear Cave still has a great deal of charm. The area near the cave is sunny and powerful. There is a trail to Bear Cave, but it is rough and unmarked. The cave is 200 yards above Bear Creek on the south side of Dinosaur Mountain, is hard to see from the Bear Canyon Trail and can be difficult to find. The cave is in the bottom of the south face of the Northern Dinosaur Egg, which is the larger and higher of a pair of rocks that form the southern end of the second tier of rocks of Dinosaur Mountain. The second tier also contains Mallory Cave.

To reach Bear Cave, hike 0.25 mile west up Bear Canyon on the main Bear Canyon Trail. Pass the second tier of rocks that contains the Northern and Southern Dinosaur Eggs. Deep cracks in their east faces mark both of these rocks. From Bear Creek, hike up the gully west of the second tier. After 200 yards, move east and cross a small pass between the Southern and Northern Dinosaur Eggs. Bear Cave is 100 feet farther east and you can see it from the pass.

You can also reach Bear Cave by hiking up the gully east of the second tier although this approach is more difficult. From Bear Creek, hike uphill under the east face of the Southern Dinosaur Egg to the base of the Northern Dinosaur Egg. Find and climb an easy 15-foot Class 2+ pitch that angles back south. Bear Cave is a few feet away from the top of this pitch.

A hundred feet south of Bear Cave, some cave like spaces are under large boulders at the base of the north face of the Southern Dinosaur Egg. Small people with large imaginations are best suited for entering a peculiar passage a few feet west of Bear Cave.

Fumbledeedum (5.0–5.2)

If, when you hike west on the Bear Canyon Trail, you keep careful track of the gullies between the first, second, third and fourth tiers of rock on the south side of Dinosaur Mountain, you will discover an extra gully and, apparently, an extra tier of rocks. For a few hundred feet up out of Bear Canyon, there is indeed an extra rib of rock between the third and fourth tiers. Higher up, this extra rib blends into the third tier but the extra gully narrows to a ramp and continues. This extra gully and ramp is the route Fumbledeedum, which is recommended as an adventuresome hiking and scrambling route up Dinosaur Mountain.

Fumbledeedum is fun. It is full of little surprises, holes and cruxes, but never reaches the stature of a roped rock climb. It is the hardest hiking route described in this book. The eastern boundary of Fumbledeedum is composed of the rocks Fee, Fi, Fo and Fum. The route is important for rock climbers because the descents from the summits of Fi and Fo end up in the Fumbledeedum gully, and you can only enter or exit Fumbledeedum in a few places. The Bowling Alley is immediately west of Fumbledeedum.

After you locate the Fumbledeedum gully, head up the easy lower stretch until you are under an ugly sloping cave. You can easily bypass it to the west (easy Class 3). Scramble across an area where the gully seems to disappear. Soon the rock Fee will appear above you. While still below Fee, you can escape Fumbledeedum to the west (Class 1) or the east (Class 4).

Above, the route begins to narrow into a ramp, but a large black cave interrupts this process. Charge forth into the blackness, scramble up and wiggle through a nifty hole (Class 3) to easy ground above. You can bypass this cave-hole on the west (Class 3) or east (Class 4), but you should enjoy the hole. Above the hole, Fumbledeedum becomes a real ramp, and the Fee–Fi col is not far beyond. From the Fee–Fi col you can escape east (Class 1), but not west.

Follow the ramp as it sneaks underneath the steep west face of Fi, and reach a cruxy little area below the Fi–Fo col. Either climb it directly via a 10-foot Class 4 wall or find a sneaky route which ends with another hole (Class 4). Both of these routes involve some exposure. From the Fi–Fo col, you cannot easily escape either east or west.

Follow the ramp upward under the west face of Fo, and overcome a tricky five-foot chockstone (5.0–5.2). There is no exposure below this move as you are buried in the bowels of the ramp, so you might as well go for it. Above this chockstone, you will wind up through some large holes and pick your way to the Fo–Fum col. From this col, you cannot escape to the east, but a short Class 3 downclimb to the west allows you to escape into the Bowling Alley.

The Fumbledeedum ramp continues on under the west face of Fum where you must overcome one more Class 4 move. Then, walk up through a final large hole to emerge at the top of the route at the Fum–Dum col. This col is on the Mallory Cave to Dinosaur Mountain Route. You can easily move west into the Bowling Alley and follow it north up to the top of Dinosaur Mountain.

Bear Canyon Trail

Bear Canyon is the major canyon between Green Mountain and Bear Peak. The Bear Canyon Trail starts from the Mesa Trail at a switchback 0.33 mile south of Bear Canyon. The trail is 1.8 miles long and gains 1,000 feet to its end near the western boundary of the Boulder Mountain Park.

There are several ways to reach the start of the Bear Canyon Trail. The most obvious is to follow the NCAR Trail to the Mesa Trail, then hike south on the Mesa Trail to Bear Canyon, and continue south for another 0.33 mile to the start of the Bear Canyon Trail. The other approaches utilize either Wildwood Road or Stony Hill Road. Hike west on the dirt service road on the north side of Bear Creek and join the Mesa Trail. One hundred yards west of the junction with the Mesa Trail, the road crosses to the south side of Bear Creek and climbs southeast. Stay on the road for 0.33 mile to the start of the Bear Canyon Trail.

From the Mesa Trail, the Bear Canyon Trail heads 100 yards north, then turns west into the canyon at a power substation. This point is on the south side of Bear Canyon, several hundred feet above the bottom of the canyon, and there is a magnificent view of the rocks on Dinosaur Mountain from here. As the trail climbs gently west on the south side of the canyon, these rocks will pass silently in review.

After 0.35 mile the gently rising trail reaches the bottom of the more steeply climbing canyon and crosses to the north side of Bear Creek. After another 0.3 mile, the trail crosses back to the south side of the creek near the bottom of the long south ridge of Green Mountain. The trail continues to wind up the canyon to reach the start of the Bear Peak West Ridge Trail near the western park boundary.

Yuri Pass Trail

This short, unmarked trail provides a nice alternative to the dirt service road in lower Bear Canyon. It starts on the north side of the power substation west

44

of Wildwood Road and climbs 0.35 mile west to a small pass between Yuri
Point and the NCAR Mesa. The 5,980-foot summit of Yuri Point is an enjoyable side trip from the pass and provides a good view. Also, from the pass a
side trail climbs north to NCAR. The main Yuri Pass Trail descends 150 yards
west from the pass and rejoins the dirt service road.

Shanahan Trails

The Shanahan Trail starts from Lehigh Drive and ascends gently west up a dirt
road to reach the Mesa Trail. You can also reach the lower Shanahan Trail from
Cragmoor Road. A half-mile west of Lehigh Drive, the lower Shanahan Trail
forks into northern and southern branches, both of which continue to the
Mesa Trail. Using the Mesa Trail to connect the two branches of the Shanahan
Trail makes a wonderful loop hike or run.

From the northern-southern Shanahan Trail junction, the southern trail
descends 0.2 mile southeast, then winds 0.8 mile southwest and ends at the
Mesa Trail. The northern trail continues 0.6 mile straight west from the junction to the Mesa Trail. This point is 0.1 mile south of Fern Canyon and 0.4
mile south of the place where the Mesa Trail leaves the dirt service road above
Bear Canyon.

The northern Shanahan Trail does not stop at the Mesa Trail. It continues
west for another quarter mile to the bottom of the huge Flatiron called the
Slab. The large meadow here is a nice destination for a stroll. From the base of
the Slab, the trail turns north, crosses Fern Canyon, and joins the Fern Canyon
Trail. This approach to Fern Canyon is shorter than the ones that use the dirt
service road in lower Bear Canyon.

Fern Canyon Trail

The Fern Canyon Trail begins from the Mesa Trail 200 yards south of the junction of the Mesa Trail and the Bear Canyon Trail. To reach this point, see the Bear
Canyon Trail description. The Fern Canyon Trail is 1.3 miles long and gains 2,100
vertical feet to its end on the summit of Bear Peak. This route up Bear Peak, while
steeper than the Bear Peak West Ridge Trail, is very scenic and enjoyable.

The Fern Canyon Trail first climbs southwest from the Mesa Trail along a
small shady draw. It then turns south and traverses across open meadows. Seal
Rock and the Goose are the large Flatirons to the west. The trail turns gradually
west to join the northern Shanahan Trail. It then enters Fern Canyon on the
north side of the canyon. The dramatic rock that guards the entrance to the
canyon is the southern Goose Egg. The Slab is across the canyon to the south.

The trail climbs steeply up Fern Canyon to reach the 7,400-foot saddle between the Nebel Horn and Bear Peak. This stretch of the trail is shaded and can be very icy in winter. The saddle has a spectacular view of Green Mountain across Bear Canyon. Above the saddle, the trail climbs steeply up the northeast ridge of Bear Peak for 1,000 vertical feet to the summit. There is a little Class 2+ scampering near the top. The view from the summit of Bear Peak is unobstructed in all directions.

Bear Peak West Ridge Trail

This trail is the easiest way to reach the summit of Bear Peak. It starts from the Bear Canyon Trail 1.55 miles up the Bear Canyon Trail from the Mesa Trail. The Bear Peak West Ridge Trail gains 1,300 feet from Bear Canyon to the summit of Bear Peak.

The trail climbs the slopes south of Bear Canyon to reach the northwest ridge of Bear Peak, which it follows southeast to the summit. The final quarter mile is across a steep talus field where the trail is faint. The summit ridge runs north-south at the top of the talus field. Scramble up and reach the summit ridge a few feet north of the highest point.

Shadow Canyon Trail

Shadow Canyon is the large southeast-facing canyon that separates the southeast ridges of Bear Peak and South Boulder Peak. You cannot see it from Boulder, but you can see it clearly from Colorado 93 a few miles south of Boulder. The Shadow Canyon Trail leaves the Mesa Trail in two different places, then these two trails join at the mouth of Shadow Canyon. The trail then climbs up Shadow Canyon to the 8,180-foot saddle between South Boulder Peak and Bear Peak. It is easy to reach the summits of both peaks from this saddle, and this trail is the easiest way to reach the summit of South Boulder Peak. It is 1.8 miles long and gains 2,000 vertical feet to the saddle.

Two branches of the Mesa Trail leave the dirt road in lower Shadow Canyon and head north on the east side of Bear Peak. When approaching from the Southern Mesa Trail Trailhead, stay south (left) at the two eastern forks with the Mesa Trail. Follow the dirt road west as it crosses to the south side of the creek, switchbacks once, is joined by the Old Mesa Trail coming from the south, then swings north into the mouth of upper Shadow Canyon. There is a cabin here and usually water is in the creek.

When approaching from the north, leave the Mesa Trail at an old watering trough, climb southwest, swing around the end of Bear Peak's southeast ridge and descend west to reach the mouth of Shadow Canyon. This stretch of trail is part of the original Mesa Trail.

A few feet east of the creek crossing in the mouth of Shadow Canyon, the trail heads northwest up the canyon. Once into upper Shadow Canyon, it is hard to get lost as the trail is never far from the bottom of the canyon. A half-mile up the canyon are some good views of Devils Thumb soaring high on the southeast ridge of Bear Peak. It is a "long" mile from the junction at the mouth of the canyon to the saddle, but the trail is never very steep. The saddle between South Boulder Peak and Bear Peak is the end of the Shadow Canyon Trail.

Northeast Slopes of South Boulder Peak

The Shadow Canyon Trail does not go all the way to the summit of South Boulder Peak, but an established trail does continue to the summit. From the saddle between South Boulder Peak and Bear Peak, hike southwest to a large talus field, climb up it and continue south to the summit. It is 0.3 mile and 380 vertical feet from the saddle to the 8,549-foot summit.

Southwest Slopes of Bear Peak

From the end of the Shadow Canyon Trail in the saddle between South Boulder Peak and Bear Peak, contour northeast, staying on the west side of Bear Peak's steep broken south ridge. Angle up across the talus field that is at the top of the Bear Peak West Ridge Trail and climb up to the summit ridge a few feet north of the summit. It is 0.4 mile and 300 vertical feet from the saddle to Bear Peak's 8,461-foot summit.

TWO

Gregory Amphitheater

Check for closures

Gregory Amphitheater is a delightful collection of pinnacles forming a natural amphitheater that opens to the south. The Amphitheater is only a five-minute hike from Boulder, and this proximity to town plus the large number of excellent climbs makes the Amphitheater one of the most popular climbing areas on the Flatirons. Approach by following the Amphitheater Trail for 300 yards to the south side of the Amphitheater. You can approach the outside of the Amphitheater by hiking up the Amphitheater Express Trail on the east and north-facing slopes above the Gregory Canyon Trailhead. This trail leaves the main trail 150 yards south of the bridge at the start of the Amphitheater Trail, and also climbs along the west side of the Amphitheater.

The Amphitheater offers a bewildering array of climbs that can be difficult to sort out on a first visit. Take some time to understand the various summits before charging forth. Three summits and two benches form the main Amphitheater. When walking into the Amphitheater from the south, the first small summit to the east is T-Zero. The west face of the East Bench (to the right), the south face of the First Pinnacle (straight ahead), the east face of the West Bench (to the left), and the east face of the Second Pinnacle (to the left) form the main part of the Amphitheater. You can hike from the inside of the Amphitheater to the top of the West Bench by hiking west on the Amphitheater Trail, then hiking north up under the west face of the Second Pinnacle on the Amphitheater Express Trail.

The Third and Fourth pinnacles are outside and west of the main Amphitheater. They are not as popular as the main Amphitheater, but they do have several good routes that can provide relief from the crowds on the standard routes. Finally, there is the Gregory Flatironette rising out of Gregory Canyon to a summit west of the Fourth Pinnacle. This is the highest summit in the Amphitheater area.

The longest climbs in the Amphitheater do not exceed 200 feet and you can top rope many of them. I do not record exact distances on these short routes. There are several fixed bolts in the Amphitheater, and opportunities for protection are good to excellent on most routes. Enjoy.

Amphitheater Overview

1 First Pinnacle
2 Third Pinnacle
3 Fourth Pinnacle

4 Saddle Rock
5 Gregory Flatironette
6 Gregory Canyon

21 T-ZERO

It all starts here. Between this humble rock and the famous summit T2 in Eldorado Canyon is a wonderland of Flatirons. A staggering amount of rock is here, a fact that becomes clearer as you try to climb them all. T-Zero is the small but distinct summit on the southeast side of the Amphitheater, south of the East Bench. It is the first rock to the east as you walk into the Amphitheater. Although it is only 50 feet high, it is steep and provides several short routes. I describe the routes on T-Zero counter clockwise (looking down from above), from inside to outside the Amphitheater.

Descent

21D Downclimb the North Ridge Route to a notch (Class 4), then either scramble east into a gully or west into the Amphitheater. There is a secure but often unseen hole on the summit of T-Zero that you can thread with a long sling. It is a few feet south of the highest point.

211 North Ridge Class 4

This is the shortest and easiest route to T-Zero's summit. Scramble up to a notch north of the summit, then climb up the 40-foot north ridge. The Class 4 crux is just below the top.

212 West Face 5.5 *Classic*

This is the most popular route on T-Zero. It is steep, clean and readily accessible from inside the Amphitheater. Climb 10 feet up a slightly overhanging finger crack, then overcome an overhang with a horn below it.

212 The West Face of T-Zero 5.5

213 South Ridge 5.3–5.4

This is the longest climb on T-Zero. Start a few feet north of the Amphitheater Trail just before it reaches the Amphitheater. Climb the lower part of the south ridge, pass a tree branch and climb a steep 5.3–5.4 wall to reach the top.

214 East Face 5.0–5.2

Ascend a crack on the east face that is a few feet north of the summit and reach the North Ridge Route a few feet below the summit.

Variation

214V Twenty feet below the summit, leave the crack, move south and climb directly to the summit (5.3–5.4).

22 EAST BENCH

The East Bench forms the west face of the inside of the Amphitheater. The routes on the East Bench are steep, varied and enjoyable, and are most often used to reach the upper routes to the top of the First Pinnacle. Not counting

22 East Bench   23 First Pinnacle

22 East Bench
221 East Bench Dihedral 5.2
23 First Pinnacle

variations, there are 30 ways to reach the top of the First Pinnacle via the East Bench. I describe the routes on the East Bench counter clockwise (looking down from above), from inside to outside the Amphitheater.

Descents

22D1 Downclimb the Inside West Face Route (Class 4).

22D2 Ten feet below the East Bench on its north side is a bolt at the top of the Northeast Chimney Route. Rappel 55 feet down the Northeast Chimney to reach the ground outside the Amphitheater.

221 East Bench Dihedral 5.2

This route ascends the dihedral formed by the west face of the East Bench and the south face of the First Pinnacle. A three-move bridging problem halfway up is the 5.2 crux, and the rest of the route is easier. Finish the route by climbing up the easy chimney between the East Bench and the First Pinnacle.

222 Inside West Face Class 4

This is the easiest route to the top of the East Bench. If you find the easiest line, the climbing is only Class 4, but the route is steep in places. Fifty feet downhill to the south from the back of the Amphitheater and the East Bench Dihedral is a 20-foot cave in the bottom of the face, which has a smoke blackened roof. Start this route 15 feet west (left) of this hole, near some poison ivy. Angle north up the face on easy rock. Fifteen feet before reaching the East Bench Dihedral, traverse south below a steep red wall. Angle back up to the north, get into the East Bench Dihedral above its 5.0–5.2 crux, and follow the easy chimney up to the East Bench.

Variations

222V1 Before the final traverse north to the upper part of the East Bench Dihedral, climb straight up a steep eight-foot wall with a finger crack in it (5.3–5.4). Ascend ten feet up a U-shaped scoop above the wall and climb a final 15-foot corner to reach the East Bench (5.0–5.2).

222V2 Before the final traverse north to the upper part of the East Bench Dihedral, traverse 10 feet south on a down-sloping 8-inch wide ledge to reach a small ridge (5.0–5.2). Climb north along this small elegant ridge to reach the East Bench (5.0–5.2).

223 Inside Southwest Face Class 4

This is a longer climb than the Inside West Face Route and is often done in two pitches. This route follows a line 25 feet southeast of the Inside West Face Route. Scramble to the notch between T-Zero and the East Bench. Climb north along a small Class 4 ridge to get onto the main southwest face of the East Bench. Angle north across steep but easy Class 4 rock and enter a large gully. You can see this gully from the ground and it has some holes at the back of it that are formed by several massive chockstones on top of the East Bench. Scramble up to the north end of the gully and worm up through the holes between the chockstones to reach the East Bench (Class 4).

Variations

223V1 Fifty feet downhill to the south from the back of the Amphitheater and the East Bench Dihedral Route is a 20-foot cave in the bottom of the face, which has a smoke blackened roof. A popular and more difficult start to the Inside Southwest Face Route begins 25 feet southeast (right) of the cave entrance. Climb straight up 15 feet of 5.3–5.4 rock to reach easier rock above.

223V2 From the large gully below the chockstones, climb the gully's short east-facing wall to reach a small steep ridge and follow it up to the East Bench (5.0–5.2). This is the same ridge that is the top part of Variation 2 with the Inside West Face Route.

223V3 From the large gully below the chockstones, climb up the gully's steep west face to reach the East Bench (5.3–5.4). Combining Variations 1 and 3 makes a steep direct 5.3–5.4 route to the East Bench.

224 Northeast Corner 5.0–5.2

This seldom-climbed route reaches the East Bench from outside the Amphitheater. A lower subsidiary summit is east of the East Bench. From the south side of this subsidiary summit, get into the south-facing gully between the sub summit and the east face of the East Bench. Ascend this gully to the

22 East Bench
221 East Bench
   Dihedral 5.2
222 Inside West Face
   Class 4
223 Inside Southwest
   Face Class 4

notch between the sub-summit and the East Bench (Class 4). Turn west (left) and ascend the 40-foot northeast corner of the East Bench (5.0–5.2). The hardest moves are on the east face near the top.

Variation

224V You can reach the notch between the sub-summit and the East Bench from the north. Fifteen feet east of the start of the Northeast Chimney, climb a slightly overhanging rotten red wall for 20 feet to reach the notch (5.0–5.2).

Extra Credit

224EC From the notch between the sub-summit and the East Bench, climb a short west face to the top of the sub-summit (Class 4). This summit has a good view of the east face of the First Pinnacle.

22 East Bench
23 First Pinnacle
225 Northeast
     Chimney 5.3
225V Divertissement
     5.7

225 Northeast Chimney 5.3

This chimney separates the East Bench from the First Pinnacle on the outside of the Amphitheater. Climb 65 feet up the chimney, passing three chockstones en route, to reach the East Bench. The first chockstone is the hardest (5.3) and squeezing up past the last chockstone can be difficult with a pack on. An eye-bolt is ten feet below the East Bench.

Variation
225V Divertissement 5.7

Above the first chockstone, traverse north (right) onto the steep east face of the First Pinnacle, climb straight up, and overcome an overhang (5.7) to reach the juniper tree on the upper part of this face.

23 FIRST PINNACLE

This summit forms the steep south face of the inside of the Amphitheater. It is most often climbed from the top of the East Bench.

22 East Bench
23 First Pinnacle
233 Southeast Face 5.4
234 Juniper Crack 5.5

235 Pizza Pie Crack 5.5
236 Northeast Corner 5.4
237 Upper West Ridge Class 4

Descents

23D1 Downclimb the West Ridge Route (Class 4).

23D2 From the summit eyebolt, rappel 110 feet east to reach the ground outside the Amphitheater.

23D3 From the summit eyebolt, rappel 45 feet southeast to the East Bench or 55 feet to the eyebolt at the top of the Northeast Chimney Route. Follow one of the descents from the East Bench.

The following routes start on the East Bench. I describe them in a sequence from left to right as viewed from the top of the East Bench.

231 Upper South Face 5.4

From the top of the chimney between the East Bench and the First Pinnacle, get onto the south face of the First Pinnacle and traverse 12 feet west (left). Climb up a small curious dihedral to the summit area.

232 McCrumm's Crack 5.4

This time-tested crack is 5 feet west of the southeast corner of the First Pinnacle. Either reach the lower part of the crack from the chimney between the East Bench and the First Pinnacle, or step across the top of the chimney to a 5-foot block, climb to the top of this block, and step west (left) into the crack. The route angles up slightly west (left) and the hardest moves are right below the top.

233 Southeast Face 5.4 *Classic*

With the addition of a bolt, this route has evolved as the most popular and easiest way to get from the East Bench to the summit of the First Pinnacle. Step across the top of the chimney between the East Bench and the First pinnacle and get on top of a 5-foot block (5.2). Climb 30 feet up a shallow scoop with a bolt halfway up and arrive at the summit by the eyebolt (5.4).

234 Juniper Crack 5.5

Step across the top of the chimney between the East Bench and the First Pinnacle, then traverse 12 feet north to a point below a juniper tree (5.2).

Climb south (left) of the juniper tree and ascend a 5-foot crack above the tree (5.3). When the crack ends, make the crux 5.5 move up a smooth slab to reach the summit.

235 Pizza Pie Crack 5.5

Step across the top of the chimney between the East Bench and the First Pinnacle, then traverse 12 feet north to a point below a famous juniper tree (5.2). Stay below the tree and continue north for 8 more feet. Climb up past a flake, make the crux 5.5 move up the crack above the flake, and continue up easier rock to the summit.

236 Northeast Corner 5.4

This route is 3 feet north of Pizza Pie Crack. Step across the top of the chimney between the East Bench and the First Pinnacle, then traverse 12 feet north to a point below a very famous juniper tree (5.2). Stay below the tree and continue north for 10 more feet to the northeast corner. Climb up the east face of the corner to the top (5.4).

237 West Ridge Class 4

This is the easiest way to reach the top of the First Pinnacle, and it is often used as a descent route. The start of the route is on top of the West Bench, at the southwest corner of a small west face below a large block. This point is in hiking territory. Climb up the west face on large holds (Class 4), pass south of the large block (exposed Class 4) and continue east to the highest summit with the eyebolt.

Variation

237V Climb around the large block on its north side (exposed 5.0–5.2).

Extra Credit

237EC Climb to the top of the large block from the east (Class 4).

24 WEST BENCH

The West Bench is the broad saddle between the First and Second Pinnacles. A 100-foot east face is on the inside of the Amphitheater that leads to the West Bench and someone must have climbed every inch of this face. An eyebolt is

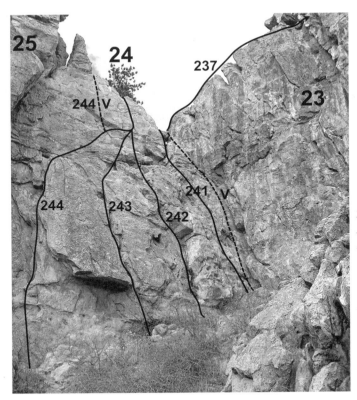

23 First Pinnacle
24 West Bench
25 Second Pinnacle
237 West Ridge
      Class 4
241 West Bench
      Dihedral 5.0–5.2
241V 5.4
242 Direct West
      Bench 5.6
243 The Slot 5.6
244 The Inset 5.6
244V 5.7

on top of a large boulder a few feet west of the West Bench, other anchor possibilities are plentiful and the face below the West Bench is popular for top roping. You can hike to the West Bench from the west on the Amphitheater Express Trail. The following routes are all on the east face of the West Bench and I describe them in a sequence from north to south.

241 West Bench Dihedral 5.0–5.2

This is the easiest climbing route to the West Bench and it is often used as a descent route. Start 5 feet south of the dihedral between the West Bench and the First Pinnacle, and climb cracks south of the dihedral. The easiest line may be difficult to find on a first encounter with this route, especially if downclimbing.

Variation

241V Climb directly up the dihedral (5.4).

242 Direct West Bench 5.6

This petite test piece ascends a delicious line up the east face of the West Bench. Start 15 feet south of the dihedral between the West Bench and the First Pinnacle. Climb 20 feet up steep rock past some reassuring handholds to a small left-angling dihedral (5.4). Climb 10 feet up the dihedral using a combination of holds above and below it (5.6). From the top of the dihedral, step north (right), climb straight up and reach the West Bench by climbing up a thin finger crack (5.6).

243 The Slot 5.6 *Classic*

This popular route ascends a direct line up the middle of the east face of the West Bench. Start 22 feet south of the dihedral between the West Bench and the First Pinnacle below a sharp-edged roof 10 feet above the ground. Climb a foot-wide crack on the north edge of the roof, continue up over an awkward bulge, angle north (right) and reach the West Bench by climbing up the well-used finger crack at the top of the Direct West Bench Route.

244 The Inset 5.6

Start 40 feet south of the dihedral between the West Bench and the First Pinnacle. This point is below a 20-foot wide inset on the lower part of the face a few feet south of a sharp edged roof 10 feet above the ground. Climb up the north side of the inset, climb above the inset to a ledge, angle north (right) and reach the West Bench by climbing up a now famous finger crack.

Variation

244V From the ledge above the inset, climb directly up another thin 5.7 crack.

25 SECOND PINNACLE

This striking summit forms the upper east face of the inside of the Amphitheater. A little higher than the First Pinnacle, it provides the longest climbs in the Amphitheater. The routes on this popular rock are all excellent. I describe the routes in a clockwise sequence looking down from above, from the inside to the outside of the Amphitheater.

25 Second Pinnacle
251 East Face 5.7
251V1 5.7
251V2 Approach from
    West Bench

Descents

25D1 A fixed eyebolt is on the summit. Rappel 75 feet northwest to reach the ground not far from the West Bench.

25D2 From the summit eyebolt, rappel 62 feet west down the Northwest Corner Route.

25D3 Downclimb the Northwest Corner Route (5.1).

25D4 From the summit eyebolt, rappel 160 spectacular feet east to reach the inside of the Amphitheater.

251 East Face 5.7

This is a wonderful climb on the steep east face of the Second Pinnacle. It is 180 feet long and is commonly done in three short pitches. Start 15 feet north of a large tree near the bottom of the east face. This point is 40 feet downhill to the south from the start of the Inset Route on the West Bench.

Do a nifty hand traverse south, then climb up a crack behind a block to reach a comfortable ledge between the large tree and the face above. It is convenient to belay on this ledge. The original route climbed directly up from the ledge but a branch of the tree, which has grown considerably since the route was first done, now touches the rock here and makes this direct ascent more difficult. Climb up a delicate 5.7 slab south of the branch and reach easier rock above. Angle up to the north, then traverse straight north to reach a secure stance below a vertical north-facing red dihedral (5.3–5.4). From the stance below the red dihedral, angle up to the south of the dihedral, then climb straight up steep exposed rock to the summit of the Second Pinnacle (5.6). This is the most dramatic finish in the Amphitheater and it would be a good one in any domain.

Variations

251V1 You can do a more difficult finish by climbing directly up the vertical north-facing red dihedral (5.7).

251V2 You can enjoy the upper part of this route by traversing onto the east face from the top of the West Bench. From the top of the West Bench, down-climb east, get onto a ledge and follow it south to the stance below the red dihedral.

252 South Face 5.2 *Classic*

This is the longest and finest 5.2 climb in or near the Amphitheater. The climb is steep, clean, and you can do it in two or three pitches. The bottom of the South Face Route is only a few feet north of the Amphitheater Trail and is just outside the Amphitheater proper. The bottom of the route has a 20-foot slab below a 3-foot wide chimney. A 15-foot wide bowl is a few feet farther west.

Climb up the 20-foot 5.2 slab and ascend the unique 3-foot wide 5.2 chimney above. Continue 30 feet up some easier rock to the bottom of the steep upper face. Climb this upper face near its eastern edge. It offers several opportunities to peer east down into the Amphitheater. The lower section of this face is broken and provides steep, enjoyable Class 4 climbing. Higher, ascend 20 feet up a south-facing 5.2 slot that ends below the final steep headwall. Traverse 10 feet west (left) (5.0–5.2) and climb straight up to the summit (5.0–5.2).

Variation

252V You can start the South Face Route by climbing up the 15-foot wide bowl a few feet west of the initial 3-foot wide chimney. Climb up into the bowl, traverse south near its top, and climb back east above the bowl to reach the steep upper face (Class 4).

253 Southwest Face Class 4

This route provides an easy tour up the steep southwest face of the Second Pinnacle. Thirty feet west of a 15-foot wide bowl at the bottom of the south face is another bowl with two chockstones wedged above it. Scramble up for 20 feet under the chockstones and climb a wide Class 4 slot for 20 feet to an eyebolt. Continue straight north from the eyebolt on easy rock and climb a short Class 4 wall just below a tree. Scramble 100 feet up the broad easy gully above the tree (Class 3) and join the Northwest Corner Route in a notch 30 feet west of the summit. Climb the last 30 feet to the summit on the steep west face (Class 4).

Variation

253V You can start this route by climbing the 15-foot wide bowl 30 feet east of the initial bowl with the chockstones above it. Climb up into the 15-foot wide bowl, traverse south near its top and angle northwest up to reach the Class 4 wall below the tree (Class 4).

254 Second Pinnacle
Northwest Corner 5.1

254 Northwest Corner 5.1

This is the shortest route to the summit of the Second Pinnacle. It is commonly used as a descent route. Start the route 50 feet southwest of the West Bench. The 75-foot route ascends an obvious crack system on the northwest side of the pinnacle. The first move is the 5.1 crux and the rest of the climb is Class 4. The route reaches the summit a few feet north of the highest point and the summit bolt.

Variation

254V Shortcut 5.4

Like many shortcuts, this one is longer and harder. Halfway between the Amphitheater Trail and the start of the Northwest Corner Route, climb east up a short steep 5.4 wall with good holds to the ramp on the upper part of the Southwest Face Route. Scramble north up this Class 3 ramp to the notch 30 feet west of the summit and join the Northwest Corner Route.

Extra Credit

254EC Ginseng Pillar Class 4

Halfway up, the route passes a notch between the main summit and a lower summit to the west called Ginseng Pillar. From the notch, climb an amusing 15-foot east face to the top of Ginseng Pillar (Class 4), then climb back down into the notch.

255 North Face 5.6

This route climbs the short steep north face of the Second Pinnacle. Start from the south end of the West Bench and stem up the obvious but tricky groove. This route is easily top roped.

26 THIRD PINNACLE

This broken slab is outside and west of the Amphitheater. The rock has many small bushes on it, but it has a dramatic summit pinnacle. This summit is higher than the Second Pinnacle.

Descent

26D Downclimb the east face of the summit pinnacle (5.3), then scramble north and west to the ground.

26 The Summit block of
    the Third Pinnacle from
    the south
261V2 5.7

261 Halls of Ivy 5.3

This route ascends the central part of the east face below the summit pinnacle. A south-facing dihedral separates the central and northern parts of the east face. Climb up the broken Class 4 face south of this dihedral to a bench that is north of the summit pinnacle. Traverse south and climb 15 feet up the beautiful fist-sized crack on the east face of the summit pinnacle to the top (5.3).

Variations

261V1 Climb the northern part of the east face to reach the bench north of the summit pinnacle (5.0–5.2). This section of the east face has a nasty overhang 30 feet up that you can climb on its north end near a tree (5.0–5.2). Continue up an interesting 5.0–5.2 crack above the overhang, pass another tree, and continue up the Class 4 face above to reach the bench.

261V2 For more excitement hike around to the west side of the dramatic summit pinnacle and climb an overhanging 5.7 crack to the top.

26 Third Pinnacle
27 Fourth Pinnacle
261 Halls of Ivy 5.3
261V 5.0–5.2
262 South Ridge 5.6

262 South Ridge 5.6

This 300-foot route ascends a south-facing ridge that starts a few feet north of the Amphitheater Trail and connects with the west side of the Third Pinnacle. The 5.6 climbing is in the first 80 feet, with the rest of the route being much easier. Start at the low point, make a 5.6 move to get onto the smooth face, and climb this tricky southeast face for 30 feet (5.5). The rock above is steep and the next 50 feet require thoughtful 5.3–5.4 climbing. The ridge above is much easier. Scramble north to a small summit and do an awkward exposed downclimb off its northwest corner via a horn (5.0–5.2). Cross a delectably exposed stretch of ridge and continue scrambling north to hiking territory on the west side of the Third Pinnacle. If you are possessed with summit fever, scramble around to the east face of the final summit block and climb up a beautiful 15-foot fist sized crack to the tippy top (5.3).

27 Fourth Pinnacle
271 East Face 5.6 S
272 Halls of Poison Ivy
5.0–5.2

27 FOURTH PINNACLE

This pinnacle is 150 feet west of and higher than the summit of the Third Pinnacle. The lower part of the east face is steep and has several small overhangs on it. The upper part of the east face has a large gully above a steep headwall. This rock provides some offbeat routes that see very little traffic compared to the more popular routes in the Amphitheater proper.

Descent

27D A few feet north of the summit is a large crack. Climb 45 feet west down this crack system to reach the ground (steep Class 4).

271 East Face 5.6 S

This exciting route ascends the tricky lower part of the east face and gets into the large gully on the upper part of the face. The route's crux is getting up into the gully. This problem apparently attracted aid climbers long ago as there are three bolts on the steep south-facing wall below the gully. The free route starts at the bottom of the main part of the east face and ascends the slab near the south side of the face. The rock gets steeper and more difficult as you approach the gully. Sneak up a tricky 20-foot section that finishes on the water polished rock below the gully (5.6). Once on top of the difficulties you can look down on the old bolt ladder.

The first 20 feet of the gully are 5.3–5.4 but the difficulty eases to Class 4 farther up. An overhang caps the upper end of the gully so your climb is not yet over. Climb up to the overhang and climb onto the east face south of the gully near a bush (5.0–5.2). Get past the bush and romp to the top (Class 4).

272 Halls of Poison Ivy 5.0–5.2

In addition to having an exciting patch of poison ivy on a ledge part way up, this crafty route ascends a ramp system south of the main part of the east face. Start 30 feet south of the start of the East Face Route and climb up slabs under an overhang (Class 4). Angle 20 feet south to reach the ledge with the poison ivy on it (5.0–5.2). You can avoid the ivy by doing a devious climb to the south. Above the ivy ledge, ascend an interesting 5.0–5.2 crack on the east face of a now well-formed south-facing dihedral. From the top of this crack, scramble back east to reach the summit.

28 GREGORY FLATIRONETTE

This rib is 200 yards west of the Amphitheater and you can easily see it from Baseline Road. This rib is continuous from Gregory Canyon to the Amphitheater Trail and it has a spectacular summit. The rib sees very little traffic, which is surprising considering its proximity to the popular Amphitheater. From the summit of this rock you will be ruler of the Amphitheater as this is the highest summit in the Amphitheater area.

To approach the North Ridge Route, start up the Saddle Rock Trail. Leave the trail before it swings to the west side of the Gregory Flatironette and hike up to the low point of the rock. To approach the South Ridge Route, follow the Amphitheater Trail west for 200 yards from the Amphitheater. The south ridge is the last rib of rock the trail passes before it turns southwest.

Descents

28D1 Climb down the north side of the summit block, scramble 100 feet south and escape to the southwest through the southernmost of two fat-man frenzy holes (Class 4).

28 Gregory Flatironette
281 North Ridge 5.0–5.2

28D2 Climb down the north side of the summit block, scramble 100 feet north and escape to the east (Class 4).

281 North Ridge 5.0–5.2

This surprisingly long climb starts at the lowest point of a scruffy ridge below the main piece of rock. Scramble 100 feet along this ridge, and without leaving the rock get onto the main east face. The path of least resistance from here consists of a series of traverses to the south (left) interspersed with blasts upwards at appropriate points. After 300 feet of this, you will reach the upper end of the main Flatironette, but don't stop here. Continue scrambling along the now much easier rib for several hundred feet to a surprisingly exposed summit. This is the highest summit in the Amphitheater area, and it overlooks the junction of the Saddle Rock and Amphitheater Trails.

282 South Ridge Class 4

This 300-foot ridge is more of a mountaineering experience than a rock climb. Get onto the low point of the southern end of the rib, which is only 2 feet north of the Amphitheater Trail. Scramble up and climb a little Class 4 headwall. Scramble north (Class 3) and climb a clean 50-foot Class 4 headwall that is the crux of the route. Scramble up to the north, do a short downclimb en route, and reach the pinpoint summit.

29 SADDLE ROCK

Saddle Rock is the distinctively shaped rock on the skyline north of Green Mountain. It is halfway between Gregory Canyon and the summit of Green Mountain. Saddle Rock is made of granite and is the only granite rock included in this guide. The north-south canyon east of Saddle Rock is called Contact Canyon, and it marks the contact line between the sandstone Flatirons and the granite rocks farther west. Contact Canyon is west of the Gregory Flatironette.

Saddle Rock is made up of two summits with the namesake saddle in between. The lower, northern summit is the richer of the two. Approach via the Saddle Rock Trail, which reaches a ridge 200 yards north of Saddle Rock.

29 Saddle Rock

Hike north from the trail to a point overlooking the broken south side of Saddle Rock. From this point, scramble down to the west, then hike north to reach the south side of Saddle Rock. The higher southern summit is an easy scramble from the south. The easiest way to reach the saddle is to hike north below the southern summit, then hike up into the saddle from the west. You can also reach the saddle by traversing a ledge on the east side of the southern summit. From the saddle, you can easily reach the northern summit on a large ledge east of the summit block. The low point of the rock is on the north side of the northern summit and you can easily reach it by hiking down to the north on the west side of the rock.

The visual appearance of Saddle Rock is more exciting than its climbs. This strange rock is broken and friable, and while there are many places where you can climb upwards, Saddle Rock offers very little worthwhile climbing. I describe routes that capture Saddle Rock's best offerings.

Descents

29D1 From the northern summit, scramble down to the south into the saddle between the two summits. Hike down to the west, then up to the south staying west of the southern summit. Stay west of another broken cliff area and reach the Saddle Rock Trail.

29D2 From the southern summit, scramble down to the south. Hike up to the south, stay west of a broken cliff area and reach the Saddle Rock Trail.

291 Northeast Face 5.0–5.2

The most coherent part of Saddle Rock is the northeast face of the northern summit. Scramble up a scruffy area and find the 1-foot high painted letters "JERSEY" on the bottom of this face. Scramble up a gully north of the letters to a small notch near a prominent tree on the north side of Saddle Rock. Angle 60 feet southwest (right) across a nice 5.0–5.2 slab and reach the North Ridge Route above its crux. Romp up to the northern summit.

292 North Ridge Class 4

This 260-foot route is the longest climb on Saddle Rock. This route's redeeming feature is the great view of the high peaks to the west. Start at the northwest corner of the northern summit and climb the wide blocky ridge for 120 feet to a ledge below some steeper rock. Continue up the steeper but still easy rock and pass the Class 4 crux, which is 40 feet above the ledge. Romp up to the northern summit.

293 West Face 5.7

Start at the bottom of the West Dihedral and climb 60 feet up the steep 5.0–5.2 wall north (left) of the dihedral to a ledge below a vertical section. Climb up the vertical section (5.7) and continue up 5.0–5.2 rock to the summit ridge.

Variation

293V You can escape below the vertical section by traversing north on a ledge behind a flake to reach the north ridge below its steep upper portion.

294 West Dihedral Class 4

In the middle of the northern summit's west face is a broken 200-foot high dihedral system directly below the summit. With a little route finding, this dihedral provides a Class 4 climb that is the easiest route on the west face of the northern summit. Start up the dihedral, and after 50 feet, angle south (right) to a broken ridge. This maneuver avoids a vertical step in the dihedral. If you climb up under the vertical step, then traverse south and make a few 5.0–5.2 moves to reach the ridge. In the upper part of the dihedral, angle north (left), follow the main dihedral system, and reach the summit ridge 30 feet north of the summit. Some loose rock is in the upper part of the dihedral.

Variation

294V Instead of angling back to the north and climbing the upper part of the main dihedral, continue straight up a smaller dihedral (Class 4) and climb a steep exciting 5.3 finish directly to the highest point. You can avoid the steep finish at the last second by traversing north to easier rock.

295 Southern Summit North Face 5.0–5.2

From the namesake saddle between the two summits, climb an 80-foot 5.0–5.2 pitch west of a smooth slab on the southern summit's north face.

Variation

295V East of the smooth slab on the north face is a left angling groove. Make a few awkward 5.5 moves to get up into the groove, climb it (Class 4), and reach the summit from the east.

THREE

First Flatiron

31 FIRST FLATIRON

This is the northernmost of the three great Flatirons above Boulder. The First Flatiron is a huge rock, and the routes on it are some of the longest on the Flatirons; they are excellent and justifiably popular. Because of their position, the North Arête and summit of the First yield spectacular views of the high peaks to the northwest. The exposed position and wonderful view provide an alpine setting that sets the First apart from the other Flatirons.

The summit of the First is quite a bit south of the low point of the Flatiron. Because of this, most routes on the east face end up on the North Arête and follow it to the summit. This is fortunate in that the joys of the North Arête can be savored after a variety of starts. The First is a difficult Flatiron to escape from. This plus the size of the rock make it a serious undertaking. Most escapes are best accomplished by executing a forward retreat, and I describe several variations that can aid this process. Remember that the summit of the First can be a very exciting and dangerous place during an electrical storm.

A route junction knob 600 feet above the Flatiron's low point is where three of the major routes converge. This knob is 200 feet below the North Arête. The North Arête route is described first followed by the lower face routes.

Approach the First Flatiron by following the Chautauqua Trail from the Kinnikinic Trailhead. This trail intersects the Bluebell Baird Trail 20 feet north of a good trail leading 300 yards west to the low point of the First Flatiron. You will see the low point of the First Flatironette on the north (right) side of a gully, 200 feet before you reach the bottom of the First.

Descents

31D1 From a fixed eyebolt on the summit, rappel 100 feet west to the ground.

31D2 Rappel 25 feet west to a large but exposed ledge, then either continue rappelling, or downclimb 30 feet south to a second eyebolt. From the second eyebolt, rappel 60 feet south to the ground.

THREE | FIRST FLATIRON

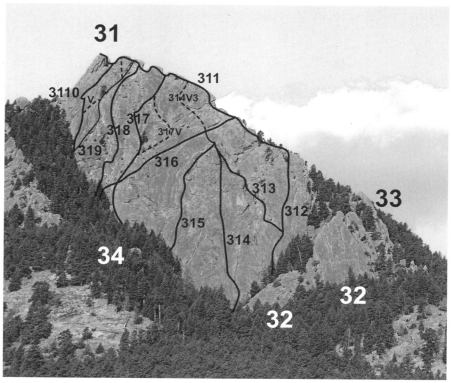

31 First Flatiron
32 First Flatironette
33 The Spy
34 Macbeth
311 North Arête 5.4

312 East Face North Side 5.2
313 East Face Gully 5.5
314 East Face Center 5.6 S
315 Butterfly 5.7 S
316 Baker's Way 5.4

317 Fandango 5.5
318 Zigzag 5.7
319 Atlanta 5.4
3110 Hubris 5.4

31D3 Downclimb the Southwest Face Route (5.2). This is a tricky exposed downclimb, and the easiest route is difficult to find, especially on the lower part of the face. To do it, downclimb 25 feet west to a large ledge (exposed Class 4). Descend south down ramps and ledges to an eyebolt. Continue southeast down ramps, and reach the ground by an old tree near the rock (5.2).

311 North Arête 5.4 *Classic*

This route is one of the finest Flatiron classics, and anyone who enjoys moving over rock should climb it. On the ridge, you can climb to the music of the high

31 First Flatiron
311 North Arête 5.4

316 Baker's Way
314V3 5.5–5.6

peaks to the northwest, and a yodel seems to carry forever. The 5.4 rating refers to one short crux with most of the climbing being much easier. The 650-foot long Arête breaks naturally into six moderate length pitches.

You can enjoy the North Arête without climbing the lower face. The easiest approach to the start of the North Arête is to follow the Saddle Rock Trail for 200 yards past its upper junction with the Amphitheater Trail, then angle up the slope to the southeast to reach the northwest side of the Flatiron. If your hiking approach starts near the low point of the First, stay east of the First Flatironette as the gully between the First and the First Flatironette is not a hiking route. Hike up along the northwest side of the Flatiron until the west face begins to overhang. The start of the route is the highest place where it is easy to get onto the ridge.

Climb easily onto the ridge from the west, make a 5.0–5.2 move over a step, follow the ridge above and reach a secure stance after 80 feet. Easy Class 4 climbing leads up along the ridge for 100 feet to a secure stance below the second step, which you can see overhead. Just like the more famous North Ridge of Everest, the second step poses a more serious problem than the first step. It is the hardest move of the route and it is 5.4. A wonderful handhold is tantalizingly out of reach above the edge of the step.

Beyond the second step, climb 200 feet of amiable 5.0–5.2 and Class 4 rock to the quartz knob pitch, which has the final 5.0–5.2 moves of the route. A unique quartz knob with a flat top lives where it is most needed. This quartz knob is standing the test of time well. Beyond the quartz knob headwall is a final headwall, the east face of which is Class 4 on its south side and 5.0–5.2 on its north side. Climbing is easy to the false summit. From the false summit, descend south into a notch and climb a northeast-facing ramp to the true summit.

Variation

311V From the bottom of the final northeast-facing ramp below the summit, climb directly up the north face of the summit block via an awkward 5.6 slot.

312 East Face North Side; to bottom of North Arête 5.2; including North Arête 5.4

This 700-foot five-pitch climb is north of the major gully below the bottom of the North Arête. Although graded a little easier than the North Arête, this route is more consistent in its difficulty. You can walk off from the top of this section of the face, so you can do this route by itself or combine it with the North Arête.

The standard start for the north side of the east face is 120 feet uphill to the north from the low point of the Flatiron. Start just above a south-facing dihedral/overhang that bars easy access onto the face. Look for a 4-foot, horizontal horn that is 10 feet out onto the face. You can also get onto (or escape) the face 130 feet farther up the gully to the north by climbing a tree next to the rock. I don't recommend this start, since the poor tree is already worn out and would not appreciate the extra traffic.

Start even with the horn, make a few delicate 5.2 moves south to get to it, then angle up to the north (right) on Class 4 rock to a ledge above the escape tree. The second pitch continues straight up to a good ledge (5.0–5.2) that angles up to the southwest (left) and provides access into the large gully. Cross this ledge, stay north (right) of the large gully and continue straight up for three more first-class pitches to the ridge. Either walk off the rock at this point, or hike 150 feet uphill to the south to the start of the North Arête and follow it on to the summit.

313 East Face Gully 5.5

The great gully that splits the east face of the First has attracted climbers for years. You must cross it to climb from the easier rock on the north side of the east face to the route junction knob and North Arête, both of which are south of the gully. The gully is not very hospitable, and like most gullies, rock fall can be a problem. Snow clings to it long after the rest of the face is dry and the rock is polished and smooth. This route provides a different kind of Flatiron challenge.

Follow the East Face Right Side route for two pitches, then angle 75 feet up to the southwest (left) along an obvious crack to the north side of the gully. It is two long pitches or three shorter pitches from this point to the route junction knob.

Above the entrance point to the gully is a tricky stretch of Flatiron rock. The easiest way to do it is to stay on the north (right) side of the gully, using holds on the gully's north wall until you reach easier rock (5.4). You can also make a 5.5–5.6 friction move to the south (left) into the center of the gully, then head straight up. Either way, continue up the 15-foot wide gully and reach some rubble-strewn ledges where the gully starts to widen into its large upper section.

Above these ledges, stay on the south (left) side of the gully and climb 100 feet up polished rock (5.4). Rock scars here indicate that when rocks do come down the gully, they ricochet off this section. Also, this is exactly where snow lingers. Above this section, look sharp for the exit from the gully, which is to the south (left).

Escape the gully by climbing a short steep wall up into a slot (5.0–5.2). Although steep, this exit has good holds and is the best way to escape the gully to the south. Many parties have continued past this exit hoping for a better exit higher up, but this choice leads into more difficult climbing.

From the top of the easy escape slot, climb 100 feet up to the route junction knob (Class 4). For the easiest route from this knob to the North Arête, climb 200 feet straight up and join the North Arête below its 5.4 crux. Follow the North Arête to the summit.

Variations

313V1 From the entrance to the gully below the tricky section, you can avoid the gully and stay on the face to the north (right) of the gully (5.0–5.2).

313V2 Before exiting the gully to the south, you should consider the problems of escaping from the center of this huge face, and this variation may come in handy when executing a forward retreat. Part way up the polished section along the south (left) side of the gully, an easy ledge system leads diagonally across the gully to its north side. This ledge system is 40 feet below the south side exit wall. Follow this ledge system for 50 feet across the gully, then climb 20 feet up the north (right) side of the gully to a spot where it is easy to escape the gully to the north. Follow the final 80 feet of the East Face North Side

Route to the place where you can walk off to the west. This escape is the easiest way out of the gully, and if you find the easiest route, it is Class 4.

313V3 From the route junction knob, angle 200 feet up to the south (left), then climb 30 feet up a weird but fun flake-gully combo (5.5–5.6). Continue 100 feet up the gully above the combo (5.3–5.4) and join the North Arête above its 5.4 crux. If you are quick and the Arête above is jammed with people, this shortcut can be used to pass people!

314 East Face Center 5.6 S *Classic – Top Ten*

This climb is a Flatiron classic of the First magnitude. The route's commitment to the center of this great face is unrelenting for the first six pitches. It is 12 pitches from the low point of the face to the summit, making this one of the longest climbs above Boulder. The most difficult and committing pitch is the first one, with the route gradually tapering off in difficulty above.

Start at the low point of the face, angle up slightly to the north (right) and follow a vague rib just north of a shallow gully (5.6). After 80 feet, angle left up an incipient crack across the gully. Finish the pitch on the south side of the gully at a large slingable flake. This 125-foot pitch is consistent 5.5–5.6 and except for a bolt, protection is difficult.

Start the second pitch by moving a few feet south (left), then climb 100 feet straight up to a ledge with a tree (5.3–5.4). On the third 130-foot pitch, angle left (5.0–5.2) then climb straight up (5.3–5.4). On the fourth and fifth pitches, engage the imposing steeper rock in the center of the Flatiron. This rock is easier than it looks and these two 5.0–5.2 pitches are full of yodeling moves.

The sixth pitch is also 5.0–5.2 and takes you to the route junction knob where this route joins Baker's Way coming in from the south and the East Face Gully Route coming in from the north. Above the knob, climb 200 feet straight up to join the North Arête below its 5.4 crux and follow that route to the summit.

Variations

314V1 If you start north of the low point of the face, the natural lines tend to diverge from the East Face Center route and join the East Face Gully Route.

314V2 If you start south of the low point of the face, you will end up in a gully that angles back north to join the East Face Center Route near the top of its third pitch. This gully starts near the top of the Witch's Cabin, a huge block resting against the south side of the Flatiron 200 feet above its low point. This is a considerably easier alternative to the first three pitches of the East Face Center Route.

314V3 From the route junction knob, angle 200 feet south (left), then climb 30 feet up a weird but fun flake-gully combo (5.5–5.6). Continue 100 feet up the gully above the combo (5.3–5.4) and join the North Arête above its 5.4 crux. If the ridge above is jammed with people and you are quick, you can use this shortcut to pass people!

Escapes

314E1 It is difficult to escape from the middle of the First Flatiron. From the vicinity of the route junction knob, the first choice is to descend Baker's Way. Baker's Way is the small gully that actually forms the route junction knob and separates it from the rest of the Flatiron. This gully drops into steep rock to the south and east of the route junction knob. The Baker's Way ledge angles across the face 75 feet above the route junction knob. Climb south down this ledge system and rappel 50 feet south from a tree to reach the ground.

314E2 From the route junction knob, your second escape choice is to climb up to the North Arête and either downclimb the first pitch of that route (5.0–5.2) or rappel 60 feet west to the ground. The large gully below the bottom of the North Arête prevents easy escape from the route junction knob to the walkoff point at the top of the north side of the east face.

315 Butterfly 5.7 S

This devious route is seldom climbed. It offers three pitches of harder than average Flatiron before reaching the route junction knob. The start of the route is on the south side of the Flatiron, 40 feet west of the top of the Witch's Cabin, which is a huge block resting against the south side of the Flatiron 200 feet above its low point. Start up a small gully and after 40 feet, leave the gully and get onto the face south of the gully. Continue straight up across a checkerboard pattern and belay below the steep rock above. Overcome the crux overhang above (5.7) and continue up on tricky rock. Pass a tree and angle up to the north (right) to reach the route junction knob. See the East Face Center Route for routes beyond this point.

Variation

315V An alternate start for Butterfly is 350 feet above the low point of the Flatiron, 120 feet above the top of the Witch's Cabin. Start south of a broken south-facing dihedral system, which is the first significant south-facing dihedral system encountered when hiking up along the south side of the Flatiron. Climb east-facing slabs south of the dihedral system, then angle up to the north (right) where the dihedral system is broken into a series of shorter steps

(5.3–5.4). Work up to the north and join the regular route below the crux 5.7 overhang.

316 Baker's Way 5.4 *Classic*

This beautiful time-tested climb is the easiest summit route on the east face of the First. The route follows a ledge system that goes diagonally up to the north from half way up the south side of the Flatiron to a point just above the start of the North Arête. The 5.4 rating refers to the crux on the North Arête. Baker's Way starts with a few moves of 5.0–5.2, and the rest of the route below the North Arête is Class 4. It is 400 feet across the face to the North Arête.

To approach Baker's Way from the bottom of the First, continue up on the access trail around the south side of the Witch's Cabin, scamper up a short rocky section on the trail and continue up some switchbacks south of the Flatiron. Don't be lured onto the rock too soon. It is several hundred feet from the top of the Witch's Cabin to Baker's Way. The trail comes within a few feet of the start of Baker's Way, which is below a steep 40-foot wall with two trees above it.

Climb the 40-foot wall to the two trees (5.0–5.2). This wall is the crux of Baker's Way and the rest of the climbing to the North Arête is much easier. A bewildering array of possibilities is above the two trees. Fandango continues straight up and Baker's Way is to the north (right). Seventy feet north of the two trees, overcome a 5-foot southwest-facing wall, and follow the now obvious ledge system up to the north. Pass 75 feet above the route junction knob, a raised knob in the center of the face, and join the North Arête below its 5.4 crux. Follow the North Arête on to the summit.

317 Fandango 5.5

This fun 1,000-foot route offers a direct line on the complicated south side of the First. The route I describe is different in its middle portion from the Fandango route that has been described in other guides, since I believe that my route provides a cleaner, more amenable way across this part of the face. I describe the original Fandango route as Variation 1. A word of caution: The crux of my Fandango route can be difficult for people shorter than 5 feet 8 inches tall.

Start 200 feet below the start of Baker's Way, below a 50-foot wide slab south of a south-facing dihedral system. This is the second south-facing dihedral system that you encounter when hiking up along the south side of the First.

Climb 200 feet up the slab south of the dihedral to some trees (Class 4). These are the trees above the initial wall of Baker's Way. Cross Baker's Way at the trees and climb 165 feet up the slabs above, angling slightly north to reach some blocks just beyond two large trees (Class 4). These are the largest of several trees on this section of the face and you can easily see them from the first 150 feet of Baker's Way. When viewing the First from Bluebell Shelter, these trees appear to be near the center of the east face.

Above the large trees, climb 140 feet up the slab above (5.0–5.2). This slab is south of a new, 8-foot high, south-facing dihedral. This slab and the pitch end where this dihedral joins the Zigzag dihedral to the south. This is a spectacular stance. Climb the 8-foot high, south-facing wall of the dihedral (5.5). This wall is the crux of the route and is best accomplished by traversing east across the wall on some chin-up bar holds. It is easier for tall people to reach these holds from the slab below.

Above the crux wall, angle 70 feet up to the north to a crack on the face south of yet another south-facing dihedral system (5.0–5.2). Follow the mellow crack up this beautiful dihedral for 140 feet to the North Arête (Class 4). You will reach the North Arête at the notch below its quartz knob pitch. Continue 300 feet along the North Arête to the summit.

Variations

317V1 This is the original Fandango route. This line follows the main water-polished dihedral system all the way to the North Arête. From the trees on Baker's Way, follow Baker's Way up to the north for 70 feet. At the point where Baker's Way climbs a 5-foot southwest-facing wall and heads north, continue up the now well-formed dihedral system for 30 more feet to a steep broken area. Climb up through the steep broken area (Class 4) and reach a ledge that is 30 feet north of the blocks above the two large trees on the "new" Fandango route. This is the ledge of Variation 3. Forty feet above this ledge is the crux east-facing overhang of the "old" Fandango. Climb through this small overhang at a 2-foot wide slot (5.5). Continue up attractive 5.3–5.4 rock for a pitch below the now large southeast-facing wall of the main dihedral. Join the "new" Fandango one pitch below the North Arête.

317V2 After the first 200 feet of this route, follow Baker's Way. Although longer, this makes an easier start for Baker's Way and you can reach the North Arête with Class 4 climbing.

317V3 From the large trees 165 feet above Baker's Way, angle up to the north (right) along an obvious ledge system (Class 4). The 5.5–5.6 flake-gully combo that is Variation 2 of the East Face Center route is 175 feet from the trees. The bottom of the 5.4 crux of the North Arête is 50 feet farther up the same ledge system.

317V4 One hundred feet below the North Arête, leave the mellow Class 4 crack and angle up to the southwest across the smooth hard to protect face (5.6). Join the North Arête south of the quartz knob pitch.

318 Zigzag 5.7

This difficult six-pitch route up the dihedral-ridden south side of the First follows a line less than 100 feet south of Fandango. Start at the base of a slab 30 feet southwest from the start of Baker's Way below a large south-facing dihedral system and a broken east-facing overhang south of the dihedral system. This dihedral system is the barrier that the first pitch of Baker's Way overcomes, and the intimidating broken overhangs are called the Kamikaze Roofs.

On the first 80-foot pitch, climb straight up slabs, pass a 5.4 crux and 15 feet farther reach a secure belay stance next to a hidden thread below the Kamikaze Roofs. On the second pitch, traverse 20 feet straight north (right), step north (right) around the end of an overhang (5.6) and climb up the Zigzag dihedral (5.2) to a sketchy belay stance, or move south (left) to a tree. On the third pitch, climb 120 feet up the dihedral (5.2) to a belay by a 4-inch crack below another overhang, which is the route's crux. On the fourth pitch, climb straight over the north (right) end of the overhang (5.7), climb 100 feet, pass under a flake and reach the North Arête south of the quartz knob pitch. Climb two pitches along the North Arête to the summit.

Variation

318V Start up Atalanta and traverse north to reach Zigzag below the upper 5.7 overhang. This start shortens the climb and avoids the Kamikaze Roofs.

319 Atalanta 5.4

This unusual four-pitch climb high on the south side of the First sneaks up a tiny dihedral 100 feet south of the major Zigzag dihedral. There is one short 5.4 crux and the rest of the climb is easier. Start 230 feet southwest from the start of Baker's Way below a low-angle groove leading onto the face. This is the first easy place to get onto the rock above Baker's Way.

Climb 30 feet northwest up the groove, climb directly up past some small trees, and get into a tiny dihedral with a 10-foot wide east face. Follow the diminutive dihedral, cross some red rock, and climb a short 5.4 step in the dihedral's east face, which is the route's crux. Continue up the dihedral to a large tree that you can see from the start of the route, and continue up the larger broken dihedral. Follow the path of least resistance and reach the North Arête 80 feet northeast of the false summit.

Variation

319V A hundred feet below the North Arête, angle south (left), get onto the east face of the false summit and climb directly up this enjoyable 5.0–5.2 face to the false summit.

3110 Hubris 5.4

This 500-foot route, the southernmost and shortest route on the east face of the First, ascends the southernmost dihedral on the face that turns into the gully between the false summit and main summit. If you follow the easiest line on this smooth water polished route, the difficulty is 5.4, but it is easy to stray onto harder climbing and Hubris will test your ability to read Flatiron rock. This route is also exposed to rockfall from Atalanta's loose upper gully.

Start at the same place as Atalanta and climb 100 feet directly up the face (Class 4). Above these introductory slabs, follow the now well-formed dihedral system. The difficulty increases to 5.0–5.2, and at the 200-foot level, there is a 30-foot 5.4 crux. The easiest climbing is sometimes in the dihedral and sometimes on the face south of the dihedral. Above the 5.4 crux, continue up the dihedral (5.0–5.2) to a point south of Atalanta's large tree. Above this point there is a discontinuity in the dihedral.

To avoid an overhang, traverse 15-feet south (left) (5.3–5.4) to an area of smooth rock at the entrance to the upper gully between the two summits. Traverse 15 feet straight south (left) (5.0–5.2), duck under a small bulge and reach easier rock. Angle north up a tiny Class 4 ramp that turns into a crack system 10 feet south of the smooth upper south-facing dihedral. Climb the crack system for 80 feet (5.0–5.2) to the notch between the false summit and the main summit.

Variations

3110V1 After 100 feet, climb the south-facing wall of the dihedral (5.0–5.2) and join Atalanta below the crux of that route.

3110V2 The Hippomenes Connection 5.3–5.4

Below the discontinuity in the dihedral and before the traverse at the smooth section, climb the dihedral's south-facing wall (5.3–5.4) and join Atalanta at the large tree above the crux of that route. This is the highest place to escape Hubris before engaging the smooth upper gully between the two summits.

3110V3 Instead of traversing to avoid the smooth section, climb straight up on smooth 5.6 rock.

31 First Flatiron
3111 Southwest Face 5.2

3111 Southwest Face 5.2

The shortest easiest route to the summit of the First Flatiron is usually used as a descent route, but is a worthwhile climb by itself. You can climb it in one long pitch, but it is more convenient to break the climb into two shorter pitches using the rappel bolt part way up as an anchor. An old gnarled tree right next to the south face marks the start of the route. Climb 15 feet straight up near the tree, continue 20 feet up the wall, then angle 90 feet west (left) on ramps and grooves to the lower rappel bolt (5.2). It is 55 feet from this bolt to the summit. Climb into a small notch directly west of the summit (Class 4). The last 25 feet up the west face to the summit are steep and exposed, but the Class 4 moves utilize holds that resemble chin-up bars.

Variation

3111V You can start this climb 40 feet downhill to the east from the old gnarled tree. This start lengthens the climb and increases its difficulty to 5.3.

31 First Flatiron
32 First Flatironette
33 The Spy

321 East Face 5.0–5.2
322 South Ridge 5.0–5.2

32 FIRST FLATIRONETTE

The First Flatironette is an independent rock sitting below the north side of the First Flatiron. It has two distinct gullies separating the larger, more impressive northern piece from the rest of the rock. The climbing on the First Flatironette is mellow and the rock is close enough to Boulder to be climbed in a lunch hour (if you are quick). Follow the approach for the low point of the First Flatiron and find the low point of the First Flatironette a few feet north of the trail, 100 feet east of the low point of the First Flatiron.

The First Flatironette is often the first piece of Flatiron rock touched by hikers, and you can find them sunning themselves and enjoying the feel of solid rock on the broad lower ledges of the South Ridge. People often hike up the gully between the First Flatiron and First Flatironette with the intent of hiking around the First. This doesn't work as this gully rapidly turns from hiking to 5.0–5.2 climbing in a water polished, unpleasant hole. A good trail in the lower part of this gully is used by all the people who have made this discovery. Stay east of the First Flatironette when hiking around the First.

Descent

32D From the summit, walk west then north for 60 feet until you bump into another rock. This rock is the Spy. For a hiking descent from here, hike uphill to the west, go around the top of the Spy and descend under its north face. For a scrambling descent, turn east and hike down into the small gully between the Spy and the First Flatironette. This gully soon ends at the top of a 100-foot face where the lower parts of the two rocks are joined. Climb 100 feet down the obvious Class 4 crack.

321 East Face 5.0–5.2

This is a shorter climb than the South Ridge but it provides more 5.0–5.2 climbing. From the low point of the First Flatironette, hike north along the bottom of the east face, passing both gullies, to the bottom of the main piece of the First Flatironette. Pick a suitable starting point and climb directly up 350 feet of wonderful rock to the summit. Near the top is a neat checkerboard pattern in the rock that invites you to climb it.

322 South Ridge 5.0–5.2

This is a fun climb on solid rock and provides great views of the mighty First Flatiron soaring overhead. Start at the low point and ascend Class 4 rock to the ridge above. An easier start is just around the corner to the west. Once on the ridge, joyous easy climbing leads you upward for 200 feet to a notch at the top of the southern gully on the east face. You can walk west from this point into the gully between the First Flatironette and the First Flatiron.

Above the first notch, climb 30 feet (Class 4) to a second notch at the top of the northern gully on the east face. Above this notch the climb becomes more serious and gives you a good chance to understand the difference between Class 4 and 5.0–5.2. If you feel uncomfortable with this difference, then escape the rock to the west from the second notch.

From the second notch, climb north onto the east face of the main piece of the First Flatironette. Climb 200 feet along the south edge of this piece, passing a nice 5.0–5.2 section, to reach the summit.

Variation

322V You can reach the first notch by climbing the southern gully on the east face. This gully is Class 3 except for a troublesome chockstone, which you can pass by climbing 30 feet of Class 4 rock on the face to the north.

31 First Flatiron
33 The Spy
331 East Ridge 5.0–5.2

33 THE SPY

The Spy is a distinct little finger of rock just north of, and higher than, the First Flatironette. A ridge of rock 370 feet long, it's upper portion is less than ten feet wide. The hillside below the short steep north face drops rapidly down into Gregory Canyon and the exposure along this narrow rib is dramatic. On this humble rock, you can quickly feel suspended high over Boulder. In spring and summer, late afternoon sun beams in on the north face of the Spy, which makes this a beautiful place to be near sunset. Approach the Spy by hiking uphill to the north along the bottom of the east face of the First Flatironette. The lower part of the Spy is connected to the First Flatironette.

331 East Ridge 5.0–5.2 *Classic*

This climb is rated the same as the First Flatironette, but the prospect of falling off the ridge in any of three different directions makes this a more serious proposition than the First Flatironette. Start north of the scrambling descent crack described with the First Flatironette, and climb up 120 feet on the connected part of the east face to a 5-foot vertical step. This narrow step marks the point where the Spy becomes distinct from the First Flatironette. The step is easiest on its south side (5.0–5.2), but it also goes on its north side (5.3–5.4).

Above this first step, tiptoe 100 feet up the increasingly spectacular ridge to a smooth, steep bulge. This bulge is the crux, and the exposure is fierce here. Move up on small holds near the north edge of the ridge (5.0–5.2) to easier rock above. The stance above this smooth bulge is 270 feet above the ground. A final 100 feet of Class 4 take you to a spectacular summit, then down and up again to a second summit.

Descent

331D From the south end of the summit block, find the tantalizingly close but overhung descent to the west. The path of least resistance to overcome this gravity-prone problem is to jump (J3). Once you are off the rock, hike down to the east under the north face of the Spy.

34 MACBETH

This overgrown boulder is on the south side of the First Flatiron, uphill to the southwest from the top of the Witch's Cabin. It is sometimes mistaken for the Witch's Cabin, which is a giant block resting against the bottom of the First. Macbeth is an independent rock that is visible from Baseline Road. It has a 100-foot east face which provides a quick Class 4 scramble. The exposed summit is a good place to study the lower south side of the First Flatiron. You can walk off to the south from the summit or continue scrambling for another 150 feet up a broken ridge. A tour of the alcove and hole on top of the Witch's Cabin combined with an ascent of Macbeth makes an unique off-trail workout.

35 SUNSET FLATIRONETTE

This rock is a short distance west of the First Flatiron, and ambitious people hiking around the back of the First often reach its summit. The Sunset Flatironette is not visible from central Boulder, but you can see it from NCAR and Flagstaff. The summit of this rock, like the west face of the First, will bask gloriously in the late afternoon sun long after the rest of the Flatirons are in shadow.

The south ridge of this rock provides a climb of surprising length and quality, and this climb makes a nice addition to an ascent of the First or Second Flatirons. To approach the bottom of the rock, hike up past the south side of the Second Flatiron, then angle uphill to the north and find the bottom of the rock hidden in the trees. From the west side of the First, hike downhill to the south along the base of the east face of Sunset Flatironette. Pass a false bottom and continue on down to the low point of the rock.

Descents

35D1 Downclimb the East Face Route. From the highest point, scramble directly east, downclimb 30 feet of Class 4 rock and scramble northeast to easier ground.

35D2 For a Class 3 scrambling descent that avoids the Class 4 downclimb, scramble south from the summit and scramble east down a gully full of jumbled features. This gully drops off lower down, so you have to be clever. Escape the gully to the north, scramble up a few feet on sharp holds and join the direct descent route below its Class 4 crux. Scramble northeast to easier ground.

351 Chase the Sun 5.4 *Classic**

I recommend this 600-foot climb up the south ridge of the Sunset Flatironette. Late in the day a climber on this route can play tag with the setting sun. If the shadow seems to be climbing the ridge faster than you are, take heart, since you will catch the sun on the summit. This ridge also provides good views of the north side of the Third Flatiron.

Start at the rock's low point, move west (left) past a horn and gain the ridge above. Follow the ridge for a pitch to a notch. The second pitch follows the ridge to another notch at the base of a steep headwall. Traverse east (right) around a small corner (5.3–5.4) and ascend steep rock on good holds up into a large basin. Figure a way to climb out of the basin (5.3–5.4) and climb easier rock for 200 feet to the false summit. An easy but exposed traverse leads north to the highest point. On a clear day you can see the high peaks from the Arapahos to Longs Peak.

352 Pack Rat 5.7

This grubby but technique-testing 70-foot route ascends the steep west face of the Sunset Flatironette. Climb up some obvious V-slots and pass three little cruxes. The last crux, which is half way up the face, is the hardest. Easier rock leads up to the summit ridge. Climb 30 feet north to the summit.

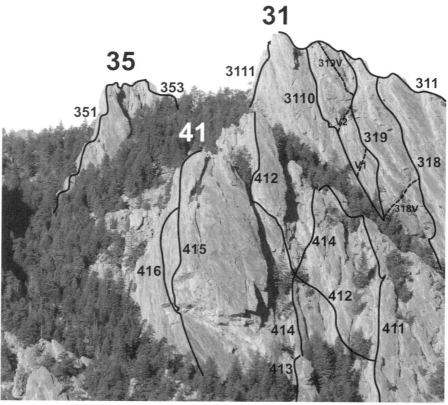

31 First Flatiron
35 Sunset Flatironette
41 Second Flatiron
351 Chase the Sun 5.4
353 East Face Class 4
3111 Southwest Face 5.2
311 North Arête 5.4
318 Zigzag 5.7

319 Atalanta 5.4
3110 Hubris 5.4
411 Freeway Class 4
412 Free For All 5.6
413 Second Flatironette East Face Class 4
414 Dodge Block Class 4
415 Southeast Ridge 5.7
416 South Sneak Class 4

353 East Face Class 4

This is the easiest way to reach the summit of Sunset Flatironette. This short climb is usually used as a descent route, but it provides an exciting extension to hikes in the area, and the summit provides an excellent view of the high peaks to the northwest. From the hiking saddle west of the First Flatiron, hike

31 First Flatiron
35 Sunset
     Flatironette
352 Pack Rat 5.7

west, scramble up a grove past a tree, and scramble 15 feet west to a small ridge northeast of the summit tower, which you can now clearly see. Scramble south along this ridge to the summit tower. The difficulty to this point is easy Class 3, but it's about to get harder. Using some sharp holds, scramble up, then south (left) to a small stance below a steeper wall above (Class 3). Climb 30 feet up this wall to the summit. You can either use some sharp holds in the center of the face or balance up a groove a few feet to the south (Class 4).

36 THE DEVIATIONS

Two small Flatironettes are southwest of the Sunset Flatironette. The lower one is the smaller of the two, and the upper one has several deep cracks on its steep east face. The rock on both of these Flatironettes is friable and unpleasant to climb on. The lower Deviation provides a 150-foot Class 4 climb on its east face that arrives on the summit from the north. The upper Deviation has a large central chimney splitting its east face. The highest summit is just north of this chimney. Ascend 140 feet up the chimney into a deep notch (5.3–5.4). Scramble west out of the notch and climb 20 feet up the west face of the summit tower to the south of the deep chimney (Class 4). From the south summit, step north across the top of the chimney and climb the top 20 feet of the northern summit's east face (5.3–5.4).

36 The Deviations

FOUR

Second Flatiron

41 SECOND FLATIRON

The middle of the three great Flatirons above Boulder is considerably lower and more broken than its stately neighbors. Its summit is formed by a large rectangular block appropriately named the Pullman Car that sits impressively above the east face. The Pullman Car is separated from the rest of the east face by 30 feet of vertical rock. The South Block is a similar but much larger block forming the south edge of the Flatiron. It is below and south of the Pullman Car.

Because of its broken appearance, the Second Flatiron has received far less attention than the First and Third; however the Second contains a great deal of excellent scrambling and climbing. It is home to three of the finest and longest Class 4 routes above Boulder. The easiest route from the low point of the rock to the summit requires more difficult climbing than the east face of the Third. The Second also has two large unusual arches.

To approach the Second Flatiron, start at the Kinnikinic Trailhead, and hike 0.75 mile south up the fire road to the Bluebell Shelter. From the trail sign southwest of the shelter, hike 200 yards west, then southwest on the Royal Arch Trail to a trail junction. Leave the Royal Arch Trail and go northwest on the Second and Third Flatiron access trail. Follow this access trail to the edge of a north-facing talus field, hike west across the talus field and turn right at another trail junction where the Second and Third Flatiron access trails split. Follow the Second Flatiron access trail to the bottom of the rock.

411 Freeway Class 4 *Classic*

This delightful easy 800-foot route does not go to the top of the Pullman Car, but follows the obvious ridge angling across the east face from south (lower left) to north (upper right). Start at the lowest point of the Flatiron, climb 250 feet straight up, get onto the central ridge as it becomes well formed and follow it diagonally up to the north (right). The South Block and the Pullman Car will be sailing overhead, and if your imagination is good, you can pretend that you are climbing one of the great routes on the Chamonix Aiguilles. At the 600-foot level a steep-sided notch on the Freeway Route on the Second Flatiron above Boulder will break your reverie.

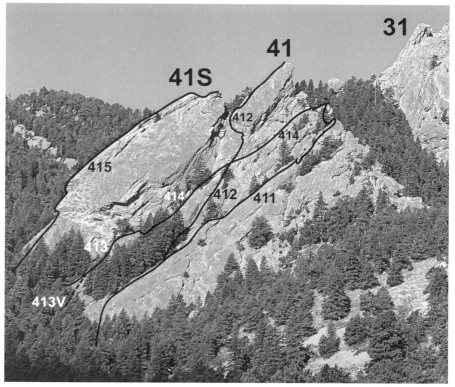

31 First Flatiron
41 Second Flatiron – Pullman Car
41S Second Flatiron – South Block
411 Freeway Class 4

412 Free For All 5.6
413 Second Flatironette East Face Class 4
414 Dodge Block Class 4
415 Southeast Ridge 5.7

A few feet south of and below the small summit that forms the notch is a passage to the rock beyond. Jumping may be the easiest way to overcome the gap. Jumping, while not a recommended climbing technique, seems innocent and safe enough at this notch. Go ahead and indulge yourself; take a flying leap.

Beyond the notch climb a slab with a tree. Soon after you will reach the north edge of the Flatiron and can peer down to the ground 20 feet below. It is not easy to reach the ground from this point however, so keep climbing. One more pitch up the mini block above will bring you to a place where the climb really seems to be over. From this point it is simple to walk west and north. Those possessed with summit fever can hike west underneath the upper north face of the Pullman Car and climb the West Face Route to the true summit of the Second Flatiron (5.0–5.2).

Descent

411D Escape from the middle of this route is difficult, so finish the route to the north side walkoff. From the summit of the Flatiron, use one of the descents described with the West Face Route.

412 Free for All 5.6

This 1,000-foot route is the easiest way to climb from the low point of the Second Flatiron to the summit without sneaking around and climbing the west face of the Pullman Car. Most of the route is Class 4, but two tricky pitches that reach the elevated east face of the Pullman Car increase the rating to 5.6. Unlike most other routes on the Second, this route climbs very directly from the low point to the summit. This fact, along with the two interesting leads near the top, makes this a recommended climb.

Start at the low point of the Flatiron and climb 250 feet straight up, just like the Freeway Route (Class 4). At this point you will be on the long ridge of the Freeway Route angling up to the north. Free for All and Freeway diverge here, but before you charge ahead, take a moment to view the arch high on the edge of the South Block to the southwest. You can bag this arch while climbing the Southeast Ridge or South Sneak Routes on the South Block.

Leave the Freeway ridge and continue west straight up easy rock leading to the Flatiron's central broken area. There are many possibilities for easy ascent in this area, but the cleanest route ascends small ridges and faces (Class 4) north of the major gully descending from the north side of the Pullman Car. Since you are headed for the base of the Pullman Car, you must cross this gully. Cross the gully 300 feet above the Freeway ridge, then climb 50 feet to some ledges below the east face of the Pullman Car. These ledges are on the Dodge Block Route.

The east face of the Pullman Car will now be looming steeply overhead, and you can no longer ignore the Pullman Car's difficulties. Climb straight up steeper rock, climb a 5.2 slot, a delectable exposed 5.6 face move and a curious tongue-like 5.2 flake. This is a spectacular, 70-foot section, and at the base of the vertical east face of the Pullman Car, you will better understand the Second Flatiron.

Traverse straight south (left) on exposed Class 4 rock directly underneath the vertical face above, angle southwest and enter the gully between the Pullman Car and the South Block. Hike and scramble 60 feet up this gully. Climb 30 feet of tricky 5.4 rock on the south face of the Pullman Car and reach its east face. Climb 120 feet up the south edge of this small east face to the summit (Class 4). This is a spectacular finish.

Escapes

412E1 After 250 feet, you can follow the Freeway Route (Class 4).

412E2 After 250 feet, you can traverse south and follow one of the descents described with the Second Flatironette.

412E3 Before you engage the difficulties of the Pullman Car, you can follow the great escape of the Dodge Block Route.

412E4 Once in the gully south of the Pullman Car, you can hike west up this gully and avoid the last pitch.

Descent

412D From the summit of the Second Flatiron, downclimb the West Face Route (5.0–5.2).

413 Second Flatironette East Face Class 4

Unlike the distinct First and Third Flatironettes, the Second Flatironette is really part of the Second Flatiron. You can climb it as if it was a separate rock, or you can use it to start other routes on the Second Flatiron. I include it here as a route on the Second Flatiron.

The Second Flatironette is located south of the gully running down the entire east face of the Second Flatiron separating the Pullman Car from the South Block. This 250-foot Flatironette is nestled below and east of the northern corner of the huge overhang on the east face of the South Block.

To approach the Second Flatironette, hike 200 feet uphill southwest (left) from the low point of the Second Flatiron. After passing the bottom of the Freeway ridge, the Second Flatironette will appear. It is marked by a 10-foot step 200 feet up. If you hike past the Second Flatironette, you will be staring up at the huge east overhang of the South Block.

This route makes a suitable objective for a noontime run and scramble. Start the climb 25 feet up to the south from the low point of the Flatironette. Moderate Class 4 climbing will take you up near the rock's south edge. The 10-foot step 200 feet up looks like it could be difficult but it goes easily via a slot-block combination near its south edge (Class 4). The small but distinct summit of the Second Flatironette is not far beyond the step.

Variation

413V For those looking for more excitement, start at the lowest point of the Flatironette and climb straight up (5.6). Thirty-five feet up, pass a short head-wall at an appropriate place near the center of the rock. Continue straight up, then slightly left to join the easy south edge 100 feet off the ground. This pitch is consistent in its difficulty and is a recommended Flatiron pitch at the 5.6 level. It is also a good example of how 5.6 rock can live only a few feet away from Class 4 rock on a Flatiron face.

Descents

413D1 (Class 3) From the top of the Second Flatironette, look at the Third Flatiron and you will see a cluster of three trees 50 feet away on this line. Head over to these trees and descend through them. From the lowest tree, move 10 feet south and descend easy red slabs to the ground. These red slabs are below the north end of the huge east overhang of the South Block.

413D2 (Easy Class 4) Get off the summit block and climb down some grooves southeast of the Second Flatironette. These grooves reach the ground just below the 10-foot step on the east face.

413D3 (Hard Class 4) What appears to be a hiking gully leads down along the north side of the Second Flatironette. This is the gully that separates the Pullman Car and the South Block. It has a huge chockstone wedged in its lower end and is not hikeable all the way to the ground. A few moves on polished rock will take you around the north edge of the chockstone.

414 Dodge Block Class 4 *Classic*

This is another delightful route that ascends 700 easy feet across the east face of the Second Flatiron. It always flirts with difficulty but never engages it. Like the Freeway Route, Dodge Block is not a summit route, but angles across the face from south to north as it dodges the South Block and Pullman Car.

Start this route by climbing the East Face Route on the Second Flatironette. From the top of the Second Flatironette, look up the Second Flatiron and you will see a slender blockette north of a polished gully on the north side of the South Block. Get off the top of the Second Flatironette, scramble down to the north, and engage the bottom of the slender blockette. Ascend this rib near its south edge for 300 feet until the impressive east face of the Pullman Car looms overhead and difficulties greater than Class 4 seem inevitable.

The charm of this route is its clever Class 4 escape from this apparent trap. One hundred feet below the steep east face of the Pullman Car, angle up to the north (right) on easy rock. Look sharp for a good place and traverse straight north across the gully north of the Pullman Car. The south-facing wall of the gully at the level of the traverse looks improbable but it goes easily. This escape out of the gully is just below the bottom of the east face of the Pullman Car.

After leaving the gully behind, climb a final 100 feet up to the northwest (right) and finish in another small gully. This will leave you at the same walk off on the north side of the Flatiron that is the top of the Freeway Route. Either walk away from it all or hike up and climb the West Face Route to the summit of the Flatiron (5.0–5.2).

Escape

414E In the early going, you can escape this route by getting to the top of the Second Flationette and using one of the descents described from there. After you climb the slender blockette, your best escape is to finish the route to the north side walkoff.

Descent

414D From the summit of the Second Flatiron, use one of the descents described with the West Face Route.

415 Southeast Ridge 5.7

This route overcomes the south side of the great overhang on the east face of the South Block. Hike south (left) from the low point of the Flatiron and find the smooth slab below the great overhang. Start at the southeast corner of this slab and climb 160 feet up its south edge to a belay just below the south edge

415 Southeast Ridge 5.7   416 South Sneak Class 4

of the overhang (Class 4). On its south edge, the overhang is broken into two overhangs separated by a short steep face. On the second pitch, climb over some spooky flakes to overcome the first barrier, climb the steep face above and move south (left) to avoid the upper overhang (5.7). Either climb a 5.7 wall directly west of the upper overhang to reach the southeast ridge or climb 160 feet up a 5.3–5.4 ramp and join the South Sneak Route where it traverses north to reach the southeast ridge. Once on the South Block's slabs above the overhangs, the climb becomes much more simple. Head up the southeast ridge to the summit of the South Block. Be sure to look for the skyline arch along the way.

Escape

415E From the belay below the crux pitch, you can follow the South Sneak Route (Class 4).

Descent

415D From the summit of the South Block, scramble northwest (Class 3) to the top of the gully between the South Block and the Pullman Car. Hike northwest to the base of the West Face Route on the Pullman Car. From here you can hike down either side of the Flatiron.

416 South Sneak Class 4

This clever 700-foot route ascends the south side of the South Block. Like most of the routes on the Second, this route is not a true summit route since it finishes on top of the South Block. Like Dodge Block, this route flirts with the difficulties of the South Block, then avoids them at the last second. Approach this route by hiking south (left) from the low point of the Flatiron to the large slab below the South Block's east-facing overhang.

Start at the southeast corner of this slab and climb 160 feet up its south edge to a belay just below the south edge of the overhang (Class 4). The Southeast Ridge Route heads up the steep rock above, but the South Sneak Route avoids this difficulty by angling southwest (left) onto a ramp. Ascend this Class 4 ramp for 150 feet as it sneaks along below the South Block's southeast ridge. The ramp is water polished and this section is the route's crux. When the ramp finally opens into a broken area near a large tree, take advantage of a weakness in the South Block's south face. Traverse 100 feet north (right) on low angle rock, cross another ramp, and get onto the southeast ridge of the South Block (Class 4). Follow this Class 4 ridge for 300 feet to the summit of the South Block. Part way along you will encounter a large arch that you can scramble across.

Escape

416E From the broken area before the traverse to the southeast ridge you can continue west across the broken area to a shoulder and hike west.

Descent

416D From the summit of the South Block, scramble northwest (Class 3) to the top of the gully between the South Block and the Pullman Car. Don't descend east into this gully, since it drops off lower down. Hike northwest to the base of the West Face Route on the Pullman Car, which you may choose to ascend to the summit of the Flatiron (5.0–5.2). From the bottom of the west face of the Pullman Car, the access trail is a few strides north.

417 South Face 5.0–5.2

Climb 70 feet up the Pullman Car's steep south face, angling back and forth up a series of ramps, and arrive abruptly at the summit of the Second from the south. This is not the same pitch as the last pitch of Free for All, which is 100 feet east.

41 Second Flatiron – Pullman Car   417 South Face 5.0–5.2

418 West Face 5.0–5.2

This route ascends the west face of the Pullman Car and has the distinction of being the shortest route to the summit of any of the three major Flatirons. Although short, the route is steep and exposed. Climb 15 feet up a crack near the center of the small face. When the rock overhangs above, traverse 10 feet north (left) and climb 15 feet up some exposed moves near the north edge of the face to reach the summit.

Descents

418D1 Downclimb the West Face Route (5.0–5.2).

418D2 Rappel 40 feet west or 100 feet north.

41 Second Flatiron
   – Pullman Car
418 West Face
   5.0–5.2

FIVE

Third Flatiron

51 THIRD FLATIRON   *Closed 2/1 – 7/31*

The Third Flatiron, the third large Flatiron counting from the north, is the finest rock above Boulder, and is one of the finest climbing rocks anywhere. When all the obscure routes have been found and climbed, the Third will still stand supreme as the monarch of all the Flatirons. Climbing the Third is like viewing a full moon; you don't have to work very hard to see the light.

Like the Grand Teton, Rainier, Denali, Aconcagua and Everest, the Third is the most sought after climb in its domain. The Third sees as much climbing activity as the rest of the Flatirons put together. The climbs on the east face are long and retreat is difficult. The descent from the summit is longer and more complicated than any other Flatiron. With a coating of snow, the rock becomes devilishly difficult. Don't ignore these facts in your rush to climb the big one.

This great rock is only a few minutes hike from Boulder, and those who live nearby are indeed privileged, but the privilege has often been abused. For years the rock carried the hundred-foot letters **C U**. The letters always got a fresh coat of paint on some random night, and the acronym always seemed to be highly visible for important football games. Before a game with Oklahoma, rivals closed the **C** to an **O**. On another occasion, an **I** appeared, spelling **I C U**. Full scale paint wars erupted, with both painters and paint removers doing their thing. Through all of this it was the rock that suffered. Mercifully, the current level of eco-consciousness is sufficient for people to enjoy the rock in less damaging ways.

The Third has seen plenty of other silly behavior. The rock has been climbed with no hands, naked and on roller skates. The east face has been soloed in about 7 minutes and the summit has been reached from Bluebell Shelter in 17 minutes. It is also common to do a round trip climb of the Third from Baseline Road in less than an hour, but the record for this event is closer to a half hour. The third has been skied. The list goes on and on. In addition to the paint wars, the rock had a large flake dynamited from it! Once, a brightly painted 55-gallon drum was hauled to the top, and it subsequently fell down the length of the east face. The summit is recovering from memorial plaques and cement register holders. The rock has been badly scarred and will recover very slowly. Please leave no trace of your passage.

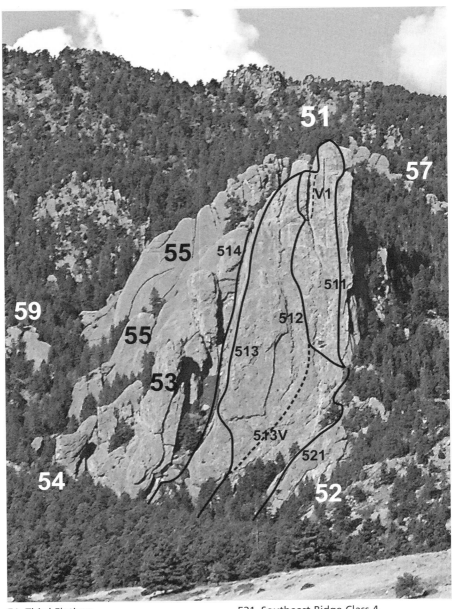

51 Third Flatiron
511 East Face North Side 5.3–5.4
512 East Face 5.2
513 East Face South Side 5.2
514 1911 Gully 5.4
52 Third Flatironette

521 Southeast Ridge Class 4
53 Queen Anne's Head
54 W.C. Field's Pinnacle
55 Ironing Boards
57 Jaws
59 Eyes of the Canyon

Approaches to the Third Flatiron

51A1 Approach to the north side
and the standard East Face Route

From the Kinnikinic Trailhead, hike 0.75 mile south up the fire road to the Bluebell Shelter. From the trail sign southwest of the shelter, hike 200 yards west, then southwest on the Royal Arch Trail to a trail junction. Leave the Royal Arch Trail and go northwest on the Second and Third Flatiron access trail. Follow this access trail to the edge of a north-facing talus field, hike west across the talus field and stay left at another trail junction where the Second and Third Flatiron access trails split. Continue southwest on the Third Flatiron access trail past some slabby boulders. Finally, following cairns, boulder-hop south to reach the north edge of the Flatiron. The regular route starts from a ledge called the East Bench that is 500 feet above the lowest point of the Flatiron. The East Bench is the highest easy access onto the east face. From the center of the talus field, an access trail continues uphill underneath the north face to the west side of the Flatiron.

51A2 Approach to the
lowest point of the Third Flatiron

From the Bluebell Shelter, follow the Royal Arch Trail southwest for several hundred yards. As this trail passes beneath the Third, it turns west and enters Bluebell Canyon. Fifty feet before the Royal Arch Trail crosses to the south side of Bluebell Canyon, leave it and hike steeply uphill to the west on a smaller trail. Stay south of the low point of the Third Flatironette and navigate past some large boulders to the bottom of the Third Flatiron.

51A3 Approach to the
southwest side of the Third Flatiron

From the Bluebell Shelter, follow the Royal Arch Trail into Bluebell Canyon south of the Third. Continue for a few hundred yards as the trail climbs west along the south side of the canyon. Look north for W. C. Field's Pinnacle with its hammerhead summit, as the approach to the west side of the Third is west of this summit. The approach gullies are east of the Ironing Boards, which are large smooth slabs west of the Third. A long rib of rock stands between the Ironing Boards and the southwest side of the Third. This rib runs all the way from Bluebell Canyon to the saddle west of the Third. Although it is innocuous on its east side, this rib has a steep west face that prevents hiking between the gullies on either side of it. There are two approach routes, one east and one west of this rib. Before you leave Bluebell Canyon, you must decide which gully to ascend.

The easiest way to reach the saddle west of the Third stays west of the long rib. Before the Royal Arch Trail's first long switchback up the hill south of

Bluebell Canyon, look sharp for a small side trail leading northwest into Bluebell Canyon. This departure point from the Royal Arch Trail is west of the place where the summits of W. C. Field's Pinnacle and Queen Anne's Head are visually aligned. Cross Bluebell Canyon and get into the broad hiking gully between the Ironing Boards and the southwest side of the Third. Hike north up this gully and reach a hiking saddle west of the Third. From this saddle, climb east up a 10-foot Class 3 wall to reach the saddle immediately west of the Third.

The more difficult approach, but the one that gives access to many of the west side routes on the Third, stays east of the rib. Leave the Royal Arch Trail before the summits of W. C. Field's Pinnacle and Queen Anne's Head are visually aligned. Follow a side trail down and cross Bluebell Canyon. Get into the gully between the rib and the west face of W. C. Field's Pinnacle, which is southeast of the much higher massif of the Third, and hike northwest up this gully. Three short scrambling pitches are required to ascend this gully. The first is halfway up and is the most exposed. Climb a water polished Class 4 slab near the west edge of the rib. Near the top of this pitch, a less exposed variation is a few feet east (Class 4). The second scrambling pitch is 200 feet farther up the gully and is below the start of the Southwest Chimney Route. This Class 4 pitch is more difficult than the first crux, but it is safely buried in the gully and is not exposed. The final Class 3 scramble is 200 feet beyond and ends in the saddle immediately west of the Third.

Descents from the summit of the Third Flatiron

51D1 Three rappels from fixed eyebolts will take you from the summit to the ground. Directions are attached to each eyebolt. From the summit, rappel 40 feet south into the South Bowl. Walk a few feet south and rappel 50 feet south to the exposed Friday's Folly Ledge. This ledge is in the middle of a large, steep face and you must take care to not rappel past the ledge. Two eyebolts are on Friday's Folly ledge. Make a few exposed moves west and find the second bolt around a corner. Rappel 70 spectacular feet to the ground. The eastern bolt on Friday's Folly Ledge requires a two rope, 140-foot rappel to the south to reach the ground. At least one fatality has occurred because of confusion over these two bolts.

51D2 Downclimb and/or rappel the Southwest Chimney Route. This 5.2 route is 500 feet long and can be difficult to find. If rappelled, this descent requires three rappels plus some scrambling. This is the shortest reasonable downclimbing route from the summit to the ground. See the description of the Southwest Chimney Route for details.

51D3 Downclimb the East Face Route.

511 East Face North Side 5.3–5.4   *Closed 2/1 – 7/31*

You can climb this 900-foot route in six long pitches. Both the difficulty and proximity to "big air" increase the closer you climb to the startlingly abrupt north edge of the east face. This general line with its many variations is recommended as an alternative to the often-crowded East Face Route.

Start at the same place as the East Face Route and head straight up, staying within 50 feet or less of the north edge of the face. At the 200-foot level you can climb a pretty nut-eating finger crack. After 380 feet, a large ledge system will be directly below the old painted **U**. The climbing to this point is no harder than 5.2. The path of least resistance above this point is to climb up near the south (left) side of the **U** (5.0–5.2). As an alternative, you may climb 50 feet of unprotected 5.7 rock near the north (right) edge of the **U**, which is only a few feet from the edge of the face. Above the **U**, continue straight up. Some nice 5.3–5.4 climbing is near the north edge of the face and easier rock is 50 feet south (left). If you stay near the north edge of the face you will intersect Kiddy Kar Ledge at a spectacular notch above the northwest face. The last airy pitch follows a vague 5.2 crack above the notch and arrives on the summit from the north.

512 East Face 5.2 *Classic – Top Ten*   *Closed 2/1 – 7/31*

This is the regular route on the Third and it is the most traveled rock route near Boulder. It is *the* classic Flatiron route and is one of the finest easy climbs in the country. Anyone who enjoys moving over rock should climb it.

The 950-foot route is commonly done in seven or eight pitches. If you follow the easiest line, most of the climb is Class 4 in difficulty. There are two short stretches of 5.2 climbing, one on the first pitch, and one on the last pitch. This route follows the six fixed eyebolts on the face. Follow the approach route to the north side of the Flatiron and start the climb from the highest ledge, where it is easy to walk south and get onto the east face.

There are two ways to start onto the face. The easiest way is to climb 7 feet straight up, then traverse 12 feet straight south (left) on some good footholds (Class 4). Most people miss this start and traverse south first, then head up (5.2). Once on the face, angle 50 feet up to the southwest (left) and pass the first bolt. This bolt is not usually used for a belay, but it protects the 5.2 traverse across the gully to the south. You must cross this smooth water polished gully, and the best place to cross is only 10 feet above the level of the first bolt. Climb over a short wall on the gully's south side and climb up 30 feet to the second bolt. This first pitch is 140 feet long.

The second pitch goes 120 feet straight up to the vicinity of the third bolt (Class 4). When this third bolt was placed, it was above a comfortable ledge formed by a large flake. This flake was dynamited from the face in 1957, and the bolt is now difficult to reach and use. A flake 30 feet south of the bolt provides a secure alternate belay anchor.

The third pitch continues straight up the face for another 120 feet to the fourth bolt, which is above a nice ledge (Class 4). The fourth pitch angles up slightly to the south (left) for 140 feet to the fifth bolt. The fifth bolt is not easily seen and parties who continue straight up from the fourth bolt often miss it. On this fourth pitch, you will start to climb over splattered paint from the old painted **C** above.

The fifth pitch angles north (right) across the old painted **C** and reaches the sixth and final bolt after 120 feet (Class 4). This bolt is near the upper northern corner of the **C** a few feet south of the large gash that splits the upper part of the east face.

The sixth pitch stays on the east face south (left) of the gash. From the sixth bolt, angle up slightly south and overcome a steep wall (Class 4). Continue up 150 feet across handhold-ridden rock to some flakes that you can use for an anchor. There is no bolt here. You can reach the summit from here with a 165-foot rope, but since you must cross the gash, it is more convenient to break the remainder of the climb into two shorter pitches.

On the seventh pitch, continue 50 feet straight up, angle 10 feet northwest and traverse neatly to the top of a large chockstone wedged at the top of the large gash (Class 4). This point is at the entrance to the South Bowl. There is a 2-foot wide horizontal ledge called Kiddy Kar Ledge that traverses across the east face north of the gash.

The 90-foot long eighth pitch is the finest pitch of the climb. Walk north on Kiddy Kar Ledge for 15 feet, then climb 40 feet straight up the face to a deep one-foot wide crack (Class 4). Traverse a few feet south (left) along this crack and finish the pitch near the exposed southeast corner of the face (5.2). This is a beautiful finish to a grand summit.

Variations

512V1 From the sixth bolt, climb down into the gash, descend for 6 feet, and climb out onto the east face to the north (right) of the gash. Climb 165 feet up the east face north of the gash to Kiddy Kar Ledge. A 165-foot rope just reaches on this pitch and the second may not have enough rope to downclimb to the easy access onto the face to the north of the gully below the sixth bolt. There are at least two other more difficult ways to escape the gully to the north, slightly above the level of the sixth bolt. This pitch is mostly pretty Class 4 with a few 5.0–5.2 moves 20 feet below Kiddy Kar ledge.

512V2 From the sixth bolt, climb down into the gash and scramble up it. This gash is full of loose rock and you should take care to not bombard climbers below. Overcome two chockstones on your trip up the gash. The second chockstone is awkward 5.2 and this may be the hardest move on the climb. Near the top of the gash you will be under the large chockstones that form the secure stance at the south end of Kiddy Kar Ledge. Climb up a smooth dark slab under these chockstones and emerge into the South Bowl a few feet west of Kiddy Kar Ledge.

512V3 Greenman's Crack 5.3

This ramp angles up to the west on the south side of the summit block. The bottom of the ramp is in the South Bowl a few feet west of Kiddy Kar Ledge. The top of the ramp is at the summit rappel bolt. The ramp is 90 feet long with the most difficult climbing near the top. An unprotected fall from this ramp would have serious consequences for either the leader or the second; however you can easily protect the pitch.

512V4 West Door 5.6

This exposed pitch from the South Bowl to the summit is rarely climbed. Scramble up to the far west end of the South Bowl and climb 10 feet up a steep south-facing crack system to the highest ledge that traverses under the west side of the summit block (5.6). Traverse north on this small ledge onto the west face of the summit block and climb up a short west-facing wall to the summit.

513 East Face South Side 5.2 *Classic*   *Closed 2/1 – 7/31*

If the regular East Face Route on the Third is the best beginner's climb in the country, then this route must be a close second. This route has long been coveted as a less crowded alternative to the East Face Route. You can climb this 1,200-foot route in eight pitches with a 165-foot rope. The protection is adequate, but there are no fixed eyebolts on this route.

Start at the lowest point of the Flatiron and follow an obvious but tiny ridge that angles up to the north for 80 feet (Class 4). At a convenient place, leave this ridge and head straight up the Flatiron on steeper 5.0–5.2 rock to a small tree 165 feet above the ground. A prominent overhang cuts horizontally across the southern half of the east face at the 300-foot level. The second pitch angles up to the south (left) to a belay near the south end of the long overhang (5.2). Thirty feet below this stance, you can escape (or gain) the rock by moving south into 1911 Gully. On the third pitch, climb south of the overhang and follow ramps just south of the east face. Move north (right) onto the main east face and climb to a large ledge. Follow the south edge of the Flatiron for 500 feet to the subsidiary summit known as the Dog's Head (Class 4–5.2). Descend north from the Dog's Head and climb 250 feet to the summit of the Third. The last pitch is the same as the East Face Route.

Variation

513V You can start at the low point of the Third, angle north (right), climb straight up the face and join the East Face Route after 600 feet (5.2). This start will lengthen an ascent of the East Face Route by 600 feet.

514 1911 Gully 5.4   *Closed 2/1 – 7/31*

This gully and chimney system lies immediately south of the main east face of the Third. The lower part of the route is in the gully between Queen Anne's Head and the Third. This gully has a lot of poison ivy in it, but is worth enduring, since the climbing in the chimney above the gully is compelling and satisfying.

To reach the start of this route, follow the approach to the low point of the Third, then hike downhill to the south to the slabs between Queen Anne's Head and the Third. An alternate approach is to follow the Royal Arch Trail for 150 feet past the point where it crosses to the south side of Bluebell Canyon. Leave the trail, cross Bluebell Canyon, and hike north up the hill, skirting the base of Queen Anne's Head to the slabs at the start of the climb.

It is not obvious where to start this climb since this is a large area of slabs with many possible starts, most of which don't work out very well. The easiest and best start is in a crack system at the lower south end of the slab system. This start is only a few feet north of Queen Anne's Head. Climb this crack system for 100 feet to easier ground (5.0–5.2). Above this, hike 150 feet to a jumble of boulders, crawl north through a hole, move north to the edge of the Third and climb up along it. Above this, 250 feet of pure hiking up the now broad gully will take you to the base of the obvious chimney immediately adjacent to the Third.

The climb up this chimney is fun and you can accomplish it in three leads of 140 or 150 feet each. The rock is water polished, but not insanely so, and the chimney is largely free of loose rock. Climb up some easy slabs, then continue up steeper 5.0–5.2 rock. Above this, climb two steep 5.4 cruxes that are separated by easier climbing. The deep upper chimney contains enjoyable 5.3–5.4 climbing.

The top of the 1911 Gully is in a notch that is also at the top of the Southwest Chimney on the west side of the Flatiron. From this point, you may descend the Southwest Chimney for 120 feet to the ground or follow the upper part of the Southwest Chimney Route to the top of the Third. Continuing to the top of the Third will add three more pitches plus some scrambling. For details about these pitches, see the Southwest Chimney Route.

515 South Chimney 5.5   *Closed 2/1 – 7/31*

You can combine this hidden 300-foot climb with other routes higher up to make a nice ascent on the southwest side of the Third. You can do the climb in two 150-foot pitches or break it up into three pitches of 80, 70 and 150 feet. This once popular route now sees very few ascents.

Do not confuse the South Chimney Route with the Southwest Chimney Route farther north. The South Chimney is a steeper and more difficult route than the Southwest Chimney. The start of the South Chimney Route is 30 feet beyond the first smooth crux of the approach gully under the southwest side of the Third. Above this point is a large south-facing dihedral-chimney system. This is the route.

The chimney does not extend all the way down to the approach gully and the first crux of the route is getting up into the chimney. Climb 80 feet up the

515 South Chimney
    5.5
515V 5.5

steep narrow west-facing wall directly below the chimney (5.5). The bottom of the chimney is flat and makes a comfortable and secure belay stance.

The overhanging chimney above looks improbable as it narrows to 7 inches but it is not as hard as it looks. Climb up into the chimney, then step neatly west to the outside edge of the chimney on some surprise footholds that are underneath the obvious crux. Stay outside the now 7-inch wide chimney, stem past the crux (5.5), and get into the easier secure upper chimney. The dramatic notch at the top of the chimney is 20 feet past the crux. This notch is 150 feet above the ground and 70 feet above the stance in the bottom of the chimney.

Stem out of the notch and climb a steep smooth southeastern-facing wall (5.4). At a suitable place, move north and get onto the easy east face above and follow it to a small summit, which is 150 feet northwest of the notch. Fifteen feet north of this summit is the notch above the Southwest Chimney and 1911 Gully. Either continue up the Southwest Chimney Route or descend the lower part of that route to the ground.

Variation

515V You can start the climb by stemming up the dihedral south (right) of the regular start then traversing north into the bottom of the chimney (5.5).

516 Southwest Chimney 5.2   *Closed 2/1 – 7/31*

This is the shortest easy climb to the summit of the Third Flatiron. This route would be more popular if it were located elsewhere, but it is tucked away on the backside of a monarch surrounded by grander lines, and does not receive the attention it deserves. It is used mostly as a descent route, since this is the easiest way to downclimb from the summit to the ground. The route has two fixed eyebolts and can be rappelled, which is a good alternative when the regular rappel route is crowded.

To reach the route, follow the approach for the south and west sides of the Third, and hike up the gully closest to the Third. Two hundred feet past the first slick crux of this approach gully the otherwise steep west face of the Third relaxes into a broken area with a chimney on its north edge. This is the route. The start of the climb is above the second scrambling pitch of the approach gully, and you can easily reach it by traversing south from a point north of the route. You can also reach this point from the notch directly west of the summit by scrambling and hiking 200 feet south down the approach gully.

You can reach the summit of the Third in three long pitches plus some scrambling, but it is more convenient to break the climb into four pitches. Start up the chimney or the face just south (right) of the chimney (5.0–5.2). The chimney is a little harder but more secure than the face. After 100 feet, pass a large chockstone by climbing a 20-foot south-facing 5.2 wall.

516 Southwest
Chimney 5.2

This effort will leave you in the notch at the tops of both the Southwest Chimney and the 1911 Gully. The easiest way to proceed from the notch is to downclimb 15 feet east into 1911 Gully, move north onto a ramp and climb this ramp 30 feet west to a fixed eyebolt (Class 4). You can also climb directly from the notch to the eyebolt (5.2). This eyebolt is 150 feet above the ground.

From the eyebolt, hike 100 feet north up a gully with an overhang above it. When the hiking ends, turn northwest and climb 140 feet up a ramp to another eyebolt (Class 4). This ramp is known as Slipslide Ledge, and although it is easy, it is not far from a rather large drop to the southwest. Slipslide Ledge connects the lower southwest face to the upper east face.

From the eyebolt at the top of Slipslide Ledge, move north through a lucky hole called Fat Man's Frenzy. Short slim people sometimes observe that you would have to be very fat to get stuck in this hole. People over six feet tall usually feel awkward while crawling through it. If Fat Man's Frenzy were not there it would be much more difficult to get from the top of Slipslide Ledge to the top of the Third. The north end of Fat Man's Frenzy is in the South Bowl. Scramble east through the bowl, downclimb a short boulder problem and emerge onto the east face at Kiddy Kar Ledge. Either climb the last pitch of the East Face Route or the Greenman's Crack Variation from here to the top.

517 Winky Woo 5.4 S *Classic*   *Closed 2/1 – 7/31*

This is a wonderful 200-foot climb up the vertical bucket-hold-infested wall north of the Southwest Chimney. Protection is lacking, but the climbing is still joyous. Start at the base of the Southwest Chimney and climb 30 feet straight up the vertical wall north (left) of the Southwest Chimney (5.4). Angle north (left) across the now slightly less than vertical pot-holed wall (5.4) and work out a belay after 120 feet. Climb 80 feet up the slightly easier wall above to a point near the bottom of Slipslide Ledge (5.3). From here either continue up or down on the Southwest Chimney Route. Continuing on the Dog's Head Cutoff is also a possibility.

516 Southwest Chimney 5.2   517 Winky Woo 5.4 S

518 Dog's Head Cutoff 5.4 *Closed 2/1 – 7/31*

This is not a base to summit route but rather a time-tested pitch that you can combine with other routes to provide an unusual tour on the southwest side of the Third. The pitch climbs from the bottom of Slipslide Ledge to the summit above, which is known as the Dog's Head.

Climb 40 feet up Slipslide Ledge, then climb onto the vertical wall above via a chin-up bar hold in a hole (5.3–5.4). Descend a few feet southeast along a precarious ramp, then traverse 30 feet east across a steep wall (5.4). Step neatly up into the notch between the Dog's Head and the rest of the Third. From this notch, continue on the East Face South Side Route to the summit of the Third.

Variation

518V A 7-inch crack separates the Dog's Head from the rest of the Third. Small people can squeeze up this crack (5.6), but large people usually look askance at this possibility.

519 Falcon's Fracture 5.8 *Closed 2/1 – 7/31*

This once popular 150-foot route is now seldom climbed. It ascends a south-facing dihedral south of the large southwest wall on the west buttress of the Third. The route is 120 feet south of and below the saddle immediately west of the Third. A tree on a ledge halfway up marks the route. Climb easily to the tree by doing a 50-foot, ascending traverse from the northwest (5.0–5.2). Climb the dihedral above the tree, and continue up a narrow chimney (or the face to the left) to a belay shelf 75 feet above the tree (5.8). Continue east up an easy crack to the bottom of Slipslide Ledge and join the Southwest Chimney Route.

5110 Friday's Folly 5.7 *Classic – Top Ten* *Closed 2/1 – 7/31*

This ultra-classic one-pitch route ascends the north edge of the large southwest-facing wall on the west side of the Third. The vertical wall, good rock and superb position yield a climb that is larger than life. From the saddle immediately west of the Third, scramble up 15 feet and scramble a few feet south on a ledge to the start of the climb. This ledge is at the bottom of the third rappel on the standard rappel route.

You will meet the challenge immediately. Make some 5.7 moves up to the right on the west face, and step around the corner onto the exposed southwest face. Welcome to Friday's Folly. Follow a crack that angles up slightly to the

51 Third Flatiron
5110 Friday's Folly
5.7
The climber is on
Friday's Folly Ledge.

right, overcome a small overhang on good holds (5.7) and either follow another right angling crack or climb the face left of it. After 90 spectacular feet, reach the spacious Friday's Folly Ledge that is equipped with two eyebolts.

From Friday's Folly Ledge, you can rappel 70 feet west to the ground from the westernmost of the two eyebolts. It is 140 feet to the ground if you rappel south from the eastern bolt. To continue the climb, move to the east end of the ledge, do an ascending traverse south across a small wall below an overhang and arrive at the top of Slipslide Ledge (5.0–5.2). Continue on the Southwest Chimney Route.

5111 Saturday's Folly 5.8+   *Closed 2/1 – 7/31*

This difficult 75-foot route ascends the direct west buttress of the Third. The climb ascends the west-facing wall that has a prominent crack 50 feet up. It is

51 Third Flatiron
5110 Friday's Folly
    5.7
5111 Saturday's
    Folly 5.8+

near the line of the third rappel from the bolt at the west end of the Friday's Folly Ledge. This climb is easily top roped, but since it is on a popular rappel route, traffic jams are likely. Start at the same place as Friday's Folly, climb straight up and follow the path of least resistance to a position below the headwall with the crack in it. Climb up the beautiful wall a few feet south (right) of the crack on small holds. Traverse 5 feet north (left) to the top of the crack, get into a v-groove and climb up it to the west end of Friday's Folly Ledge.

52 THIRD FLATIRONETTE   *Closed 2/1 – 7/31*

This rock is below the northeast side of the Third. Unlike the prominent First Flatironette, people often overlook the Third Flatironette since you cannot see it from central Boulder. However, it provides a recommended climb in a scenic setting that does not require much commitment. To approach the Third Flatironette, follow the approach for the low point of the Third Flatiron. The trail leading to the low point of the Third passes 30 feet from the low point of the Third Flatironette, which is 100 feet east of and below the low point of the Third Flatiron. You can add 500 feet to your ascent of the Third Flatiron by first climbing the Third Flatironette, and this is a good warm-up.

521 Southeast Ridge Class 4   *Closed 2/1 – 7/31*

Start at the low point of the rock and cruise 300 feet up the ridge to a nice summit that is overhung on its west side. The most difficult climbing on this ridge is in the first 100 feet. This ridge provides a foreshortened but awesome view of the Third soaring overhead and you can examine Queen Anne's Head to the south. From the first summit, descend 30 feet along the north edge of the east face (Class 4) and move north to hiking territory. Either walk away from it all, or hike west and climb another 100-foot pitch to a second summit (Class 4). From the top of this rock you can also walk away, or hike west and tackle a final 100-foot east face (Class 4). A ten-foot descent off this summit brings you to the starting point for the Third's East Face Route.

53 QUEEN ANNE'S HEAD   *Closed 2/1 – 7/31*

Queen Anne's Head is the large pinnacle located near the lower southeastern corner of the Third. It forms the southern boundary of the lower part of 1911 Gully and soars above the Royal Arch Trail as the trail begins to climb into Bluebell Canyon. Your ascent of the east face of Queen Anne's Head is likely to attract the attention of hikers. To approach Queen Anne's Head, follow the Royal Arch Trail for 100 yards past the point where the trail crosses to the south side of Bluebell Canyon. Leave the trail, drop down 40 feet, cross the canyon and hike northwest uphill to the base of the rock.

531 East Face 5.4 *Classic*   *Closed 2/1 – 7/31*

This is a highly recommended four-pitch climb on steeper than average Flatiron rock. An overhang 50 feet above the low point blocks easy access to the upper face. Start 50 feet south of the low point at the bottom of a south-facing dihedral formed by Queen Anne's Head and some addendum slabs to the south.

Climb 80 feet up the dihedral (5.3) and pass a short 5.4 crux. Continue up easier rock to a good belay at the 150-foot level. On the second pitch, climb

51 Third Flatiron
53 Queen Anne's Head
54 W.C. Field's Pinnacle
531 East Face 5.4
58 Morning After

120 feet of Class 4 rock, then climb an obvious break to the south. This break leads to the main east face of Queen Anne's Head and a large comfortable ledge system. A hundred and twenty feet above this ledge is a small overhang, which is the crux of the route. From the comfortable ledge, climb the 5.4 slabs to the south edge of this small overhang and work out a marginal belay. There is a thread here, which is not visible until you reach it. From this stance, traverse 10 feet north directly above the small overhang (5.4) and get into a crack system that splits the upper part of the face. Climb this delightful 5.3–5.4 crack for 75 feet, pass a knob and continue up a 75-foot 5.0–5.2 face to the summit. This vantage gives a unique view of the Third Flatiron.

Variation

531V From the stance at the south edge of the small overhang, continue straight up a small 5.6 dihedral to easier rock above.

Descent

531D *This is a dangerous rock to be on top of without a rope.* Using a hole that you can thread with a nine-foot sling as an anchor, rappel 105 spectacular feet down the north face to the ferns of 1911 Gully. There is a ramp system 50 feet below the summit, and for a one-rope descent, you can rappel to the ramp, then climb down it to reach 1911 Gully. Either continue up the 1911 Gully Route, or descend the lower part of that route to the ground. If descending, you can overcome the route's lowest slab with a 40-foot rappel off a tree.

54 W.C. FIELD'S PINNACLE   *Closed 2/1 – 7/31*

This 200-foot pinnacle is below and directly south of Queen Anne's Head. When viewed from the east it has a distinctive hammerhead shape and a steep

51 Third Flatiron
54 W.C. Field's
    Pinnacle
541 A Very Ament
    Slab 5.8
541EC 5.0–5.2

east face with several small overhangs on it. The pinnacle looks spectacular and difficult from the Royal Arch Trail. The West Face Route on this pinnacle was popular decades ago, but it is now the east face that attracts most of the attention. To approach the east face, leave the Royal Arch Trail southeast of the pinnacle, drop down and cross Bluebell Canyon to reach the base of the east face. To approach the west face, leave the Royal Arch Trail a little farther along, cross Bluebell Canyon and hike up the gully west of the rock.

Descents

54D1 Rappel 75 feet west to the ground.

54D2 Downclimb the West Face Route (exposed 5.4).

541 A Very Ament Slab 5.8 *Classic*   *Closed 2/1 – 7/31*

This beautiful and difficult two-pitch climb ascends the east face of the pinnacle. Steep rock, solid protection, sharp holds and a knife-edge summit combine to create a classic. Start at a tree on the north side of the east face north of a 2-foot overhang.

Climb 120 feet up a clean Class 4 slab, which becomes 5.0–5.2 near its top. Traverse north (right) and climb over a steep step (5.5). Eight feet north of the step is a 1-foot wide pothole near the north edge of the east face. This belay stance has a unique view of Queen Anne's Head and the Third Flatiron.

The second 80-foot crux pitch climbs the steep overhang-ridden upper face to the summit. From the pothole, angle 20 feet southwest to a bulge (5.4) and prepare for the route's crux. Climb a dicey 5.8 crease a few feet south (left). There are only two 5.8 moves. Above the crease, continue 15 feet straight up steep rock to a small overhang (5.3–5.4). Step north (right), then climb 10 feet to the final overhang (5.3–5.4). Traverse 5 feet south, climb past the final overhang (5.5) and climb 25 feet up 5.0–5.2 slabs to reach the spectacular summit ridge.

Extra Credit

541EC The Class 4 slab on the first pitch is a huge arch. The inside provides a cave-like 5.0–5.2 scramble, and if you want to be really weird, you can do the first pitch of this route from underneath! From the southeast corner of the east face, scramble up into a gully and continue up under the huge slab. Climb a classic Class 4 layback, make a few 5.0–5.2 moves and climb out a hole to the north side of the east face.

542 West Face 5.4   *Closed 2/1 – 7/31*

This is the easiest route to the summit of W. C. Field's Pinnacle. The climb is short, exciting and exposed. Hike up the gully west of the summit to a point northwest of the summit. Climb 30 feet up a west-facing wall to a ridge northwest of the pinnacle (Class 4). Descend 20 feet southeast along this ridge to a notch directly below the summit (Class 4). Climb 20 feet up the steep northwest corner of the summit block and do a hand traverse south under the summit overhang (5.0–5.2). The exposure is fierce here. Make a final crux move up to the south to gain the summit ridge (5.4). The highest point is 15 feet back to the north.

54 W.C. Field's
    Pinnacle
542 West Face 5.4

55 IRONING BOARDS   *Closed 2/1 – 7/31*

These smooth slabs west of the Third Flatiron are awesome when seen from
the summit of the Third. Many alpinists have arrived on top of the Third,
observed the Ironing Boards and known in their hearts that there is a lot more
to Flatiron climbing than the Third Flatiron.

The Ironing Boards provide the smoothest slab climbing above Boulder.
There is very little protection on these routes, so they are serious undertakings.
There are two Ironing Boards and they both rise north of Bluebell Canyon.
The Western Ironing Board is the higher and steeper of the two. Also, a narrow
continuous rock rib between the two main Ironing Boards connects with Jaws
to the north and forms a continuous rock barrier from Bluebell Canyon to the
canyon between the Second and Third Flatirons.

Approach by following the Royal Arch Trail until it starts to switchback up
on the south side of Bluebell Canyon. Leave the Royal Arch Trail and follow a
small trail leading northwest into the canyon. Cross to the canyon's north side

35 Sunset Flatironette
51 Third Flatiron
55E Eastern Ironing Board
551 Smooth 5.6 S
552 Que Rasca 5.8 S
55W Western Ironing Board

553 Crescent 5.5 S
554 Smoother 5.7 S
56 Green Thumb
561 East Face 5.4
613 Woods Quarry

and bushwhack to the low points of the rocks. The low point of the Eastern Ironing Board is within 200 feet of the Royal Arch Trail and the Western Ironing Board is 400 difficult feet farther west up Bluebell Canyon. When headed for the Western Ironing Board, be sure to stay south of the low point of the rock rib between the two Ironing Boards. The bottom of the Western Ironing Board is 100 feet west of this rib.

Descents from the Eastern Ironing Board

This is a dangerous rock to be on top of without a rope.

55D1 From the north end of the flat ridge below the vertical step, rappel 50 feet west to reach the large gully between the Eastern and Western Ironing Boards. For a hiking descent from here, hike north uphill, cross a saddle and descend north of Green Thumb to reach the west side of the Third Flatiron. From the bottom of the rappel, you can hike southeast down the gully to a jam of massive boulders that extends completely across the gully. Do a short downclimb on the slab on the west side of the gully (Class 4) or work out a devious zigzag route down through the boulders (Class 4).

55D2 From the north end of the flat ridge below the vertical step, rappel or climb 80 feet down a crack on the east face to the lowest tree, then rappel 150 feet down the east face to the approach gully.

Descents from the Western Ironing Board

55D3 Continue scrambling northwest until you can scramble west to reach hiking territory. From here, it is easiest to hike down to the north on the west side of Jaws to the canyon between the Second and Third Flatirons.

55D4 Scramble northwest and rappel or downclimb the 5.0–5.2 chimney 10 feet south of Green Crack. This chimney is on the west side of the rock.

551 Smooth 5.6 S   *Closed 2/1 – 7/31*

This three-pitch route is in the center of the smooth east face of the Eastern Ironing Board. The line is plumb, the rock is pure and this is the extant Flatiron climb. From the low point of the rock, hike northwest up along the bottom of the east face and scramble to the top of a large boulder near the east face. Start 30 feet north of this boulder.

On the first 130-foot pitch, climb straight up north of a thin disappearing crack, continue 45 feet above the end of the crack and find a meager belay (5.3–5.4). The second 130-foot pitch contains the route's 5.6 crux. To do it, climb straight up to a steeper slab, climb straight up the steep slab on a series

55E Eastern Ironing Board
551 Smooth 5.6 S

552 Que Rasca 5.8 S

of knobs (5.6) and reach a niche in the ridge. Follow the much easier ridge north to the top of the climb on a flat stretch of ridge below a vertical step.

552 Que Rasca 5.8 S   *Closed 2/1 – 7/31*

This four to six-pitch uber-climb ascends the southeast ridge of the Eastern Ironing Board. Two of the pitches are serious and unprotected. If you start near the low point of the rock, climb two or three Class 4 pitches to reach a small summit below the first great sweep of smooth rock. You can reach this area in one long pitch by starting on the east face north of the gully separating the lower slabs from the smooth upper face.

On the first serious pitch, climb a smooth east-facing slab south of a prominent crack and arrive at the top of a small pinnacle on the southeast ridge (5.7). Welcome to the Ironing Boards. On the next 160-foot pitch, follow the southeast ridge to a belay at a small flake. The last and most serious pitch is 165 feet long. Climb steeply up the ridge above the belay (5.8) and climb the now easier ridge to a small flat summit. A vertical step in the ridge beyond blocks further upward progress; this is the top of the climb.

Escapes

552E1 From the small summit below the first 5.7 pitch, downclimb east into a large gully. Go west under a large chockstone, wiggle down a narrow chimney and reach the ground on the west side of the rock.

552E2 From the notch north of the summit on top of the first 5.7 pitch, rappel 40 feet west to reach the ground.

553 Crescent 5.5 S   *Closed 2/1 – 7/31*

This three-pitch route ascends the center of the east face of the Western Ironing Board via a long, northward-curving, crescent-shaped crack. Either climb this crack or the face north (right) of it. You can achieve protection in

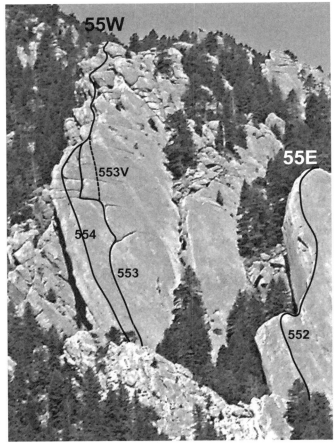

55E Eastern Ironing
     Board
552 Que Rasca 5.8 S
55W Western Ironing
     Board
553 Crescent 5.5 S
553V 5.6
554 Smoother 5.7 S

this flaring crack with pieces 4 inches or larger, but the face is difficult to protect. If you choose the crack, it is 5.4 for the first 120 feet to a spot where you can place protection. The crack is 5.5 for the next 40 feet to a spot where you can rig a belay. Continue up the crack, which is now curving north, for another 120 feet to another belay stance. To aid your ascent of this famous crack, there are lots of small face holds on the right side of the crack and you can use a combination of stemming and face climbing moves; you do not need to oomph up the crack. On the third 155-foot pitch, leave the main crack, climb directly up smaller cracks, traverse 30 feet south (left) and climb a big crack to the ridge (5.4). Scramble northwest up the much easier summit ridge.

Variation

553V On the third pitch, climb straight up the smooth face to the ridge (5.6).

554 Smoother 5.7 S   *Closed 2/1 – 7/31*

This exciting three-pitch route ascends the southern section of the east face of the Western Ironing Board. Climb straight up the slab between the crescent-shaped crack and the southern edge of the east face. After three poorly protected pitches, scramble northwest up the much easier summit ridge.

555 Green Crack 5.4   *Closed 2/1 – 7/31*

This short chimney on the west face of the Western Ironing Board can be difficult to find. A hiking saddle on the west side of the Western Ironing Board separates Bluebell Canyon from the canyon between the Second and Third Flatirons. Green Crack is 150 yards down to the south from this saddle. It is an 18-inch wide chimney capped by a chockstone. At the entrance to the chimney is a saddle-horn-shaped handhold. Ten feet south of Green Crack is an easier 5.0–5.2 chimney. Wiggle up the 18-inch wide chimney past the handhold to a bench (5.4). Make another 5.4 move past a bulge to reach the upper part of the chimney and continue up to the summit ridge. It is 90 feet from the ground to the summit ridge. This is a thoughtful little route.

56 GREEN THUMB   *Closed 2/1 – 7/31*

This summit is the highest point of the Eastern Ironing Board. It is directly west of the Third Flatiron. Although the Eastern Ironing Board and Green Thumb are physically connected, the vertical step in the southeast ridge of the Eastern Ironing Board provides a logical separation of routes. Approach by hiking to the west side of the Third Flatiron and continuing west from there.

Descents

56D1 Downclimb the summit block (5.0–5.2) and scramble 100 feet south. Rappel 60 feet west from a tree to reach the ground. For a hiking descent from here, hike north uphill, cross a saddle and descend north of Green Thumb to the west side of the Third Flatiron. From the bottom of the rappel, you can hike southeast down the gully to a jam of massive boulders that extends completely across the gully. Do a short downclimb on the slab on the west side of the gully (Class 4) or work out a devious zigzag route down through the boulders (Class 4).

56D2 Downclimb the summit block (5.0–5.2) and scramble down to the southeast. Downclimb a grubby 5.0–5.2 ramp system on the north side of the east face to reach the ground not far west of the Third Flatiron.

561 East Face 5.4   *Closed 2/1 – 7/31*

Pick a suitable starting point and climb this broken east face for 200 feet to the broad, easy summit ridge (5.4). Climb the exposed summit block at the north end of this ridge via its short east face (5.0–5.2).

562 Green Corner Right 5.8+   *Closed 2/1 – 7/31*

This 50-foot route ascends the beautiful south-facing dihedral a few feet south of the summit on the west face of the rock. This route was the original Green Crack, and its history and location have been confused in earlier guidebooks.

57 JAWS   *Closed 2/1 – 7/31*

This long rock rib northwest of the Third Flatiron rises out of the valley between the Second and Third Flatirons and has a northern exposure. The rib is well named as there are many notches separating little tooth-like Flatironettes. Because of its northern exposure, the rock is festooned with lichen. To approach Jaws, hike up the canyon between the Second and Third Flatirons and find the bottom of the rock lurking in the trees.

571 North Ridge 5.0–5.2   *Closed 2/1 – 7/31*

This rock rib provides over 800 feet of grubby excitement. The many notches will give you lots of practice in overcoming Flatiron notches. Halfway up there is one that may give you fits. To preserve the 5.0–5.2 rating, climb east below

57 Jaws   571 North Ridge 5.0–5.2

it. Also, this route will give you plenty of practice in moving to the left.

The first summit you come to is the top of Jaws, and this summit is also the highpoint of the rock rib between the Eastern and Western Ironing Boards. Abandon this summit and head west to a higher pinpoint summit. This summit is west of and considerably higher than the top of the Third and is the highest point of the Western Ironing Board. I do not recommend this climb, but like the shark, it still holds a macabre fascination.

Descent

57D You can escape the rock either to the east or west at many points along the way, and both summits have Class 4 downclimbs to the east and north.

58 MORNING AFTER

This small elegant Flatiron is southwest of the Third Flatiron on the south side of upper Bluebell Canyon. It has had many names over the years, including *The Thing* and the *Needle's Eye*, a name that refers to the peculiar hole in the summit or perhaps to the distinctive U-shaped slab standing out on the upper part

58 Morning After
581 East Face 5.7
581V 5.6
59 Eyes of the Canyon
591 Sight Flight Class 4
592 Blinded 5.4

of the east face. The name Morning After has also been perverted to *Mourning After*. Whatever the name, this rock has an excellent route on its east face.

Approach by following the Royal Arch Trail until it starts to switchback out of Bluebell Canyon. After a few of the initial short switch backs, leave the trail and hike several hundred yards west up the steep hillside to the bottom of the rock. En route, stay south of some small Flatironettes called Eyes of the Canyon. From the bottom of the east face of the Morning After, you can see a distinctive overhang running across the entire face 150 feet up.

581 East Face 5.7 *Classic*

This clean enjoyable 480-foot climb breaks naturally into four or five pitches. The belay anchors are bombproof and the protection is adequate. Start at the lowest point of the north edge of the east face. Climb up and angle slightly south (left) into the middle of the face, then head straight up to a large tree 20 feet below the large overhang. This first pitch is 140 feet of thoughtful 5.3–5.4.

Overcome the overhang above the tree via the obvious crack. There are one or two 5.7 moves and this overhang is the crux of the route. The protection is excellent here. You can use another large tree 20 feet above the overhang for a belay. Climb another 50 feet of Class 4 rock to a large ledge system with many trees. Climb 50 feet up an interesting fist-sized 5.0–5.2 crack to a final, lonely tree. From this highest tree, climb the left side of the raised U-shaped slab on the upper part of the face for 150 feet of 5.0–5.2 to another spacious ledge. Climb a final 50-foot 5.0–5.2 slab to reach the summit.

Variation

581V From the large tree covered ledge above the crux overhang, you can climb 30 feet along the right side of the raised U-shaped slab on the upper part of the face, then move south (left) back into the center of the face (5.6).

Descents

581D1 From an anchor point at the west end of the hole in the summit, rappel 50 feet south to the ground.

581D2 Climb 60 feet east down a ramp on the south side of the rock and climb 20 feet southwest down some peculiar flakes to the ground (5.0–5.2). Instead of escaping down the flakes you can also continue down the ramp for another 50 feet to the ground (5.3–5.4). The gully on the south side of the Morning After is not hikeable. For a hiking descent, go down underneath the north side of the rock.

59 EYES OF THE CANYON

These small Flatironettes do not attract much attention as they silently watch over Bluebell Canyon. From the summits you can watch with them. The highest summit provides an astonishing view of the southwest side of the Third Flatiron.

The higher three summits are all connected and are located 150 feet north of the Morning After. The highest summit is much lower than the summit of the Morning After. The east face of the upper trio of rocks is broken into two pieces with the northern piece being the larger and higher. Above its summit is the small freestanding highest summit.

A fourth rock is buried in the depths of Bluebell Canyon much lower than the upper trio. A fifth rock is above and it also rises out of Bluebell Canyon. For the upper trio of rocks use the approach for the Morning After. The low points of the two pieces of the main east face are 100 and 160 feet north of, and slightly downhill from the low point of the Morning After.

591 Sight Flight Class 4

This luminescent 350-foot route ascends the east face of the northern piece and continues on to the highest summit. The northern part of this tiny face provides enjoyable Class 4 climbing on good rock while harder climbing is a few feet away on the slab to the south. After 300 feet, there is a broken summit area, and the highest summit, a 10-foot boulder perched on top of a peculiar formation, is just beyond. Scramble across some boulders and climb an obvious crack up the 50-foot lichen covered north face of the peculiar formation. Move east and overcome the final summit boulder on its east side. The flat summit is a good place for a picnic. Bring your camera.

Descent

591D Downclimb to the boulders below the north face of the peculiar formation, and scramble west to hiking territory.

592 Blinded 5.4

This 200-foot route ascends the east face of the smaller southern piece of the main east face. The first 100 feet are Class 4, and the upper 100 feet is a smooth slab that provides some 5.4 moves. A lot of lichen is on this face.

Descent

592D From the west end of the summit, leap across a gap to hiking territory.

593 Lichen Wars 5.6

Buried deep in the cool recess of Bluebell Canyon is a narrow east face that provides a surprising 400-foot climb. With its northern exposure, this rock has been growing a healthy crop of lichen for years. It is waiting for you. If you are looking for something bizarre and different, this is it. Just before the Royal Arch Trail starts to switchback up out of Bluebell Canyon, a strong side trail leads northwest into the canyon. Follow this trail for 200 feet as it starts northwest, then swings west into Bluebell Canyon. The lowest point of the climb is 10 feet north of the trail, a few feet south of the intermittent Bluebell Creek.

Start at the low point of the rock and climb a deceptive, smooth lichen-covered slab for 100 feet (5.6). This is the crux of the route and you can avoid it by hiking farther west and engaging the face higher up. Above the initial 5.6 slab, the climbing moderates to 5.0–5.2, but lichen still lurks. Stay near the northern edge of the east face for 200 feet and reach a ledge at the top of a broken area. You can escape here by walking off to the south. Above this ledge is a conglomeration of four summit blocks which all lean against each other. There are large gaps between the bottoms of the blocks, but it is easy to climb over their tops. From the escape ledge, continue 30 feet straight up (5.0–5.2), step across the first gap and continue 40 feet up a final Class 4 slab to a funky summit. The lichen moderates near the summit, and the view from the summit will convince you that the war is over.

Descent

593D Scramble west down across the tops of two more summit blocks (Class 3), continue west over the last block, and reach the ground on its west side (easy Class 4). The last move is over lichen-infested rock.

510 WILLY B

This spire is uphill to the southwest from the Morning After. It has a very narrow east face and is a freestanding pinnacle of considerable stature in spite of its small size. This summit is one of the most difficult Flatiron summits to reach. This rock is not for the casual Flatiron scrambler, but it provides rewarding climbs for those competent at the 5.7 and 5.8 levels.

Follow the approach for the Morning After and continue west uphill on the south side of the Morning After. The Willy B has several hundred feet of scruffy preliminary slabs below the main spire. The start of both routes is on the rock's south side, so when approaching, stay south of the preliminary slabs. You can climb up these slabs, but they are out of character with the clean, difficult climbing on the main pinnacle.

58 Morning After
510 Willy B

5101 East Face 5.8 S

Descents

This is a dangerous rock to be on top of without a rope.

510D1 Rappel 80 feet west to the ground. To reach the ground in 80 feet, rappel directly west over the final horn. Rappelling down the north face of this final horn requires a 90-foot rappel.

510D2 Do two shorter rappels to the west to reach the ground. A secure thread is on a ledge halfway down.

5101 East Face 5.8 S

This three-pitch climb ascends the narrow part of the east face of the pinnacle. The crux is getting onto the narrow part of the east face above an overhang that blocks easy access to the upper part of the face. There is very little protection for the crux pitch, and this is a serious route.

Get onto the lower east face from the south, climb a 120-foot 5.0–5.2 slab, pass a tree and get on top of a large block at the base of a south-facing dihedral. Climb a 10-foot south-facing wall at the bottom of the dihedral and get onto the narrow east face (5.8). This wall is the route's crux. Climb 80 feet up the narrow east face to some horizontal cracks and work out a belay (5.6). There is very little protection on this pitch. The east face is wider above the south-facing dihedral. On the last pitch, climb 110 feet up 5.0–5.2 slabs to the flat top.

5102 Swing Time 5.7

This is the easiest route to the summit of the Willy B. While it is easier than the more often climbed East Face Route, it is still a serious undertaking since a fall from the crux can leave the second dangling on the steep south face. You can do Swing Time in three moderate length pitches. The route uses a prominent ramp on the south side of the upper east face to solve the difficulties of the upper part of the rock.

Get onto the lower east face from the south, climb a 120-foot 5.0–5.2 slab, pass a tree and get on top of a large block at the base of a south-facing dihedral. On the second pitch, climb 40 feet up the south-facing dihedral (Class 4), do an ascending traverse (5.3) south (left) to a corner at the bottom of the ramp and work out a belay. On the final pitch, climb 20 feet up the ramp (Class 4), climb the steep 8-foot south-facing wall above the ramp and get onto the main east face (5.7). These moves are the crux of the route. Once onto the main east face, climb 110 feet up 5.0–5.2 slabs to the flat summit.

SIX

Fourth Flatiron

61 FOURTH FLATIRON

When climbing out of Bluebell Canyon on the Royal Arch Trail, you are still in the realm of the Third Flatiron, which towers above and dominates your view. You can see and hear climbers on the east face and on the rappel ledges. As you follow the Royal Arch Trail over Sentinel Pass and drop into the valley to the south, you enter a new realm—the realm of the Fourth Flatiron. The sounds of birds replace climber's calls, and glimpses of rocks through the trees replace expansive views. In the cool recess at Tangen Spring, you are close to thousands of feet of rock, but you can easily forget about it for a few minutes in this verdant place.

The array of rocks here may be a bit bewildering on a first visit to this realm, since the Fourth and Fifth Flatirons are almost Jovian in their dominance. The Fourth Flatiron alone has ten satellite rocks tucked in its shadows. The easier climbing on these rocks has received scant attention, and you can spend many days exploring and climbing here and never see another climber.

The Fourth Flatiron is broken into three major pieces with two large south-facing gullies separating them. You cannot see these gullies from central Boulder, and the Flatiron appears to be contiguous. Because of its disjoint nature, the regular route on the east face provides an almost alpine experience with many varied pitches. There are corners, tiptoe faces, elegant ridges, traverses, cracks, and a huge gash for you to walk through. While you can climb each piece of the Fourth by itself, the East Face Route that ascends all three pieces is a Flatiron classic.

To approach the Fourth Flatiron, follow the Royal Arch Trail over Sentinel Pass and descend to the south. When the trail begins to climb again, look west above the trail. This is the Fourth Flatironette. Stay on the trail, climb steeply west for another 150 feet, and the trail will pass within kicking distance of the bottom of the lowest piece of the Fourth. You can see a large south-facing cave 200 feet up. An alternate approach is to follow the Woods Quarry Trail, follow a small trail steeply west from the south end of the quarry and join the Royal Arch Trail 150 feet south of Sentinel Pass.

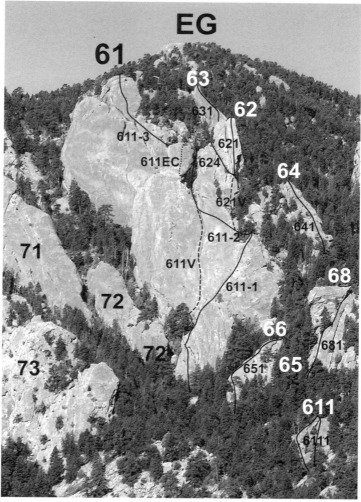

EG East Green Mountain
61 Fourth Flatiron
611-1 East Face First Piece 5.4
611-2 East Face Second Piece 5.4
611-3 East Face Third Piece 5.4
611V 5.4
611EC 5.3–5.4
62 Green Mountain Pinnacle
621 East Face 5.6
621V 5.0–5.2
624 Fern Alley Class 3
63 Challenger
631 East Face 5.4 S

64 Last Flatironette
641 East Face Class 4
65 Fourth Flatironette
651 East Face and South Ridge 5.3–5.4
66 Lost Flatironette
68 The Hammerhead
681 Yodeling Moves Class 4
611 Downclimb
6111 East Face Class 4–5.2
71 Fifth Flatiron
72 Tangen Towers
73 The Regency

611 East Face 5.4 *Classic*

This classic 10 to 12 pitch climb ascends all three pieces of the Fourth Flatiron, and each piece has some 5.4 climbing. Step off the Royal Arch Trail onto the lowest point of the rock and climb 100 feet straight up to a tree (5.0–5.2). Descend a few feet west, and climb another 90 feet into a large south-facing cave that is visible from the trail. From inside the cave you will discover that it is really an arch. Perhaps this is the Royal Arch of the future.

From the cave, move south past some intriguing potholes and climb a 5.4 crux on the south side of the cave. At this point you are only a few feet from the Tangen Tunnel hiking route. Climb easily to a large ledge 50 feet above the cave, move a few feet north onto the main east face and tiptoe 150 or 160 feet up a nice 5.0–5.2 slab to some ledges on the long summit ridge of the first piece. You will now understand the disjoint nature of the Fourth.

The first piece has a 60-foot vertical west face separating it from the second piece. Follow the southeast ridge of the first piece north for 300 feet (Class 4). This ridge is spectacular and provides good views of the second piece looming overhead. From the pointed summit of the first piece at the far northern end of the ridge, scramble west down to the ground. From this point you can hike north, but the gully between the first and second pieces is not hikeable. To continue your adventure, hike 40 feet west and engage the second piece near a large tree.

The second piece involves two long pitches plus some scrambling. Traverse 130 feet south toward the center of the second piece. Ascend only slightly on this pitch, and near its end, get into the crack below the huge gash splitting the top of the second piece. On the next pitch, ascend the crack for 150 feet to the lower end of the meadow in the gash (5.4). This crux crack is often wet, since snow lingers in the shadows of the great gash above. If the crack is wet or snowy, you can climb the rock just north of the crack (5.4). From the lower end of the meadow, scramble into the gash and walk through a verdant little paradise suitable for a summer picnic.

Walk through the upper end of the gash into the gully between the second and third pieces of the Fourth Flatiron. This gully is hikeable, and you will discover that the second and third pieces are really separate rocks. If you choose to hike southeast down this gully, be advised that it is full of poison ivy during the summer. It is much cleaner to head up to the north and then down.

To continue your climb, walk west across the gully and get onto the third piece. Climb 330 feet of Class 4–5.2 rock passing many trees and ledges. The farther south (left) you stay in this section, the cleaner and harder the climbing will be. En route, look for a nice crack that splits the otherwise smooth summit slab. From the tree at the base of this crack it is 170 feet to the top of the

Flatiron. You may also engage this crack by traversing south from easier rock on either of two ledges. However you reach it, this 5.4 crack is the prettiest pitch on the climb. As you approach the top, the crack dissolves into a 15-foot 5.4 face that takes you to a ledge only 10 feet below the summit. The summit of the third piece of the Fourth Flatiron is the least dramatic of the main Flatiron summits, but it is considerably higher than the Fifth and feels like it is several miles higher than the Third.

Variations

611V You can start near the lowest point of the second piece and angle up to the north (5.4). Either climb near the small crack below the great gash and join the regular route (5.4) or continue angling north (right) and join the East Face Route of Green Mountain Pinnacle (5.0–5.2). The low point of the second piece is not far above Tangen Tunnel.

Extra Credit

611EC The spectacular summit south of the great gash on the second piece provides an exotic addition to this climb. From the eastern end of the hiking territory in the great gash, wiggle behind or climb over a flake on the south side of the gash, traverse 12 feet east on a ledge, and get onto the east face of the southern summit. Climb the face on small holds for 165 feet to the exposed knife-edge summit. Most of the climbing on this delightful pitch is 5.0–5.2, but there are a few 5.3–5.4 moves near a 1-foot pothole 20 feet below the summit. To descend, scramble north past the highest point, sling a horn with nine feet of sling and rappel 82 spectacular feet northeast into the great gash.

Descent from the summit of the third piece

611D It is only a few feet off the west side of the summit block of the third piece, but there is an overhang. Find the spot where you can hang off some good holds, and if you are tall, reach the rock below (5.0–5.2). Move north through some boulders to hiking territory. It is a nice hike from this point to the summit of Green Mountain.

62 GREEN MOUNTAIN PINNACLE

This pinnacle is attached to the second piece of the Fourth Flatiron, but just barely. You can do a Class 3 scramble between Green Mountain Pinnacle and the rest of the Fourth Flatiron. The pinnacle forms the summit of the second piece of the Fourth Flatiron and it is north of the great gash that splits the east face of the second piece. Two more deep gashes are between the great gash and the summit of Green Mountain Pinnacle, and it is these gashes that almost separate Green Mountain Pinnacle from the Fourth Flatiron. They are connected only at the top of the middle gash.

The stately summit of Green Mountain Pinnacle has a steep, colorful north face that you can see from Boulder. Gashes interrupt the climbing on the east face of the second piece of the Fourth below the pinnacle, but the climbing on the pinnacle itself is quite clean. Approach by following the Royal Arch Trail to the end of the switchbacks on the south side of Bluebell Canyon. When the trail goes southeast toward Sentinel Pass, leave the trail and hike uphill to the southwest. Stay north of the Last Flatironette and traverse south above its summit to the north side of Green Mountain Pinnacle.

Descents

62D1 There is a fixed rappel anchor on the summit. Rappel 75 feet west to the ground.

62D2 Downclimb the Green Sneak Route (Class 4).

621 East Face 5.6

This surprising, 220-foot route ascends the entire east face of Green Mountain Pinnacle without touching the rest of the Fourth Flatiron. Directly south of the summit of the Last Flatironette is a gash named Fern Alley that is easy to scramble into, and this is the highest easy place to engage the rock. Above Fern Alley, the north face of Green Mountain Pinnacle gets organized. This is the middle of the three gashes on this part of the face. Neither of the other two gashes reaches the ground.

Hike and scramble 40 feet up Fern Alley. The crux of this route is overcoming the steep south-facing wall of Fern Alley to reach the main east face of the pinnacle. Climb 10 feet up the steep wall on some chin-up bar handholds and make a few awkward 5.6 moves north to reach easier rock. The northernmost gash appears above this point. Angle north (right) of this gash, get onto the northernmost section of east face and climb directly up this face on excellent holds to the summit (Class 4). Near the summit you will be within a few feet of the top of the steep north face.

Variation

621V You can reach the beginning of this route by getting onto the second piece of the Fourth Flatiron lower down. Start 40 feet west of the summit of the first piece, which is the same starting point for the second piece that is used by the East Face Route. Climb a few feet south, then climb 170 feet up broken 5.0–5.2 slabs to some trees. Grub up past the trees, move north (right) and step around into Fern Alley a few feet from the start of the East Face Route for Green Mountain Pinnacle (5.0–5.2). You can use this variation to include Green Mountain Pinnacle with a climb on the lower part of the Fourth Flatiron.

622 West Chimney 5.5 *Classic – Top Ten*

This is the best chimney climb near Boulder, and it provides a wonderful change of pace from regulation Flatiron climbing. The gash that splits the east face of Green Mountain Pinnacle is a deep chimney that goes through to the

62 Green Mountain Pinnacle

622 West Chimney 5.5

The author taking care of business.

west side of the rock. The chimney is only a few feet south of the summit, and you can easily see it from the bottom of the rappel directly below the summit on the north side of the rock.

From this point, scramble 30 feet into a small notch, make a few Class 4 moves into the main part of the chimney, consider your future and prepare to take care of business. From the middle of the chimney, climb 60 feet straight up, exit the chimney to the north and climb 10 feet north to the summit. The smooth-walled chimney is 3 feet wide at the bottom, 4 feet wide near the top and consistent in its difficulty. There is a crack for protection 40 feet up, but that is the only protection available in the chimney. You can top rope this beautiful pitch from the summit of the pinnacle.

623 Green Sneak Class 4

This is the easiest route to the summit of Green Mountain Pinnacle. It sneaks through the West Chimney and reaches the summit from the east. From the bottom of the rappel northwest of the summit, scramble 30 feet into a small notch and make a few Class 4 moves into the bottom of the West Chimney. Scramble east through the bottom of the chimney and get onto the east face of the pinnacle 70 feet below the summit. The last 70 feet of the east face is Class 4.

624 Fern Alley Class 3

You should do this 200-foot tour with a smile and a chuckle for partners. Fern Alley is the middle gash separating Green Mountain Pinnacle from the rest of the second piece of the Fourth Flatiron. The circumnavigation of Green Mountain Pinnacle via Fern Alley is a good objective for an evening run and scramble.

Follow the approach described for the Green Mountain Pinnacle East Face Route and get into Fern Alley. Hike 60 feet up the gully to an angular flake wedged across the bottom of the gully. Overcome this hard Class 3 obstacle, and hike into the upper sanctuary of Fern Alley, which is a cool cozy place to linger. Near the top of the alley, scramble south onto a large broken summit area (Class 3). You can walk south and peer into the deep gash splitting the second piece of the Fourth. The summit of the route is a block leaning up against the short steep south face of Green Mountain Pinnacle.

Descent

624D From the leaning summit block, scramble 50 feet west down a series of short steps to the ground (hard Class 3). This leaves you in the large hiking gully between the second and third pieces of the Fourth Flatiron. You can hike southeast down to the Tangen Tunnel Route, but beware of poison ivy lower down in this gully. It is cleaner to hike a short distance up to the north, cross the saddle between Challenger and Green Mountain Pinnacle and descend on the north side of Green Mountain Pinnacle.

63 CHALLENGER

This steeple flies future-free, high on the slopes of Green Mountain. It is west of Green Mountain Pinnacle and north of the third piece of the Fourth Flatiron. Its summit is only slightly lower than the summit of the Fourth's third piece. Follow the approach for Green Mountain Pinnacle and hike to the saddle on its west side. Challenger is west of this saddle.

631 East Face 5.4 S *Classic*

This 300-foot climb up the narrow sweeping east face of Challenger is surprising and beautiful even though there is some lichen on the rock. Start in the saddle between Challenger and Green Mountain Pinnacle and climb 150 feet to the highest tree on the east face. You will meet the challenge halfway up this pitch on a smooth 5.3–5.4 slab. Above the highest tree, ascend the north edge of the east face for 150 feet to the summit (5.4). The holds are small but plentiful. A horizontal crack halfway up this pitch provides the only protection opportunity. The hardest, most spectacular moves are just below the summit. From the summit of Challenger you can see forever.

Descent

631D Downclimb 6 feet west and step across a gap (Class 4). Continue climbing west along a fin, step across a second gap and downclimb 12 feet south to reach the ground (Class 4).

64 LAST FLATIRONETTE

This curious satellite of the Fourth Flatiron, unlike the Lost Flatironette, another of the Fourth's satellites, is visible from Boulder. The rock is a short distance north of the Fourth's second piece. The low point of the Fourth Flatironette, another satellite, is north of and slightly below the top of the first piece of the Fourth Flatiron. At first glance, this rock looks like it would not be very worthwhile, but it turns out to be fun. Approach by leaving the Royal

Arch Trail at Sentinel Pass and hiking west, staying north of the Hammerhead. From the west side of the Hammerhead, continue uphill for another 300 feet to the base of the Last Flatironette.

641 East Face Class 4

This face provides 350 feet of obscure Class 4 climbing. Start at or near the low point of the rock, climb north of a headwall, and cruise up to a second headwall that you cannot avoid. Climb the center of the second Class 4 headwall, which is easier than it looks. The summit is not far beyond with its good views of the Willy B and the Morning After.

Descent

641D From the summit, scramble 15 feet southwest and pass an eye-catching horn (Class 4). Move through some large boulders to hiking territory.

65 FOURTH FLATIRONETTE

After the Royal Arch Trail crosses Sentinel Pass, it passes under the low point of the Fourth Flatironette, climbs steeply under this rock's south face, passes the bottom of the Fourth Flatiron and continues to climb past Tangen Spring. The Fourth Flatironette has a lot of lichen, an unfriendly countenance, and I do not recommend it as an extension to running workouts. Two Move Rock and Yodeling Moves are much nicer.

651 East Face and South Ridge 5.3–5.4

Step off the Royal Arch Trail onto the low point of the rock and climb 90 feet near the south edge of the east face toward two large ponderosa pines (5.0–5.2). One of these trees grows out of the rock while the other rises from the trail directly below the south face. The section of rock below the trees is tricky 5.3–5.4. The cleanest but most exposed route is on the extreme south edge of the east face. Continue between the trees and reach the southern end of the south ridge 150 feet above the ground. Climb 150 feet northwest up varied Class 4 rock to the summit. Fifty feet below the summit, climb west of a small headwall (Class 4). The most interesting part of this climb is the 50-foot Class 4 hand traverse to the summit nestled in the trees. The views from this summit are not very exciting.

Descent

651D Scramble 50 feet south back across the Class 4 hand traverse. Downclimb past the Class 4 headwall, and 30 feet south of the headwall, scramble 20 feet west down a Class 3 escape ramp.

66 LOST FLATIRONETTE

This beguiling little rock is nestled between the Fourth Flatironette and the first piece of the Fourth Flatiron. Its summit is above the summit of the Fourth Flatironette and below the summit of the first piece of the Fourth Flatiron. Appropriately, the Lost Flatironette is not visible from the Royal Arch Trail. This rock has less lichen on it than the Fourth Flatironette and is a little more pleasant to climb on. The rock is peppered with curious and sometimes nerve-wracking knobs.

To approach the Lost Flatironette, follow the Royal Arch Trail past the Fourth Flatironette, leave the trail, and hike northwest up the gully between the Fourth Flatironette and the first piece of the Fourth Flatiron. After a few hundred feet, the bottom of the Lost Flatironette will come into view. Another way to find the Lost Flatironette is to climb the Fourth Flatironette and follow the descent described for that rock. The bottom of the Lost Flatironette is 40 feet west and slightly above the bottom of the Class 3 escape ramp off the Fourth Flatironette.

661 Southeast Ridge 5.0–5.2

This 250-foot climb is fairly consistent at the 5.0–5.2 level. Start at the low point of the rock and head 130 feet up the south side of the east face on knobby 5.0–5.2 rock to the summit ridge. The climbing eases to Class 4 as you move northwest along this ridge, but just as you think you will romp to the top, a 40-foot 5.0–5.2 slab rears up near a patch of pink rock. This slab makes a nice finish and the summit is just beyond.

Descent

661D Downclimb the 12-foot knobby lichen-covered north face of the rock (5.0–5.2).

67 TWO MOVE ROCK

This nifty little rock has often been used as a scrambling finish to various running routes in this area. Follow the Royal Arch Trail as it descends south from Sentinel Pass. The trail descends under the large West Sentinel Boulder, and 100 feet beyond passes within a few feet of the bottom of Two Move Rock. The rock is above and west of the trail.

671 Southeast Ridge 5.0–5.2

An angular boulder leaning against the base of the ridge marks the bottom of Two Move Rock and its southeast ridge. Start on or near this boulder and scramble up to a 5-foot south-facing wall. Climb the wall and get onto the main east face. A smooth slab and the two move 5.0–5.2 crux lurks a few feet above. Above the crux, continue 100 feet up the southeast ridge on enjoyable Class 4 climbing to a tiny summit, which is overhung on the west. You can either escape the rock here or continue scrambling north (Class 3) until the ridge peters out into hiking territory. This point is 100 feet west of Sentinel Pass.

68 THE HAMMERHEAD

This, the largest and most statuesque satellite of the Fourth Flatiron, is visible from almost all locations and is rather spectacular from most viewpoints to the south. The rock consists of a 400-foot east ridge that connects to a large hammerhead summit block. The east ridge connects to the north edge of the summit block while the east, south and west faces of the summit block are overhanging. It is these faces of the summit block that give the Hammerhead its character and easy visibility.

The Hammerhead is between Two Move Rock and the Fourth Flatironette, but is considerably higher than its companions. The view from the top is excellent, the rock is firm and the route described on this rock is one of the best Class 4 climbs in the Boulder area. The route is easily protected, and is a good climb for beginners.

To approach the Hammerhead, follow the Royal Arch Trail over Sentinel Pass. As the trail descends to the south, West Sentinel Boulder and Two Move Rock are west of and close to the trail. Immediately after Two Move Rock, look sharp for the bottom of the Hammerhead tucked in the trees 50 feet west of the trail. This point is north of and above the bottom of the Fourth Flatironette. From the rock's low point, you can see the great hammerhead summit block overhead, and there should be no doubt that you are on the right rock.

681 Yodeling Moves Class 4 *Classic*

This delightful route ascends a 400-foot spine to the summit block, then ascends its west face to the summit. Start at the bottom of the rock and simply head up the east ridge. Half way up you will discover a long powerful arch. With a span of 50 feet, this is the longest arch in the Boulder area. From a point on the ridge just below the arch, you can view the underside of the arch and contemplate how much weight it would take to break the thin rock on its outer edge. The main part of the arch seems quite solid, and the trip across is easy and spectacular. After 400 feet of continuous Class 4 climbing, you will reach a tiny summit from which you can look southward across a gap at the hammerhead summit block.

The easiest route to the top of the summit block is on its west face. From the top of the east ridge, scramble west for a few feet to the northwest corner of the summit block. This point is in hiking territory and you can walk away having savored the east ridge.

Near the north end of the west face is a 6-foot-high boulder propped against the base of the face. Climb up on or near it and get onto a large ledge in the middle of the steep west face. Traverse south on this ledge system and move up at strategic points (Class 4). The exposure beneath your heels will increase rapidly as you move south along this ledge. Just below the summit you can enjoy 100 vertical feet. Equally enjoyable are the chin-up bar holds along the way. With both hands sunk to the hilt on these holds, you can yodel and mock all that air. Arrive at the summit after 40 spectacular feet. The view from this summit is wonderful.

Variations

681V1 For a good view of the underside of the arch, hike up from the low point of the rock along its south side. Scramble into the gully below the summit block to a point directly below the arch. Scramble up under the lower eastern end of the arch, climb through the crack between the arch and the rest of the face (Class 4) and join the East Ridge Route below the arch.

681V2 From the top of the east ridge, step across the gap, climb the short steep north face of the summit block (5.7) and finish on the short east face of the summit block.

Descents

681D1 Downclimb back across the ledge system on the west face (Class 4).

681D2 Rig a short rappel near the northwest corner of the summit block.

69 SENTINEL BOULDERS

This is the group of five overgrown boulders that form Sentinel Pass on the Royal Arch Trail. Sentinel Pass is not a real pass, just an alleyway between two of the Sentinel Boulders. The Sentinel Boulders are on the ridge between Bluebell Canyon and the next canyon south.

The East Sentinel Boulder is 100 feet east of the pass, connected to the top of a rock called Easy Street, but this boulder throws up ferocious defenses on all sides. The easiest route on its north face provides an exciting 40-foot climb ending with a squeeze crack under the summit chockstone (5.6). There is also a route on the south face. To do it, step across a gap, traverse east across the face to reach the upper east face and ascend it to the summit (5.6). To descend, sling the summit chockstone and rappel 40-feet down the north face. Two boulders between the East Sentinel Boulder and the trail are both simple scrambles, and hikers seeking a better view often climb the one immediately east of the trail.

The large West Sentinel Boulder west of the trail has a steep east side, and this rock forces the trail to descend south of the pass. There is a short but committing 5.4 climb along the southeast edge of the West Sentinel. Descend 60 feet south from the pass, leave the trail and climb west into a notch with a tree (5.3–5.4) near the southeast edge of the West Sentinel. Climb 15 feet along the south edge of the east face (5.3–5.4), step onto the main east face, overcome a 5.4 crux and follow easier rock along the south edge of the east face to the top. It is a Class 3 descent to the west, and lost hikers looking for the trail often ascend the west side of the West Sentinel Boulder. The smaller westernmost Sentinel Boulder is an easy scramble.

610 EASY STREET

This rock, composed of two connected Flatironettes, is east of Sentinel Pass on the Royal Arch Trail. The main part of the rock is 50 feet west of Downclimb. It provides some easy fun scrambling and special views of the larger Flatirons. From the south end of Woods Quarry, hike 200 feet west, angle steeply uphill to the north and find the bottom of Easy Street in the trees 50 feet south of and slightly lower than the bottom of the extra piece at the base of Downclimb.

6101 East Face Class 4

Start at the low point of the rock, scramble up 50 easy feet and confront a headwall, which is the only difficulty on the east face. You can bypass it on the south (Class 4), the north (5.0–5.2), or climb it directly (5.5–5.6). Other starts that avoid this headwall completely are possible on both the south and north edges of the east face. Above the headwall, climb 140 feet of easy Class 4 rock to a large broken area between the two Flatironettes that form Easy Street. Above the broken area, climb another 140 feet of Class 4 rock to a weird little summit. On the last 100 feet, look for three one-foot arches. This summit is 60 feet northeast of the higher more imposing East Sentinel Boulder.

Descents

6101D1 Downclimb 25 feet east, then move 15 feet south into the gully between the East Sentinel Boulder and Easy Street (Class 4). Follow this gully west up and over a Class 4 notch to easy ground near Sentinel Pass.

6101D2 From the highest point, climb a few feet southwest to another little summit, and downclimb 25 feet west to the ground (Class 4).

611 DOWNCLIMB

This is the lowest and one of the smallest satellites of the Fourth Flatiron, but its overhanging north and west faces don't allow a simple walkoff and give the rock some character. From the summit there is an awesome view of the south side of the Third Flatiron. Downclimb is 250 yards west of and above Woods Quarry on a small ridge. From Woods Quarry, hike 200 feet west from the south end of the quarry, and angle steeply uphill to the north where you will find the bottom of Downclimb in the trees near the crest of the ridge. The bottom of Easy Street is south of Downclimb.

Descent

611D Downclimb the east face. The easiest line is near the south edge of the east face all the way to the ground (Class 4). The shortest escape is to climb 60 feet down the south edge of the east face, then angle north across the face to high ground on the north edge of the east face (5.0–5.2).

6111 East Face Class 4–5.2

There is a small extra piece of rock at the lower south end of the east face. The longest climb ascends this extra piece for 70 feet (Class 4), then overcomes an 8-foot, south-facing wall (5.0–5.2) to gain the main east face. Climb 90 feet up the south edge of the face to the top (Class 4). You can also ascend the main 140-foot east face directly. The south edge is Class 4 and the center of this small face is 5.0–5.2.

6112 West Face 5.4

Downclimb has a small but steep west face. Near the north end of this face is an obvious crack and chimney system. Ascend this oblique system for 40 feet, overcome an easy headwall and angle 15 feet north to the summit.

612 LOST SENTINELS

Two ribs of rock are below and south of the Sentinel Boulders, nestled in the recess of the canyon below the Fourth and Fifth Flatirons. These east-facing ribs are not prominent and they spend most of their time resting, lost and forgotten in the shadow of the great Flatirons soaring overhead. To approach, hike west from the south end of Woods Quarry. Shortly after the route steepens, look south and spot the Lost Sentinels less than 100 feet away.

The northern, smaller rib provides 150 feet of scrambling. As an optional exercise, you can pull over the initial overhang (5.3–5.4). You can pass a second more formidable wall on its north edge. Above this wall, 40 feet of flaky Class 4 rock leads to placid Class 3 rock. The longer southern rib has more character. It provides 200 feet of continuous Class 4 climbing, and the central portion is along an elegant edge. When scrambling along this edge in the cool of a summer evening, you can appreciate the charm of this little valley and reflect on the wonderful Flatiron parkland above Boulder. A sturdy tree marks the summit. The descents from both ribs are short and easy.

613 WOODS QUARRY

This unsightly scar on the lower east face of Green Mountain provides the smoothest slab climbing on the Flatirons, and this is an unconventional practice area. You can easily reach the quarry by hiking up the Woods Quarry Trail from the Mesa Trail. The quarry's 80-foot high east face is equipped with bolts that indicate several lines on this smooth slab. The longest most popular route is on the south side of the face and ends at a tree that provides a good anchor. This face is easily top roped, which is handy since the easiest route on it is 5.8.

614 TOMATO ROCK *Classic*

This well-named 12-foot-high boulder is hidden in the forest, 50 yards west of the Mesa Trail and 150 yards south of Bluebell Canyon. Tomato Rock stands supreme—it is one of the most difficult Flatiron summits to reach, even by its easiest route. Accept Tomato Rock as it is, and eschew cheaters who accept a boost, pile up rocks at the bottom, or worse, prop a log against the boulder. The easiest route for tall people is on the north face with the difficulty being inversely proportional to the climber's height. The difficulty is 5.8 for a six-foot climber. The easiest route for shorter people is on the southeast face and uses some holes big enough for one or two fingers (5.8). There are at least 12 routes on Tomato Rock, and some have been climbed with no hands. Once, a frustrated individual who had failed on several dozen attempts on all sides of the rock walked away in apparent defeat. Thirty feet away, this individual turned, charged the rock with a crazed roar, ran up it and two seconds later was stomping on the summit!

SEVEN

Fifth Flatiron

71 FIFTH FLATIRON

The Fifth Flatiron is just south of the multi-piece Fourth Flatiron, and is the smallest of the great Flatirons on Green Mountain. The summit, while lower than the summit of the Fourth, is still considerably higher than the summit of the Third. The east face of the Fifth is marked by a series of deep parallel cracks appropriately called the Catscratch Cracks. The low point of the Flatiron is on the northeast end of the east face, 100 yards above the Royal Arch Trail just after it passes Tangen Spring and the Lower Tangen Tower. The climbing on the Fifth is generally clean and easy, but there are some deceptive portions on the east face. The slabs near the north edge of the east face hold a lot of lichen, and it is difficult to escape from this Flatiron.

I describe four basic lines on the east face. For the Northeast Buttress, East Face North Side and Catscratch Routes, approach via the Royal Arch Trail and the low point of the rock. For the East Face South Side Route, either hike uphill from Royal Arch, staying south of two small pieces of rock, or hike up under the east face from the low point to the bottom of the southern part of the east face. The gully along the bottom of the east face holds snow through the winter, and the bottom of the Fifth is often wet.

Descent

71D *This is a dangerous rock to be on top of without a rope.* From the bolt on the summit, rappel 75 spectacular feet north to the ground. You can hike down either side of the Fifth. Hiking down the south side is easier and less brushy. On the north side, the gully between the Upper Tangen Tower and the Fifth is not hikeable. The gully between the Upper Tangen Tower and the Fourth is hikeable, but there are two 20-foot Class 4 slabs that are dangerous when wet. This gully is part of the Tangen Tunnel Route up Green Mountain.

71I Northeast Buttress 5.5

This 900-foot route is the longest and most serious climb on the Fifth Flatiron. Protection and belays are difficult but adequate on this slab. Start at the low point of the Flatiron and climb 120 feet to a secure belay stance on the north

61 Fourth Flatiron

71 Fifth Flatiron

711 Northeast Buttress 5.5

712 East Face North Side 5.0–5.2

713 Catscratch Cracks 5.0–5.2

714 East Face South Side 5.4

72 Tangen Towers

721 Lower Tanger Tower 5.5

722 Upper Tangen Tower 5.4

73 The Regency

731 El Camino Royale Class 4

74 Royal Arch

741 East Face Class 4

75 The Anomaly

751 East Face Class 4

76 The Amoeboid

761 Buckets Class 4

77 The Hourglass

771 East Face 5.0–5.2

78 The Fist

781 East Face 5.5

782 South Ridge 5.5

79 Schmoe's Nose

791 East Face 5.6

edge of the east face. You can scramble north from this stance and escape the Flatiron. On the second 140-foot pitch, climb directly over a 5.3–5.4 bulge, angle slightly south (left) and work out a belay at a series of flakes. On the third 160-foot pitch, climb two 5.5 bulges, angle south (left) and reach a sturdy tree. On the fourth pitch, angle north (right) to the ridge crest and climb it to another good belay (Class 4). Follow the north ridge for two long Class 4 pitches to the summit.

712 East Face North Side 5.0–5.2 *Classic*

This five-star, 875-foot six-pitch climb is the longest easy climb on the Fifth. The protection is adequate, the difficulty consistent at the 5.0–5.2 level and the summit ridge is beautiful. More difficult climbing lurks nearby in the first half of the climb, but if you take care to follow the easiest line, the difficulty will not exceed 5.0–5.2.

Start in a prominent foot-wide crack 15 feet south of the low point of the Flatiron. This crack becomes much deeper higher up as it parallels the north edge of the east face. It is not easy to cross this crack, so it is important to decide early which side of the crack to commit to. Also, the prospect of climbing up this crack is a grim one. Ascend the crack for 20 feet, then move onto the face south (left) of the crack. The face north of the crack is the Northeast Buttress Route, which is a more serious undertaking.

After 130 feet, you can work out a belay in some flakes 30 feet south of the big crack. From here, the route is straightforward. Climb the face south of the big crack, staying within 20 or 30 feet of it, perhaps using some smaller cracks. After 440 feet, the deep crack disappears and the face above contains several trees. After 560 feet, reach a prominent niche in the north ridge. You can reach this niche in four pitches.

The route from here to the summit is along beautiful Class 4 rock. Climb to the ridge crest and enjoy. 160 feet above the niche, reach a secure aerie right on the ridge. This is a good place to photograph your partner climbing along the crest. When ready, climb a 155-foot pitch from the aerie to the summit. The last 30 feet are classic.

713 Catscratch Cracks 5.0–5.2

This 700-foot, five-pitch route and its many variations ascends the center of the east face. On this route you can at least flirt with the deep Catscratch Cracks. The cracks are really deep chimneys and most of them are not very enticing. You can do an enjoyable face climb by staying north (right) of the cracks.

Hike 150 feet south from the low point of the Flatiron and pass a Class 3 chockstone in the approach gully. There are several places to start up the east face along the next 100 feet of the approach gully. The longest and most aesthetic route on the center of the face begins on a rib that starts 30 feet south of the chockstone in the approach gully.

Angle 300 feet south up this 5.0–5.2 rib to the center of the face. An intermediate belay is difficult to arrange in this first 300 feet, but you can solve this problem by using one of the easier starts farther south. From the center of the face there are several possibilities.

To reach the Catscratch Cracks, continue angling south for another 100 feet to a broken area below the largest chimney. If you want to climb up a chimney, you have four to choose from. If you prefer to stay on the slabs, climb 150 feet directly up the rest of the east face (Class 4) and join the north ridge near a comfortable aerie. Follow the north ridge for a final 155 feet to the summit (Class 4).

Variations

713V Many variations are possible to the line described here. You can use several different starts. By starting near the south side of the face, you can climb directly up into the broken area below the Catscratch Cracks, although this part of the face is unpleasant. An ascent of the deep central Catscratch Crack is 5.6. From the center of the face, you can proceed more directly to the north ridge and intersect it near a prominent niche. It is two long Class 4 pitches along the north ridge from this niche to the summit.

714 East Face South Side 5.4 *Classic*

This sunny 550-foot four-pitch route near the south edge of the east face is often dry when the Fifth's more northern routes are still wet. The climbing is consistent at the 5.0–5.4 level and the protection is adequate. Start from an alcove below the southern base of the east face. After an initial 160 feet of mature 5.0–5.2 rock, a prominent crack angles up to the southern edge of the east face. You can cross this crack in a number of places, and some 5.3–5.4 climbing is above the crack. A good belay stance is at the 320-foot level.

Above this stance, the face sweeps up in a series of steps between the upper ends of the Catscratch Cracks. The southern edge of the east face is not well defined at this point as the east face rolls over into a tiny but steep southeast face. The rock is steeper here and there are two nice 5.4 slabs between cracks before the climbing eases to 5.0–5.2. A large ledge is at the 480-foot level. From this ledge, you can move 20 feet north to the spectacular north ridge and follow that to the summit. From the ledge, you can do a more direct finish by climbing the final 70 feet of the east face (5.0–5.2) to join the north ridge a few feet below the summit.

72 TANGEN TOWERS

The two Tangen Towers lie nestled between the bases of the Fourth and Fifth Flatirons. Soon after the Royal Arch Trail passes the low point of the Fourth Flatiron, it climbs to Tangen Spring, which is near the low point of the Lower Tangen Tower. Hikers have long cherished this cool primal spot. The Tangen Tunnel hiking route starts above the spring, sneaks through the Tangen Tunnel under several huge chockstones, and continues up the gully between the Tangen Towers and the Fourth Flatiron. The Upper Tangen Tower is separated from the Lower by a hiking saddle, which you can reach by hiking up through the Tangen Tunnel or by hiking up the gully south of the Lower Tangen Tower. The gully between the Upper Tangen Tower and the Fifth Flatiron is not hikeable. Poison ivy lurks in these gullies.

721 Lower Tangen Tower 5.5

The Lower Tangen Tower puts up a ferocious defense for a small rock. The lower part of the tower is steep and forbidding when viewed from Tangen Spring, but the rock has a surprisingly pleasant route up it. The route starts on the upper south side via the left of two cracks that are 6 feet apart. You can reach the summit in one 120-foot pitch, or more conveniently, in two 60-foot pitches. The route's 5.5 crux is the first few moves up the crack, which is a slot at the bottom. Above the crux start, continue up the 5.0–5.2 crack for another 25 feet, then angle west (left) up an easy ramp to a secure stance on the west side of a large leaning block. Continue 25 feet up the easy ramp and climb a 10-foot southwest-facing Class 4 wall to the summit. The view from this large summit is one of the best on Green Mountain.

Descent

721D *This is a dangerous rock to be on top of without a rope.* Several secure threads and a tree are on the west end of the summit. Choose your anchor and rappel 40 feet west over a short, spectacular overhang to reach the saddle between the Lower and Upper Tangen Towers.

722 Upper Tangen Tower 5.4

The Upper Tangen Tower is larger than the lower tower. Its smooth east face provides a nice ascent on small holds. There is a lack of belay ledges on the upper part of this face. Start in or near the saddle between the two towers and climb 100 feet of Class 4 rock to a ledge with a broken-down tree on it. Sixty feet above the tree, near the north edge of the east face, there is a 5-foot flake where you can arrange a good anchor. From here, you can reach the top with a 165-foot rope by climbing straight up near the north edge of the east face (5.3–5.4). You can also climb up the center of the face and arrange an intermediate belay in a larger flake system in the center of the face. The summit is in hiking territory.

73 THE REGENCY

This large broken Flatiron east of Royal Arch is distinguished by a little teardrop-shaped summit block that is spectacular when viewed from Royal Arch or from a point just above Woods Quarry. To approach the bottom of the rock, leave the Mesa Trail 100 yards south of the small canyon coming down from the Fourth and Fifth Flatirons. Angle up south to the next small canyon to the south, hike west up this gully until the Regency comes into view and angle northwest (right) to the base of the rock.

731 El Camino Royale Class 4 *Classic*

This is one of the finest Class 4 climbs in the Boulder area, especially if you combine it with an ascent of Royal Arch. Anyone who enjoys moving over rock will savor this 600-foot route. Start at the lowest point of the rock, stay north (right) of a gully system and cruise up 250 feet to a broken area. Another 250 feet brings you to a second broken area. You can also use other, slightly harder lines south of the gully to reach this spot. Climb a 100-foot slab on the best rock of all to the spectacular summit with its awesome views of the Fourth and Fifth Flatirons. Also, if people are at Royal Arch, you will look quite heroic to them. They have been known to ask Regents to please stand on the very top so they can get a good picture!

Descents

731D1 Climb east down the upper 100-foot Class 4 slab to the second broken area and walk north.

731D2 Downclimb 20 feet east off the summit block, then move around to its west face. Climb 30 feet down the west face and get over an awkward gap (Class 4) that seems to go better if you face out. Descend east on a north side ramp, turn west and dive through a deep narrow crack. This descent leaves you at the bottom of the East Face Route of Royal Arch.

74 ROYAL ARCH

Royal Arch is one of the most visited pieces of Flatiron rock. The arch is a worthwhile hiking objective and it also provides a couple of short solid climbs. To get to the arch, either follow the Royal Arch Trail to its end, or climb the Regency east of the arch (Class 4), or hike up under the south side of the Regency and scramble up to the arch (Class 4).

741 East Face Class 4

From the lowest point of the rock, climb up 300 feet of sharp Class 4 rock to the exposed summit. This is a logical conclusion to an ascent of the Regency.

742 West Ridge 5.6

The steep west ridge of Royal Arch provides 30 feet of 5.6 excitement.

Descent

742D Climb 75 feet down the East Face Route (Class 4) and move south to hiking territory a few feet east of the inside of the arch.

75 THE ANOMALY

This rock is a satellite of the Amoeboid, which is the rock south and west of Royal Arch. This amorphous pair is south of and below the Hourglass, which is the distinctively shaped rock high on the slopes of Green Mountain below the Fist. You can climb the Anomaly by itself or combine it with the Amoeboid to enjoy 500 feet of delightful Class 4 climbing. These rocks provide easy climbing tucked away from it all.

The top of the Anomaly is even with and 200 yards southwest of Royal Arch. Approach by following the Royal Arch Trail to Royal Arch, skirting the arch on its west side, and hiking downhill to the south to the base of the Anomaly. For a more direct approach, follow the approach to the Regency, then continue hiking uphill along the south edge of that rock. Stay south (left) at two junctions where small trails head up toward Royal Arch, and as your small trail fades away, the Anomaly will appear.

751 East Face Class 4

Start near the center of this small distinctive face and climb 200 feet straight up to the top. The climbing is sustained at the Class 4 level. Some patches of lichen and moss are on this face, but you can avoid them, and other than this, the rock is clean and solid. The top of the Anomaly is in hiking territory.

76 THE AMOEBOID

Although you can see this rock from Boulder, it is easily overlooked. It lacks visual character, but does provide decent climbing. It is a few hundred yards southwest of and above Royal Arch, and southeast of and below the Hourglass. The Amoeboid's summit area is broken into a series of large boulders, and it is not convenient to just cruise up to the top. However, the main piece of rock does provide a surprising climb. To approach the Amoeboid, use either of the approaches described for the Anomaly, then hike uphill to the west along the south side of the Anomaly to the bottom of the Amoeboid. It is also easy to scamper 100 feet from the top of the Anomaly down to the south to the bottom of the Amoeboid.

761 Buckets Class 4

This 300-foot climb follows a series of natural potholes and resembles a primal ladder. Standing at the bottom of the east face you will see a curious foot-deep water groove near the center of the rock. Start just north of this groove and ascend the buckets for 250 feet (easy Class 4). Higher up, angle slightly south and get into the large gash above the water groove. Scramble and hike west up this gash between two of the Amoeboid's summits to the end of the climb. This gash is a small echo of the great gash on the second piece of the Fourth Flatiron and is a cool forgotten place high on the slopes of Green Mountain. From the west end of the gash, hike south.

There is room for more climbing on this rock. The left side of the east face is appealing and the summits on either side of the gash provide an exciting finish. Three more summits are above the end of the gash, and you can work out a notch-hopping route to ascend all three.

77 THE HOURGLASS

This well-named rock is several hundred yards above Royal Arch. Its summit is south of and even with the summit of the Fifth Flatiron. It is directly east of the Fist, which is the prominent rock on the skyline. Approach the Hourglass by hiking uphill to the southwest from Royal Arch, staying south of the Fifth Flatiron.

771 East Face 5.0–5.2

Start at an appropriate point at the bottom of the east face and climb 450 feet straight up to the summit. This face has many trees on it and consequently there are lots of pine needles on the holds and ledges. Also, the rock is loose. Considering all the wonderful climbs nearby, I cannot recommend this rock.

Descent

771D From the summit, scramble south down 40 feet of obvious Class 3 rock to the ground.

78 THE FIST

This spectacular, curious rock is prominent on the skyline of Green Mountain. It is above and slightly south of the Fifth Flatiron and its summit is a little higher than that of the Fourth Flatiron. Sometimes called the Hippo Head, it is the highest Flatiron summit on the east face of Green Mountain. The view from the summit of the Fist is spectacular, and you can look steeply down to the Third Flatiron. The climbs on this rock are varied and pleasant. The best approach for the east and north faces is to hike uphill from Royal Arch staying south of the Fifth Flatiron and north of the Hourglass. The best approach for the south side routes is to hike to Hill Billy Rock, then continue uphill, staying north of Hill Billy and south of the Amoeboid and the Hourglass.

Descents

This is a dangerous rock to be on top of without a rope.

78D1 Downclimb (5.3–5.4) or rappel 30 feet east off the summit block to a large ledge. Rig an anchor and rappel 50 feet north to the ground.

78D2 From the large ledge 30 feet below the summit block, scramble around to the west side of the summit block, rig an anchor and rappel 50 feet west to the ground.

78D3 From the summit, rappel 80 feet west to the ground.

78D4 From the large ledge below the summit block, rappel down the east face.

78 The Fist

781 East Face 5.5

782 South Ridge 5.5

77 The Hourglass

781 East Face 5.5

This 350-foot face has several horizontal ledges with trees on them and clean climbing between the ledges. You can climb the face in three pitches with the first two pitches no harder than 5.0–5.2. The third crux pitch overcomes the bulge in the upper part of the face via a nice 5.5 hand crack. The hand crack continues up the face above the bulge for an additional 40 feet to a large ledge below and south of the summit block. Climb the 30-foot summit block on its east side (5.3). There are at least two ways to overcome the difficult step at the base of the summit block. Enjoy the summit.

782 South Ridge 5.5

The 650-foot south ridge of the Fist is seen prominently from NCAR and provides an enjoyable climb. Find the low point of the rock nestled in the trees above the west side of the Hourglass. From the low point, which is below a vertical section of rock, move 20 feet east and engage the rock by climbing a crack on the east face. On the lower part of this route, stay on the east face below the south ridge, but in the middle portion of the route, and you can climb directly up the elegant south ridge.

Higher up, a beautiful imposing buttress on the ridge crest blocks easy passage. Get onto the highest ledge system that crosses the upper part of the east face and traverse north on this ledge system. Stay below the imposing buttress and join the East Face Route below its crux 5.5 hand crack. Follow this route to the summit.

783 South Ramp 5.5

This is a curious 630-foot route that follows the first ramp and gully system west of the south ridge. This sunny route breaks naturally into five or six pitches. Long after the sun has left the east faces it will be beaming in on this ramp system. From the low point of the rock, move 20 feet west to the bottom of the ramp system. The beginning of this route is a 30-foot slab marked by a distinctive water groove 6 inches wide and 4 inches deep. This groove is often wet.

Twenty feet west of this slab, you can also start up the second ramp and gully system west of the south ridge. While this system provides a nice climb for 400 feet, the ramp ends in a steep headwall, and this ramp system does not provide a reasonable summit route.

The first ramp system does go to the summit and has three cruxes interspersed with much easier climbing. Ascend the initial slab with the water groove in it. Either use the water groove or climb the slab left of the groove. The first 30 feet are 5.3–5.4, after which the angle eases. There is a tree in a meadow after 100 feet. The second crux is at the upper end of this meadow. The gully is quite steep and smooth at this point. You can avoid this spot by traversing left on an easy ledge to the crest of the ridge overlooking the second ramp system. Climb directly up this 5.3–5.4 ridge until you can traverse back into the gully below a large chockstone.

Climb through a hole below the chockstone and follow the easy loose gully to the third crux. This third crux is another smooth section of the gully that is best tackled directly (5.5). Above this awkward groove, the difficulty eases and the ramp above leads easily to the large ledge below the final summit block. Climb the summit block on its east side (5.3).

784 North Face 5.7

On the short north face, climb 50 feet up a crack system that angles up slightly to the west (right), overcome a 5.7 crux near the top of the pitch and reach the large ledge just below the east side of the summit block. Climb 30 feet up the east side of the summit block (5.3).

785 West Face 5.3

This is the easiest route to the Fist's lofty summit, and you can climb this short steep face in one 75-foot pitch. Step across a gap near the north edge of the west face and climb 60 feet straight up on small sharp holds to a large ledge below the summit block (5.3). Scramble around the south side of the summit block and climb it on its east side (5.3).

Variation

785V From the large ledge below the summit block, climb 15 feet up a lichen-covered, west-facing depression directly to the summit (5.7+).

79 SCHMOE'S NOSE

This neat Flatiron with a beat name lives high on Green Mountain north of the Fist, and above the Fifth Flatiron. The rock has a long broken lower rib capped by a bulbous summit tower etched by two overhangs that give Schmoe his nose. The route, predictably, climbs between Schmoe's nostrils, and the crux is getting past the boogers. Flatiron aficionados should not bypass the booger's dare. Approach by hiking up south of the Fifth, then moving north below Schmoe's broken lower rib. You can also approach via the Tangen Tunnel Route. Eschew the lower rib and hike up along its north side until the rock becomes coherent, and you can see the boogers looming overhead.

791 East Face 5.6

This two or three pitch climb will settle your schnoz. Where necessary, scramble up some Class 3 slabs. Either climb a 5.0–5.2 pitch or hike up under the rock's north side to the highest easy access onto the east face. Traverse onto the east face and climb 30 feet up the north edge of the face (5.3–5.4). Traverse 20 feet south across a smooth red slab to a crack and corner on the north side of the nose, and climb 25 feet up this corner to the bottom of the nostril (5.3–5.4). Now, for the moment we have all been waiting for. Grab a booger and make an awkward 5.6 move through the nostril to a commodious alcove, which offers a good belay. Climb 50 feet up the smooth unprotected face above the alcove (5.0–5.2) to a false summit. Cross a small notch, and climb 30 feet up a Class 4 slab to the summit. Honk.

Descent

791D *This is a dangerous rock to be on top of without a rope.* Climb down to the notch between the false summit and the main summit. Rig a sling around a block and rappel 60 vertical feet down the north face to the ground.

710 HILL BILLY ROCK

This is the easternmost rock north of and above the entrance to Skunk Canyon. It sits on top of a bare hillside and you can easily see it from the east. It is a good rock for beginners. Approach by leaving the Mesa Trail directly east

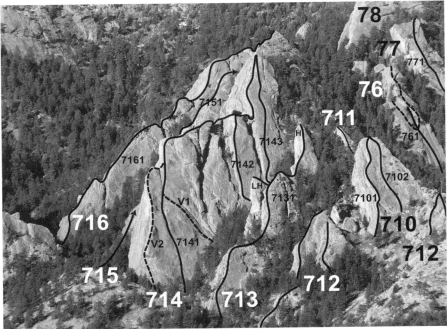

76 The Amoeboid	711 The Hobo	7141V1 5.4
761 Buckets Class 4	712 Hill Billy Flatironettes	7141V2 Southeast Ridge 5.8 S
77 The Hourglass	713 Stairway to Heaven	
771 East Face 5.0–5.2	7131 Stairway to Heaven 5.3	7142 Enchanted Devil 5.4
78 The Fist		7143 666 5.6
710 Hill Billy Rock	LH Like Heaven	715 Angel's Way
7101 East Face South Side 5.0–5.2	H Heaven	7151 Angel's Way 5.0
	714 Satan's Slab	716 Mohling Arête
7102 East Face Center Class 4	7141 East Face 5.6 S	7161 Mohling Arête 5.5

of the rock and hiking several hundred yards west to the rock. The east face of this rock is easy, and you can climb almost anywhere. I describe two obvious lines on the east face.

Descents

710D1 Rappel 60 feet north to the ground.

710D2 Climb 60 feet down the North Face Route (5.0–5.2).

710D3 Rappel 120 feet west to the ground.

710D4 Downclimb 100 feet near the north edge of the east face until you can escape to the north (Class 4).

7101 East Face South Side 5.0–5.2 *Classic*

This quaint 420-foot three-pitch climb is the longest climb on Hill Billy Rock. Start at the lowest point of the rock at the southern end of an extra piece of rock. This extra piece is attached to the lower south edge of the east face. Climb the extra piece for 140 feet past a notch to a second notch where the extra piece joins the east face of Hill Billy Rock. Follow the south edge of the east face for two more 140-foot pitches to the summit.

7102 East Face Center Class 4

Start in the middle of the east face directly below the summit and ascend 320 feet of agreeable rock to the top. This face breaks naturally into three pitches with the first pitch the hardest. The details of the proof are left as an exercise.

7103 North Face 5.0–5.2

A 60-foot pitch is on the small north face of Hill Billy Rock. Start directly below the summit and follow the obvious weakness past an awkward bulge 40 feet up, then romp to the top.

711 THE HOBO

This neat little rock is 50 yards west of Hill Billy Rock. You cannot see it from most vantage points on the Mesa Trail, but it is quite prominent when looking south from Royal Arch. Climb 120 feet up the east face on wonderful holds to a surprising exposed summit (Class 4). To descend, retreat back down the east face.

712 HILL BILLY FLATIRONETTES

There is a small Flatironette 50 feet east of the east face of Hill Billy Rock. It provides a 250-foot Class 4 south ridge and a 100-foot Class 4 east face. From its summit, you can walk north.

Just south of Hill Billy Rock are three large curious boulders. The westernmost, while ferocious on its east side, is a walk from the west. The large center boulder has an overhung summit with a large tree 5 feet away, and a 50-foot 5.3–5.4 face climb is on its north side. The easternmost boulder is the smallest, hardest and has a smooth pink east face. You can climb this boulder via an awkward 5.5–5.6 crack on its west face.

Two more Flatironettes rise out of Skunk Canyon south of Hill Billy Rock. The lower rock does not demand much attention, but does provide a 250-foot south ridge. The higher of these two rocks is larger and provides two south ridges. The westernmost is the most elegant and provides a mellow 350-foot Class 4 climb to the higher western summit. To descend from this summit, move 20 feet east, then climb north down and around an easy corner (Class 3). The eastern south ridge rises 300 feet to the lower, overhung eastern summit. To descend from this summit, climb 50 feet down the east face, then escape north.

713 STAIRWAY TO HEAVEN

When hiking up Skunk Canyon, the first big rock you see to the north is the bottom of the Stairway to Heaven. This is one of the many distinctive long ridges rising out of this canyon. The bottom of the Stairway to Heaven has a large overhang, and farther up the ridge there are three distinct summits, each higher than the last. The lowest of these three summits is a wonderful pinnacle known as Like Heaven.

7131 Stairway to Heaven 5.3 *Classic – Top Ten*

This fine 1,000-foot climb ascends the entire ridge, includes all three summits, and ends on the high point—Heaven. Because of its discontinuous nature, people with tight imaginations disparage this route, but only by overcoming discontinuities do we make the crooked straight and the rough places plain. Start at the bottom of the rock just above Skunk Canyon, climb up 5.0–5.2 rock and stay east (right) of the huge overhang. Pass a second smaller overhang on the west (5.3). This short traverse is the route's only 5.3 difficulty and you can avoid it by moving around the second overhang on the east (right) and climbing up a potholed face.

Scramble up easy rock for several hundred feet to the base of the east face of Like Heaven, which looms magnificently overhead. An obvious deep chimney splits this east face. Climb 5.0–5.2 rock right of this chimney into the notch north of Like Heaven's summit. The summit of Like Heaven is one of the finest Flatiron summits above Boulder. To reach it, climb south from the notch along the exposed 5.0–5.2 summit ridge. Return to the notch and continue north over the next easier summit to engage the final step in the stairway. Ascend the last 200 feet up an east face to Heaven.

Descents

7131D1 Hike east off the Stairway from a point below the summit of Like Heaven and also from a point 200 feet below the summit of Heaven.

7131D2 From the summit of Heaven, downclimb 40 feet north along a knife-edge ridge. Downclimb another 40 feet east to a large tree and rappel 60 feet east down a slab to the ground. You can also downclimb from the tree.

7132 Love 5.4

This beautiful higher angle route ascends the obvious dihedral on the west face of Like Heaven. Approach by hiking 400 feet up the gully west of the Stairway to Heaven to a point north of Like Heaven. Start at a large block and climb the initial 5.4 overhang. Move 20 feet south (right) and climb the handhold-rich north-facing dihedral to a notch north of the summit of Like Heaven (5.0–5.2). Climb south along an exposed elegant ridge to the summit. The view of Satan's Slab from the summit of Like Heaven is excellent, and this is a good place to preview routes on that devil.

Descents

7132D1 Downclimb back to the notch and scramble north over a second summit until you can hike east.

7132D2 To return to the base of the climb, rappel near the ascent route.

7133 Better Than Love 5.5

After surmounting the initial overhang of Love, angle north (left) to the west ridge of the summit north of Like Heaven. Ascend this beautiful ridge for 100 feet to the summit (5.5).

Descent

7133D Same as Love or continue on into Heaven.

714 SATAN'S SLAB   *Closed 2/1 – 7/31*

This is the mightiest Flatiron in the Skunk Canyon area. It is hardly visible from central Boulder, but begins to show its face from the Table Mesa area and NCAR. When hiking west up Skunk Canyon, pass the bottom of Stairway to Heaven and soon you will be staring up at Satan's Slab on the north side of the canyon. One hundred feet up is a more refined version of the Stairway to Heaven's large overhang.

Satan's Slab is made up of four main pieces. The lowest piece rising out of Skunk Canyon is the largest, smoothest and is as large as the other three pieces put together. It is this piece that gives the slab its satanic stature. The west side of Satan's slab is high and often overhanging, the home of hard climbing. Rising as it does out of the depths of Skunk Canyon, Satan's Slab is captivating to look at and contemplate. Whether climbing on this rock is enjoyable or not is a matter of opinion. The leads are long, smooth and hard to protect. This rock is not for the casual Flatiron scrambler but for hardened Flatiron leaders looking for new adventures.

Descent

714D Move south off the summit block and get into the large crack splitting the entire summit area. Scramble west through this crack to the west face of the summit block. Downclimb 40 feet north on an easy surprise ledge across the otherwise exposed west face (Class 4).

7141 East Face 5.6 S *Classic*   *Closed 2/1 – 7/31*

This is a serious eight or nine-pitch route with two long unprotected leads. It is not hard to spot, however. When approaching, look for a long dark water groove near the middle of the east face of the largest and lowest piece of Satan's Slab. From the canyon, hike 100 feet up along the base of the east face. On the first pitch, climb somewhat broken rock to a point near the bottom of the groove. On the second pitch, climb the groove to a large pothole. This groove is not a crack, but a shallow trough that only provides an illusion of safety. On the third pitch, climb 150 feet above the pothole to reach the south ridge. This pitch is also difficult to protect.

From here, follow the easier south ridge, and cross the tops of the other three pieces. The top of the second piece provides a short downclimb. After the third piece, negotiate some house-sized boulders. You can escape at this point by rappelling west down a large gully over a chockstone. The fourth piece rears impressively above the boulder field and provides a thoughtful, protectable 5.3–5.4 challenge. Climb easier rock to the summit block on the north side of a large crack splitting the summit area.

Variations

7141V1 Start from a tiny flat meadow farther north along the base of the rock. Do an ascending traverse south (left) and reach the large pothole at the top of the long water groove on the direct route (5.4). This start eliminates the water groove pitch and shortens the climb by a pitch. This variation is the easiest way to ascend Satan's Slab and still engage the lowest largest piece of the Flatiron.

7141V2 Southeast Ridge 5.8 S

Start at the low point and climb a direct line up the southeast ridge. Climb up to the small overhang, work up an awkward slot to its left and ascend a smooth wall above (5.8 S). Continue up the ridge and join the East Face Route.

7142 Enchanted Devil 5.4   *Closed 2/1 – 7/31*

This route ascends the third piece of Satan's Slab and is easier to protect than the East Face Route. It is sustained at or near the 5.4 level for seven pitches and is a highly recommended climb. From Skunk Canyon, hike uphill to the north along the bottom of the east face and pass the large smooth first piece and the narrow second piece.

Start near the center of the third piece and angle 80 feet south (left) to a large pocket in the gully between the second and third pieces. On the second pitch, climb 150 feet along the south edge of the third piece (5.4). On the third pitch, climb another 150 feet of 5.3–5.4 rock to a good stance not far below the top of the third piece. You can use small wired nuts and ingenuity to protect these three pitches. Climb a shorter fourth pitch to the top of the third piece, where this route joins the upper part of the East Face Route near the house-sized boulders.

7143 666 5.6   *Closed 2/1 – 7/31*

This clean sustained 5-pitch route ascends the fourth piece of Satan's Slab. From Skunk Canyon, hike uphill to the north along the bottom of the east face, pass the large smooth first piece, the narrow second piece, the third piece that holds the Enchanted Devil Route and continue to the southern edge of the fourth piece. Climb 90 feet on or north of the southeast ridge of the fourth piece to a tree (5.4). Climb 140 feet up the ridge to a good ledge with a crack (5.4). Climb another 100 feet up the ridge to a horizontal crack (5.4). Climb 150 feet up a beautiful smooth section, pass two diagonal cracks and reach a ledge on the ridge (5.6). Climb another smooth section (5.6), join the upper East Face Route and continue up easier rock to the summit.

715 ANGEL'S WAY   *Closed 2/1 – 7/31*

This rock rib provides one of the finest easy climbs near Boulder. Angel's Way
is a slender beautiful ridge rising over 1,000 feet above Skunk Canyon. It is
tucked 100 feet west of the steep west face of Satan's Slab. You cannot see it
from any Boulder location or even from the Mesa Trail, and that is part of its
charm. When climbing this rock, you are divorced from Boulder. The setting
feels quite alpine with Satan's Slab looming to the east and a grand view of the

G Green Mountain	77 The Hourglass	713 Stairway to Heaven
EG East Green Mountain	78 The Fist	714 Satan's Slab
61 Fourth Flatiron – Third Piece	79 Schmoe's Nose	715 Angel's Way
	710 Hill Billy Rock	716 Mohling Arête
71 Fifth Flatiron	711 The Hobo	88 Frontporch
76 The Amoeboid	712 Hill Billy Flatironettes	89 Lost Porch

often snow dusted rocks of South Green Mountain to the west. Approach by hiking up Skunk Canyon past Satan's Slab and looking sharp for the bottom of the Angel's Way 100 feet north of the trail and 100 feet west of Satan's Slab.

7151 Angel's Way 5.0 *Classic*   *Closed 2/1 – 7/31*

This 1,000-foot climb is mostly Class 4 punctuated with some 5.0 cruxes. Start at the base of the east face 40 feet east of and above the low point of the rock. Climb 100 feet up a 5.0 slab to the wonderful Class 4 ridge above. While scrambling several hundred feet up this ridge, you can see a weird headwall above. Climb this headwall via some nifty buckets on its east face (5.0). Follow the rib until you reach a summit even with the top of Satan's Slab. Downclimb from this summit and climb north up a summit Flatironette. From this angelic perch, you can look down on lowly Satan's Slab.

Descent

7151D You can escape Angel's Way in numerous places by rappelling or downclimbing east into the gully between the Angel's Way and Satan's Slab. This gully is hikeable for its entire length. You can also walk away from it all just before the summit Flatironette. From the top of the summit Flatironette, downclimb east, then north. Continuing on to Green Mountain from here makes a nice mountaineering ascent of this peak.

716 MOHLING ARÊTE   *Closed 2/1 – 7/31*

This is the westernmost of the four great rock ribs on the north side of Skunk Canyon. The ridge and climb are named in memory of Franz Mohling, who died while attempting a new route on Mt. Logan during the summer of 1982. The climb is in a beautiful setting, high in the heart of Skunk Canyon. The great ridges rising up out of the canyon all seem to be ascending toward the sky in concert with your climb. Approach by hiking up Skunk Canyon past Satan's Slab and Angel's Way. The bottom of the Mohling Arête is 200 feet west of Angel's Way, distinguished by a 50-foot low angle slab with a large overhang above it.

7161 Mohling Arête 5.5   *Closed 2/1 – 7/31*

This climb is between 1,300 and 1,500 feet long, depending on how many of the upper summits you include. This ridge is not as consistent in its difficulty as Angel's Way, since difficult cruxes punctuate long easy stretches.

Scramble up the low angle slab to a corner on the east end of the overhang where you can peer up the imposing slab above. The first pitch is a good one. Climb straight up the slab for 130 to 150 feet on consistent 5.3–5.4 rock. You can minimize the 5.3–5.4 climbing by traversing west (left) to the knobby ridge crest.

Above the first pitch, follow the broad ridge for 600 feet of Class 3 scrambling and Class 4 climbing to a rather imposing notch. A short rappel will let you down easy, but you can also downclimb into the notch near its west end by a devious little route (5.4). From the notch, a steep Class 4 pitch takes you to the base of a steeper headwall. Climb this headwall right on the ridge crest via a 10-foot 5.5 crux. After the crux, walk along the ridge for a short distance, and stare into, you guessed it, another notch.

You can also reach this notch by a route near its west end (5.3–5.4). You may be able to avoid the 5.5 crux and the downclimb into this second notch by using a ledge system on the west face of the Arête. Above the second notch, 400 feet of Class 4 climbing and Class 3 scrambling lead up a beautiful expansive slab.

At the 1,300-foot level, reach a third notch by using a ledge halfway down its 20-foot face (5.3–5.4). This notch is in hiking territory and the ridge beyond is badly broken. There are three more towers that you can climb. The highest will leave you very high over Boulder.

Descents

7161D You can escape the climb in numerous places by downclimbing and/or rappelling east. The third notch at 1,300 feet is the first place where you can hike east. You can easily scramble north from the last two towers. It is a nice hike to the top of Green Mountain from the end of this climb.

EIGHT

Dinosaur Mountain

Dinosaur Mountain is the 7,380-foot summit 0.7 mile southeast of the summit of Green Mountain, south of Skunk Canyon, north of Bear Canyon and west of the Mesa Trail. The vast array of rocks on Dinosaur Mountain can be difficult to decipher at first. The Flatirons are logically divided into four north-south tiers or layers of rock. The three eastern tiers contain almost all the Flatirons and the westernmost tier contains the summit of Dinosaur Mountain. It is generally easy to hike in the gullies that parallel the tiers, but it is often difficult to cross the tiers, especially the third one. The organization of the route descriptions on Dinosaur Mountain is different from the rest of the

8 Dinosaur Mountain	814 The Hand	823 Fi
85 Der Zerkle	816 Shark's Fin	824 Fo
86 Red Devil	817 Finger Flatiron	825 Fum
87 Unicorn	818 The Box	826 Dum
88 Frontporch	819 Backporch	827 The Rainbow
89 Lost Porch	820 Achean	828 North Ridge of
812 Der Freischutz	Pronouncement	Dinosaur Mountain

book. I describe the routes tier by tier from the easternmost (first) to western-most (fourth) tier, and from south to north within each tier. The most popular approach to Dinosaur Mountain is the NCAR Trail.

81 BEAR CREEK SPIRE   *Check for closures*

This is the imposing rock guarding the entrance to Bear Canyon on the north side of the creek. You cannot see the rock well from many of the standard viewpoints, but it is very spectacular when seen from the east end of Bear Canyon. Bear Creek Spire is the southernmost and lowest rock in the first tier of rocks on Dinosaur Mountain. While Bear Creek Spire's freestanding summit is spectacular to look at, the climbing is of dubious quality as the rock is char-acterized by lots of overhangs with rotten undersides. To approach Bear Creek Spire, walk west up the Bear Canyon service road until it crosses Bear Creek. Leave the road and follow a small trail 100 yards north of the creek to the base of the rock.

811 North Side Class 4   *Check for closures*

This 200-foot-long route is notable only because it is the easiest way to get on top of this otherwise difficult rock. From the base of the rock, scramble 150 feet up a rubble filled gully east of the rock. The route ascends an east-facing ramp on the north side of the east face. Climb 70 feet up the ramp to a large tree, climb east over an easy overhang, work up onto the upper east face, and climb easy rock to the summit.

Variation

811V You can add a little spice to this climb by moving more directly toward the east face. Instead of climbing the ramp to the large tree, climb a short north-facing wall with a small tree on it (5.3–5.4). Move up easier rock and join the North Side Route on top of the overhang above the large tree.

Descents

811D1 Twenty feet south of the summit is a notch with a large tree in it. Rappel 150 feet east down ramps and slabs to reach the rubble filled approach gully. Two 75-foot rappels will also work, using the large tree on the North Side Route as a second anchor.

811D2 Downclimb the North Side Route (Class 4).

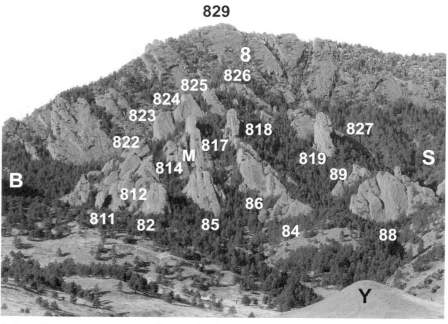

B Bear Canyon
S Skunk Canyon
829 South Green
  Mountain
82 Dinosaur Rock
85 Der Zerkle
86 Red Devil
84 Gazebo
88 Frontporch

89 Lost Porch
811 Northern Dinosaur
  Egg
812 Der Freischutz
814 The Hand
M Mallory Cave
817 Finger Flatiron
818 The Box
819 Backporch

822 Fee
823 Fi
824 Fo
825 Fum
826 Dum
8 Dinosaur Mountain
  (behind)
827 The Rainbow
Y Yuri Point

82 DINOSAUR ROCK

This is the prominent rock that you can see on the southwest skyline from the Mallory Cave Trail as it approaches the first tier of rocks. It has a rather stately, imposing appearance when seen from the vicinity of Square Rock and the Babyhorn. Dinosaur Rock is south of and lower than Der Zerkle, which is the Flatiron directly west of Square Rock. Approach by following the Mallory Cave Trail for 100 yards past Square Rock, then hike south to the base of the rock.

821 East Face 5.4 *Classic*

This is a clean, 280-foot two-pitch climb. A separate piece of Flatiron is tacked onto the base of Dinosaur Rock's east face. You can climb the separate piece (Class 4), but there is a large gap between the two rocks, so you should avoid the separate piece when starting Dinosaur Rock. Start south of the separate piece and climb 140 feet up a southeast face to some good ledges (Class 4). Fifty feet above these ledges is a small overhang on the main east face of Dinosaur Rock. On the second pitch climb up to the overhang (5.0–5.2) and avoid it to the south (left). Shaky leaders have almost fallen off this crux because of what they have seen from this unique vantage. Complete the crux sequence by following a south-facing slot for 15 feet (5.4). The climbing above this crux rapidly tapers to Class 4, and the summit is not far beyond.

Variation

821V You can do the first pitch on the north (right) side of the separate piece (5.0–5.2).

Descent

821D Downclimb the West Face Route (Class 4).

822 East Bone Class 3–4

This is not a route on Dinosaur Rock proper but rather a scrambling approach to it. The easternmost rock on the north side of Bear Canyon is Bear Creek Spire. Many people who poke their nose up into Bear Canyon leave the canyon and scramble up the gully immediately east of Bear Creek Spire. Please avoid this loose gully. The East Bone forms the eastern boundary of this gully, and this narrow rock rib provides a cleaner scrambling route out of Bear Canyon.

Find the nondescript bottom of the East Bone and ascend it for several hundred feet to hiking territory not far below Dinosaur Rock. The difficulty encountered will depend on how close you stay to the crest of the rib. The crest provides several short sections of Class 4, but you can avoid these spots and keep the difficulty at the Class 3 level. From the hiking territory at the top of the rib, either hike on, or if you desire to continue scrambling, descend 50 feet south across the gully to the west and find a 30-foot Class 4 climb onto the next rib to the west. This rib connects Bear Creek Spire with Dinosaur Rock and contains the upper part of the East Bone Route. It is difficult to ascend this rib directly from the saddle north of Bear Creek Spire, but the 30-foot Class 4 approach from the east is only a few feet north. Once on this rib, it is a simple Class 3 scramble north to the bottom of the east face of Dinosaur Rock.

Descent

822D This entire route is only a few feet from hiking territory.

823 West Bone Class 3–4

Like the East Bone, the West Bone is a scrambling approach to Dinosaur Rock from Bear Canyon. The West Bone is a short distinct rock rib immediately west of the upper East Bone that connects Bear Creek Spire and Dinosaur Rock. Approach the West Bone by hiking west up the bottom of Bear Canyon past Bear Creek Spire, then hiking uphill to the north. The bottom of the West Bone is 50 feet west of the rock saddle north of Bear Creek Spire. Don't confuse the West Bone with Dinosaur Tracks, which is the more prominent rib 100 feet farther west. If you are looking for a scrambling route in this area, then I recommend Dinosaur Tracks over the West (or East) Bone. The top of the West Bone connects with the south side of Dinosaur Rock, and the South Ramps Route provides a difficult conclusion to an ascent of the West Bone. The gully between the West Bone and the upper East Bone is hikeable and leaves you on the east side of Dinosaur Rock. The gully between the West Bone and Dinosaur Tracks leads into the Class 3–4 scrambling at the top of the Dinosaur Tracks Route that leads to the west side of Dinosaur Rock.

824 South Ramps 5.4

There are two peculiar one-pitch climbs up a pair of ramps on the south side of Dinosaur Rock. From the standard starting place for the East Face Route, move west underneath the south face and cross some easy slabs to a pair of ramps near the west end of the south face. You can climb either ramp, and they are both rated 5.4. The eastern ramp provides an interesting layback crack, and the western ramp provides a nice face climb with a tricky start. It is 120 feet up the ramps, and they join the West Face Route 60 feet below the top of Dinosaur Rock.

825 Dinosaur Tracks 5.2

Three rock ribs go from Bear Canyon to the summit area of Dinosaur Rock. The easternmost connects Bear Creek Spire to Dinosaur Rock and is the top part of the East Bone Route. The small central West Bone rib peters out northwest of Bear Creek Spire. The western rib starts 150 feet above Bear Canyon and hosts the delightful Dinosaur Tracks Route. This route is 600 feet long if you follow it all the way to the top of Dinosaur Rock. It is a good scrambling route, since most of the climbing is Class 3.

A 30-foot vertical face identifies the bottom of the route. Start around the corner east (right) of this face, and cruise up 200 feet of wonderful Class 3 rock to a little Class 4 headwall. Above this is a keyhole-shaped false summit that you can bypass to the east (5.2), and this is the crux of the route. Beyond the keyhole is a small but significant arch. At the arch, you can gain (or escape) the ridge from the west via a nifty Class 3 layback crack. Move over the arch and continue up Class 3 rock to a huge boulder that you can pass on either side. Turn east and continue up Dinosaur Rock's West Face Route.

Descent

825D You can escape the ridge in two or three places or simply walk away from it all at the base of the west face of Dinosaur Rock. From the top of Dinosaur Rock, descend the West Face Route (Class 4).

826 West Face Class 4

This short route is the easiest way to reach the summit of Dinosaur Rock. This route is the usual descent route from the summit, but many hikers have found it to be an exhilarating way to reach an exciting summit. From the hiking territory west of the summit, find and climb a 10-foot south-facing chimney. Above this is a 15-foot wall and above this is the final 20-foot west-facing wall that leads to the summit of Dinosaur Rock. This final Class 4 wall is the crux of the route.

Descent

826D Climb back down the route (Class 4).

83 SQUARE ROCK and THE BABYHORN

These two large boulders are a few feet south of the Mallory Cave Trail, 350 yards west of the Mesa Trail. They are in a meadow below Dinosaur Rock and Der Zerkle, and this is a pleasant place to play. Many climbs on Dinosaur Mountain have been delayed as approaching climbers stop to warm up on these boulders. Square Rock is shaped like a cube and is the larger of the two. It is 20 feet high on its west side and 40 feet high on its east side. The easiest route to its flat commodious summit is on the northwest corner and this route is rated 5.tree, since a tree is right next to the corner. It is much more difficult (5.8) to climb Square Rock without touching this tree. The Babyhorn is 20 feet west of Square Rock and is shaped like a newborn Matterhorn. The easiest route to its pointed summit is on its tiny east face (5.0). The south face offers a testy 5.7 problem and the smooth west face provides a tricky 5.8+ slab climb.

84 GAZEBO

This name refers to the two Flatironettes north of Square Rock and the Babyhorn. They are east of the Red Devil and the Unicorn. The two Flatironettes forming the Gazebo are connected on their northern ends, and they form a dandy little playground. The little south ridges and east faces invite scrambling and the two summits have easy downclimbs. This is a good place to eat lunch, soak up some rays or burn off a little excess energy.

85 DER ZERKLE   *East Face Closed 4/1 – 9/1*

This is the Flatiron directly west of Square Rock and the Babyhorn, and north of Dinosaur Rock in the first tier of rocks on Dinosaur Mountain. Der Zerkle has a large diagonal overhang halfway up the east face. The summit of Der Zerkle is spectacular when viewed from the Mallory Cave area and even more spectacular to sit on. To approach, follow the Mallory Cave Trail for 150 yards past Square Rock and the Babyhorn. Shortly after the trail enters the trees, it passes within kicking distance of the low point of Der Zerkle. I recommend all of the routes on this rock.

Descents

85D1 Downclimb the West Face Route (5.0). En route, you will pass a large tree that you can sniff as you give it a bear hug.

85D2 Although it is seldom done, you can do a spectacular 100-foot rappel west off the summit.

851 East Face North Side 5.7–   *Closed 4/1 – 9/1*

From the low point of the rock, hike 100 feet north along the bottom of the east face. Climb 130 feet up the slab near the north (right) edge of the rock. This 5.2 slab is Flatiron climbing at its best, and it ends on the ledge below the large overhang that cuts across the east face. From the north (right) end of the overhang, angle north and climb 15 feet up a layback crack (5.7–) to reach easier rock. You can also climb the face a few feet south of the layback crack (5.7–). Two gullies flank the summit block of Der Zerkle and your best

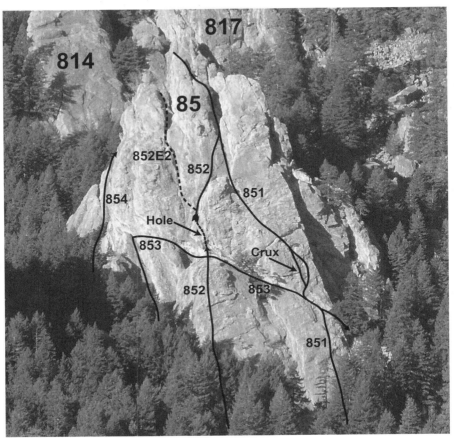

85 Der Zerkle	853 Sunnyside One 5.5–5.6
851 East Face North Size 5.7–	854 Sunnyside Two Class 4
852 East Face South Side 5.6	814 The Hand
852E2 5.1	817 Finger Flatiron

approach to the summit is from the northern gully. The slabs above the lay-back crack are 5.2 and lead naturally into the northern gully. Ascend this gully to the notch at its top and do an ascending traverse up a ramp on the north side of the summit block to reach the pinpoint summit (5.0).

Escape

851E From the ledge below the crux 5.7– layback crack, you can escape by downclimbing north along the ledge and doing a short downclimb to the ground (5.1).

852 East Face South Side 5.6 *Closed 4/1 – 9/1*

Step off the Mallory Cave Trail onto the lowest point of the rock and climb 165 feet up a wonderful 5.2 slab to the ledge below the large overhang that cuts across the east face. This slab provides a good exercise in reading Flatiron rock, and the easiest line is near the south (left) edge of the east face. Find a large rotten hole through the overhang above. The route's crux is 15 feet of 5.6 climbing through this hole, and numerous techniques have been employed in the hole depending on the size of the climber. Climb Class 4 slabs above the hole into the gully south of the summit block, from which the summit will be difficult to reach. So, if you are gripped with summit fever, angle north (right) before it's too late and get into the gully north of the summit block. Ascend this gully to the notch at its top and do an ascending traverse up a ramp on the north side of the summit block to reach the pinpoint summit (5.0).

Escapes

852E1 From the ledge below the large overhang with the hole, you can escape by downclimbing north along the ledge across the entire east face and doing a short downclimb to the ground (5.1).

852E2 Climb up to the notch at the top of the gully south of the summit block. Climb west down a Class 4 chimney to a large ledge on the west face. Hike north on this ledge and downclimb some Class 3 rock to the ground.

853 Sunnyside One 5.5–5.6 *Closed 4/1 – 9/1*

This route ascends an inviting ramp 100 feet up from the low point of the rock along its south side. The Mallory Cave Trail passes within a few feet of the bottom of this ramp. Look for a 2-foot arch part way up the ramp. Climb up for 140 feet, passing the 2-foot arch en route, to the base of a steep headwall (5.3–5.4). Forward progress may seem improbable at this point, but salvation lies to the north. Traverse north (right) to the ledge below the large overhang cutting across the east face (5.5–5.6). Either continue on the East Face South Side Route by climbing through the hole (5.6), or downclimb north along the ledge and continue on the East Face North Side Route by climbing the layback crack (5.7–). You may continue downclimbing to the north along the ledge and escape the rock. This latter alternative provides a rather curious tour of Der Zerkle.

854 Sunnyside Two Class 4

This little route exemplifies the pleasure of scrambling on the Flatirons high over Boulder. One hundred feet west of the Sunnyside One ramp, the Mallory

Cave Trail bumps into a second ramp that practically begs you to leave the trail and climb it. This is an invitation that you should not pass up. Simply climb 200 feet up the ramp on wonderful Class 4 rock. Near the top, climb around either side of a large block and move around to the west side of Der Zerkle. An orthogonal detour from here is to climb east up a Class 4 chimney into the notch south of the summit. You cannot easily reach the summit from here, but the view makes this effort worthwhile. Retreat down the Class 4 chimney to the west ledge, hike north on this ledge, and downclimb some Class 3 rock to the ground. To reach the summit from here, follow the West Face Route (5.0).

855 The Final Solution 5.8

This stimulating route follows a 50-foot vertical crack system on the lower west face of Der Zerkle. It is not a summit route. The climb starts from the Mallory Cave Trail where the trail leaves the west face of Der Zerkle and cuts west to reach the bottom of the Hand. The first half of the pitch follows a small south-facing dihedral (5.5). Halfway up there is a hole through the rock that is almost big enough to wiggle through, but this is only a variation for small sloths. Climb the exciting 5.8 finish to this pitch up the slightly over-hanging wall on the outside of the hole via some hidden buckets. Near the top you will be directly over the middle of the Mallory Cave Trail. The top of the pitch is on the upper part of the Sunnyside Two ramp.

856 Jugs 5.7

This popular 40-foot route will certainly focus your attention and has offered the question, what if you're not? Hike 50 feet north from the bottom of the Final Solution to a vertical pocketed wall. This is the route. Overcome the ver-ticality by crafting connections between the wall's numerous jug handholds, pockets and ledges. Muster a Spiderman style finish to reach the wide ledge on the upper part of the Sunnyside Two ramp. This is the top of the route. Scamper north to intersect the West Face Route.

857 West Face 5.0   *Summit Closed 2/1 – 7/31*

This route is the shortest, easiest way to reach the summit of Der Zerkle. As the Mallory Cave Trail climbs up under the west side of Der Zerkle, leave it and scramble to the saddle west of Der Zerkle's summit. Find a north-facing dihedral with a large tree halfway up it. Climb 50 feet up the west face of the north-facing dihedral to a notch northeast of the summit (5.0). Do an ascending traverse up a ramp on the north side of the summit block to reach the pin-point summit (5.0).

86 RED DEVIL

This Flatiron is north of Der Zerkle in the first tier of rocks on Dinosaur Mountain. Its east face is distinguished by a large area of red rock, and like Der Zerkle, the Red Devil has a large overhang slashing across the lower part of its east face. While it is not the cleanest or most coherent Flatiron around, the climbs on the Red Devil are excellent. To approach the Red Devil, leave the Mallory Cave Trail in the meadow west of Square Rock and angle northwest. A Flatironette called the Unicorn is connected with the bottom of the north side

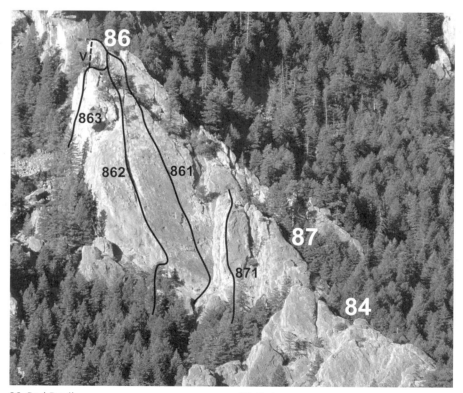

86 Red Devil
861 East Face 5.5
862 Berserker 5.7 S
863 South Face 5.4

87 Unicorn
871 Southeast Ridge 5.0–5.2
84 Gazebo

of the Red Devil's east face, forming a nice little amphitheater. To reach the low point of the Red Devil and this amphitheater, stay south of the Unicorn.

Descent

86D From the summit of the Red Devil, walk north and west.

861 East Face 5.5

This 400-foot climb ascends the red slab in the middle of the east face. You can do the climb in three long pitches. Hike northwest up the brushy gully between the Red Devil and the Unicorn to the north end of the large overhang cutting across the lower part of the east face. From here, you can get onto the red part of the east face without having to climb the overhang. Climb straight up the red slab for a long 5.5 pitch and work out a belay in the middle of this unique acre of rock. The difficulty decreases on the second pitch as you leave the red slab behind. Angle south (left) toward some large trees high on the face. On the third pitch, find the obvious passage at the southern end of a small overhang below the summit and climb the 50-foot summit block (Class 4).

862 Berserker 5.7 S

This 430-foot route overcomes the overhang on the lower part of the east face, the steep rock above it, and follows a line near the southern edge of the east face. You can best accomplish this crazy climb in four pitches. Start at the bottom of the east face and climb a 75-foot pitch to the large ledge below the overhang (Class 4–5.2). Scramble south to a small tree on the ledge below the overhang. The next 130-foot pitch is a serious, worthwhile Flatiron lead on steeper than average rock. Protection is difficult. Climb the overhang near the small tree (5.7). At least two possibilities exist for this initial challenge. Above the overhang, angle south (left) along the top of the overhang (5.6), then head up steep rock to a small flake. From here, either traverse north (right) across a smooth 5.5–5.6 slab to easier rock or continue straight up (5.5–5.6). Either way, finish the pitch in a chimney that starts and ends in this section of the face. The difficulty eases considerably above this point. Climb a jocular 150-foot 5.2 pitch to the trees near the south end of the upper overhang, and finish the climb with the 50-foot summit block (Class 4).

Variation

862V Way Berserker 5.8

A hundred feet below the summit, move south (left) and climb a silly, exposed bomb bay chimney.

863 South Face 5.4

This is a blocky one-pitch climb on the Red Devil's short steep south face. This face is prominent from the Mallory Cave Trail below the cave. Approach by following the trail to that point and hiking north to the base of the face. Climb the 5.4 face, working out a line in the obvious crack systems, and finish the pitch on a ledge with a tree. From here, move onto the east face and finish the climb with the 50-foot summit block (Class 4).

Variation

863V From the ledge with the big tree, climb straight up a smooth wall on the upper south face (5.8).

87 UNICORN

This Flatironette is northeast of the Red Devil. The gully between the Unicorn and the Red Devil is not hikeable since the two rocks are connected at their northern ends. The approach is the same as the Red Devil.

871 Southeast Ridge 5.0–5.2

This is an odd little climb that may catch your eye from the Red Devil. Start at the lowest point of the rock 100 feet downhill to the east from the bottom of the Red Devil. Zoom up 100 feet of Class 3 and another 120 feet of Class 4 to the base of the steep part of the rock. From here, follow some parallel south-facing ramps for 150 feet to a notch (5.0–5.2), and climb 20 feet west to the summit (Class 3). This humble summit provides an excellent view of the surrounding territory.

Descent

871D From the notch 20 feet east of the summit, escape by climbing north down a 10-foot Class 3 crack.

88 FRONTPORCH

This is the northernmost Flatiron in the first tier of rocks on Dinosaur Mountain. It is north of the Red Devil and east of the Backporch. This rock is as wide as it is high, and the summit is at the north end of a long summit ridge. Approach the Frontporch by following the Porch Alley Route from the

Mesa Trail up to the bottom of the east face near the southeast corner of the rock. Although Porch Alley is only a few hundred yards north of the Mallory Cave Trail, it sees much less traffic. Deer often graze near the base of the Frontporch and this is a wonderful place to rock dance. I describe four obvious routes on this amicable Flatiron.

Descents

88D1 Scramble 250 feet down the northeast ridge (Class 3) to a notch, and hike south down along the base of the east face.

88D2 From the summit, scramble 20 feet west down to a tree and rappel 40 feet west to the ground.

88D3 From the rappel tree, climb south down an awkward hidden ramp to the ground (Class 4).

88 Frontporch
881 East Face South Side 5.2
882 East Face Center Class 4
883 Tiptoe Slab 5.2
884 Northeast Ridge Class 3
89 Lost Porch

891 Southeast Ridge 5.0–5.2
820 Achean Pronouncement
714 Satan's Slab
715 Angel's Way
716 Mohling Arête

881 East Face South Side 5.2

This 600-foot climb is the longest on the Frontporch and allows you to enjoy the full length of the summit ridge. Start near the rock's southeast corner and climb 150 feet south (left) to some large trees. Either climb the difficult bulge above or stay left of the bulge and climb near the south edge of the east face. The low point of the summit ridge is 150 feet above the large trees. The summit ridge is 300 feet long and with its notches and walls is distinctly alpine. The final notch and wall will require a little thought.

882 East Face Center Class 4

This easy 500-foot climb follows a curving line up the center of the east face. Start 50 feet north of the rock's southeast corner and climb an angled rib north and west into the center of the face. Solid Class 4 climbing takes you directly to the summit.

883 Tiptoe Slab 5.2 *Classic*

This attractive slab north of the central rib invites passage. It is 400 feet directly up the slab to the summit. The difficulty is consistent at the 5.2 level, and this is Flatiron climbing at its best.

884 Northeast Ridge Class 3

This is the descent for the other routes, but since Class 3 scrambles to Flatiron summits are rare, I include it to encourage the pursuit of easy routes. From the rock's southeast corner, hike north uphill along the bottom of the east face and follow a gully up to a small notch on the northeast ridge. Turn west and climb 250 feet up the broad ridge to the top.

89 LOST PORCH

This Flatironette hides between the Frontporch and the Backporch. Its shape is a vague echo of the Frontporch, and it is difficult to see from the east. From the southeast corner of the Frontporch, hike west uphill, pass the south edge of the Frontporch and find the bottom of the Lost Porch in the trees. If you are looking for an obscure Flatironette to play on, this may be it.

891 Southeast Ridge 5.0–5.2

From the low point of the rock, climb a 150-foot east-facing slab to the summit ridge (5.0–5.2). Romp north along the summit ridge for 300 feet of Class 3, passing an occasional Class 4 problem to reach the summit.

Descent

891D Scramble 100 feet down the northeast ridge (Class 4) to the Frontporch–Lost Porch col.

810 SOUTHERN DINOSAUR EGG

The second tier of rocks on Dinosaur Mountain starts abruptly in Bear Canyon with two rocks that look like old cracked dinosaur eggs. You can easily see these rocks from the Bear Canyon Trail, but they tend to blend into the background and are not usually recognized as distinct summits. Actually, the summits of both these rocks are quite distinct and both summits require 5.5–5.6 climbing. I recommend the climbs Hatch and Rehatch for anyone looking for a little spice and adventure, but not a great deal of commitment.

The Southern Dinosaur Egg, which is much lower that its northern cousin, rises directly out of Bear Canyon, and is split into two pieces separated by a deep chimney. This egg obviously cracked a long time ago and whatever was hatched must have headed north as its tracks have been found nearby. Who knows, maybe the Backporch hatched from the Southern Dinosaur Egg, grew strong, climbed north across Dinosaur Mountain, and was starting to move out for Green Mountain when it spotted Satan's Slab right next to Angel's Way. It must be hunkered down right where it is waiting for this conflict to resolve. Personally, I hope the Backporch moves on and mates with the Third Flatiron. The results could be stunning. All this from the little old Southern Dinosaur Egg!

Ahem. To approach the Southern Dinosaur Egg, hike west up the bottom of Bear Canyon. Pass the imposing Bear Creek Spire and soon you will see the Southern Egg with its hatch crack.

8101 Hatch 5.5 *Classic*

This classy 200-foot climb ascends the obvious chimney splitting the east face of the Southern Dinosaur Egg. Ascend the crack for 75 feet to the base of a steep section (Class 4). At this point the crack deepens to a chimney, but direct ascent up it is blocked by some chockstones. If you are small you may be able to wiggle up behind the chockstones, but it is far more elegant to step neatly up on the outside (5.3–5.4). Above these chockstones, enter the chimney's sanctuary and ascend it for another 75 feet (5.0–5.2). Then, 160 feet from the ground, you will come to a large flat-topped chockstone at the top of the chimney.

The final 40 feet to the summit is the crux of this route. Step off the large flat-topped chockstone and climb directly up the steep 40-foot face north of the top of the chimney (5.5). From the broad summit you can spy on Bear Cave and look up at the much higher Northern Dinosaur Egg.

Descent

8101D *This is a dangerous rock to be on top of without a rope.* Rappel 40 feet back down the south face of the summit block to the flat-topped chockstone and climb 60 feet west down broken rock to the ground (Class 4). You can avoid the last steep 20 feet to the ground by scrambling north up a small ramp to join hiking territory 100 feet southwest of Bear Cave.

811 NORTHERN DINOSAUR EGG

This egg is higher and narrower than its southern neighbor. It is a freestanding pinnacle with steep 300-foot high south and east faces. When you see it from across the gully to the east, this rock looks quite spectacular. The route Rehatch is the longest easiest route on the rock. Bear Cave is located in the bottom of the south face of the Northern Dinosaur Egg. To approach the Northern Dinosaur Egg and the climb Rehatch, follow either of the hiking routes to Bear Cave that are described in chapter one.

8111 Rehatch 5.5 *Classic*

You can gobble up this remarkable 320-foot climb in two long pitches or break it into smaller bites. Start this climb 25 feet east of Bear Cave. Climb 150 feet up the obvious fun chimney splitting the east face (Class 4). This chimney provides a refreshing change from standard Flatiron climbing. At the top of this pitch, reach a pair of 4-foot chockstones. Above this point, the south face of the main piece of rock takes shape, and overcoming this face is the crux of this route. The south face is smallest directly above the 4-foot chockstones. Climb 20 feet up the south face above the chockstones (5.5), step right onto the narrow east face of the main pinnacle and climb this steep east face to the summit. En route there is some sharp 5.0–5.2 climbing, followed by 20 feet of harder 5.3–5.4 climbing, then a spacious ledge. The summit is 20 feet beyond this ledge. It is 150 feet from the chockstones to the summit.

Descent

8111D *This is a dangerous rock to be on top of without a rope.* There are large drops to the east, south, and west, but escape lies to the north. Scramble west over the summit and get onto a secondary ridge 20 feet west of the summit. Scramble north on this ridge, rig an anchor, rappel a few feet east, then continue rappelling 35 feet down the short steep north face into the gully below. Scramble west through a notch and descend 60 feet west down a chimney to reach the ground (Class 4).

812 DER FREISCHUTZ

This is a large Flatiron with several rich routes on it near the south end of the second tier of rocks on Dinosaur Mountain. Its summit is directly west of and considerably higher than Dinosaur Rock. Der Freischutz has a surprising 600-foot south ridge that you cannot see from the Mallory Cave Trail. There is also a smaller rock called the Overture east of and attached to Der Freischutz. To approach Der Freischutz, follow the Mallory Cave Trail as it climbs west between Der Zerkle and Dinosaur Rock. When the trail turns north, leave it and hike southwest toward the boulder-strewn saddle west of Dinosaur Rock.

Descents

812D1 From the summit, scramble north and climb 25 feet down an awkward, east-facing V-shaped ramp to some large boulders (5.0–5.2). You can also rig a short rappel over this difficulty. From the large boulders, dive through a hole and emerge north of the boulders. The gully east of here is hikeable.

812D2 Downclimb the Free Shot Route (Class 3).

8121 East Face 5.0–5.2

The bottom of this climb is not far from the Mallory Cave Trail. Find a little alcove formed by the north side of the Overture and east face of Der Freischutz. Head 300 feet straight up the rock to the broad summit area.

8122 Free Shot Class 3 *Classic*

This is a true scramblers route to a high Flatiron summit. The challenge is largely route finding. The difficulty is only Class 3 if you follow the easiest line, but it is easy to stray onto more difficult rock. The summit rewards the scram-

82 Dinosaur Rock
821 East Face 5.4
824 South Ramps 5.4
812 Der Freischutz
8121 East Face 5.0–5.2
8122 Free Shot Class 3

8123 South Ridge Class 4
822 Fee
8221 South Ridge 5.3–5.4
8222 East Face 5.5
811 Northern Dinosaur Egg
814 The Hand

bler with good views of all three tiers of rocks on the south side of Dinosaur Mountain. Start in the alcove below the east face of Der Freischutz and the north face of the Overture. Angle south (left) and get into a crack and ledge system that continues in this direction across the entire east face. You can also start this climb by climbing the Overture's east face. Follow the crack and ledge system for 200 feet up to the broad south ridge of Der Freischutz and follow it 200 feet back north to the summit (Class 3).

8123 South Ridge Class 4 *Classic*

This is the finest Class 4 climb on Dinosaur Mountain. It is 600 feet in length and steeply continuous at the Class 4 level. From the saddle between the east face of the Overture and the west face of Dinosaur Rock, hike south down a scruffy gully and pass the bottom of the Overture. The next ridge to the west is the south ridge of Der Freischutz. Look for an arch part way up. Start at the low point of the ridge and climb 150 feet to this jagged 20-foot arch (Class 4). From here, you can spot another smaller arch across the gully to the east. This is the arch on the Dinosaur Tracks Route. Continue steeply up the ridge on good holds to a little false summit. Stay west (left) of the next headwall. At the 400-foot level, a third headwall rears up and is the crux of the route. Stay west (left), and climb a slab (maximal Class 4) on good holds. Anyone bored with all this can climb a nice 5.5 pitch on the east face to the north. Above the third headwall, scramble 200 feet up the broad ridge to the top (Class 3).

813 THE OVERTURE

This is the front piece for Der Freischutz. It is of similar shape, only smaller. After reading the descriptions for Der Freischutz, the position of the Overture should be clear.

Descent

813D Downclimb 70 feet near the north edge of the east face (Class 4).

8131 East Face Class 4

Find the base of the east face southeast of the alcove at the base of the east face of Der Freischutz. Simply climb 100 feet straight up to the summit. The easiest line is near the north edge of the east face. You can use this route to access, or descend from, the Free Shot Route on Der Freischutz.

8132 South Ridge 5.0–5.2

A smaller echo of the great south ridge of Der Freischutz, I recommend this route for the small surprises it contains. From the base of the Overture's east face, hike south downhill to the low point of the south ridge. Climb 350 feet along this fairly distinct ridge to the top, passing two or three short 5.0–5.2 cruxes along the way.

814 THE HAND

This is the Flatiron south of Mallory Cave. After the Mallory Cave Trail climbs away from the west face of Der Zerkle, it passes within kicking distance of the bottom of the Hand's east face. This east face provides a fine climb with an easy descent, and it's a good one for beginning slab mongers.

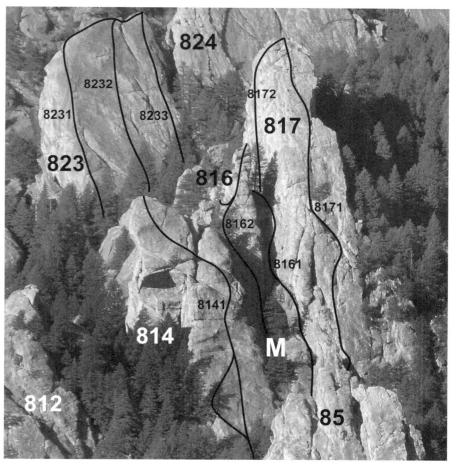

85 Der Zerkle	8161 North Side 5.0–5.2	8231 Fi Fun 5.1
812 Der Freischutz	8162 South Side 5.5–5.6	8232 Extraterrestrial 5.6
814 The Hand	817 Finger Flatiron	8233 East Face North Side 5.0–5.2
8141 East Face 5.4	8171 East Face 5.4	
M Mallory Cave	8172 Mere Wall 5.8	824 Fo
816 Shark's Fin	823 Fi	

8141 East Face 5.4

This face is a good one for anyone wishing to climb a rock with more than Flatironette status, but without a great deal of commitment. It is a 500-foot climb that you can consume in four pitches. Start at the lowest point of the rock, climb a 5.2 slab for a pitch, and either find a tree on the rock's south edge or work out a belay on the face. The next 150 feet of slightly easier enjoyable rock leads to a pair of ledges below a steep headwall. Surmount this headwall on wonderful sharp holds (5.2), and climb into the confusing world of multiple ledges and slots above. Fifty feet above the steep headwall is a ledge above which upward progress appears difficult. From the south (left) end of this ledge you can enter a deep ugly chimney, but that route is only for sloths, cavers and people wishing to escape the rock. To complete the climb on the face, go to the north (right) end of this ledge, peer down into the Mallory Cave amphitheater directly below, then climb the 5.4 bulge above. This is the hardest move of the climb. Above the bulge, climb to another spacious ledge. On the last pitch, leave the south end of this ledge, step to the south side of the sloth chimney and angle south to the broad overhung summit.

Descent

8141D From the summit, hike north into the notch between the Hand and Shark's Fin. Turn west, bend over and find a fat man frenzy hole leading west through the rock. Finding this hole is the key to a hiking descent. Once through the hole, hike 100 feet north up a gully west of Shark's Fin to the steep south face of the Finger Flatiron. Turn west, climb up a Class 3 crack and go through a small notch into the large gully between Fee, Fi, Fo, Fum and the west face of the Finger Flatiron. Hike uphill north past Finger Flatiron, descend between the Box and Finger Flatiron and head back south to the Mallory Cave Trail.

815 MALLORY FLATIRONETTE   *Closed 4/1 – 10/1*

This is the small rock directly below Mallory Cave. It is sandwiched between the lower ends of the Hand and Finger Flatiron. Visitors to the cave often perch on its twin summits. The bottom of the rock is 50 feet north of the Hand's low point, just north of a water-polished gully.

8151 East Face Class 4   *Closed 4/1 – 10/1*

Start at the low point of the rock, angle 50 feet north, then climb 130 feet of amusing Class 4 rock to either of the two summits.

Descent

8151D Scramble down the Class 3 gully between Finger Flatiron and Mallory Flatironette.

816 SHARK'S FIN
Mallory Cave Approach Closed 4/1 – 10/1

This is the phallic pinnacle directly above Mallory Cave. You can see it sailing on the skyline from many eastern locations. Its exposed summit is easy to reach; however, the approach to it is devious. Approach by hiking up the Mallory Cave Trail between the Box and Finger Flatiron. Go south around Finger Flatiron's west side and descend under Finger Flatiron's south face. For the North Side Route, descend a Class 3 crack through a small notch (Class 3) and descend into the gully between Shark's Fin and Finger Flatiron. For the South Side Route, crawl through a hole and descend into the gully between Shark's Fin and the Hand.

Descents

816D1 Downclimb the top 30 feet of the east face of Shark's Fin and return to easy ground at the top of the gully between Shark's Fin and Finger Flatiron. Hike west, ascend a Class 3 crack through a small notch, and get into the large gully between Fee, Fi, Fo, Fum and Finger Flatiron. You may hike north or south from here.

816D2 Downclimb the top 30 feet of the east face of Shark's Fin and get into the notch between Shark's Fin and the Hand. Follow the Hand's descent route from there by using the fat man's frenzy hole to the west.

8161 North Side 5.0–5.2
Mallory Cave Approach Closed 4/1 – 10/1

Eighty feet east of Mallory Cave, get onto a ramp system on the south face of Finger Flatiron, the Flatiron north of the cave. Climb 100 feet up the ramp system past a weird tree to a point above the cave entrance (Class 4). Move southwest (left) into the major gully between Shark's Fin and Finger Flatiron. Ascend the gully for 80 feet and escape the steep upper part of the gully by moving north (right) near a small tree on steep rock with good holds (5.0–5.2). Climb 50 feet west on a ramp to easy ground (Class 4) that you can reach by the devious west side approach. To continue to the summit of Shark's Fin, scramble south, stay west of the overhung summit, and emerge on the south face of the final pinnacle. Move onto the east face and climb 30 feet of exposed rock to the tippy top (Class 4).

The route above the cave is used more for access to hiking routes westward than as a summit route on Shark's Fin. For years it has been luring hikers upwards, then promptly giving them fits. It is definitely a rock climb, not a hiking route.

8162 South Side 5.5–5.6
Mallory Cave Approach Closed 4/1 – 10/1

From the entrance to Mallory Cave, step south and climb 80 feet up a convoluted chimney (5.5–5.6). This chimney ends in the short hiking gully between the Hand and Shark's Fin that you can reach by the devious west side approach. To summit Shark's Fin, climb the rock north of this gully (5.0–5.2), and climb the final 30 feet on the Fin's east face (Class 4).

817 FINGER FLATIRON

This is the long slender Flatiron immediately north of Mallory Cave. It has a nice climb up the east face, but unlike its super solid neighbors, it has some loose rock on its ledges. The upper route is above Mallory Cave. Approach by following the Mallory Cave Trail to the small amphitheater between Mallory Flatironette and Finger Flatiron.

Descent

817D *This is a dangerous rock to be on top of without a rope.* A secure but hard to see thread is on the west end of the summit area. From this anchor point, rappel 50 feet north to the ground.

8171 East Face 5.4

A more serious undertaking than the Hand, you can do this 500-foot climb in four long pitches. Start at the bottom of the rock immediately north (right) of the gully between Mallory Flatironette and Finger Flatiron. Climb straight up past a tree, over a 5.0–5.2 bulge, and continue up past several other trees. On the second pitch, avoid the loose gullies above by staying south (left). The third pitch has the 5.4 crux. Climb near the center of the face on steepening rock to a steep bulge. Climb this in the obvious crack system in the center of the face, and follow this crack to a little notch on the northern edge of the narrow face. On the fourth and last pitch, stay near the center of the face and cruise up 130 feet on good rock to the top (5.0–5.2).

8172 Mere Wall 5.8

This two-pitch climb ascends the upper south face of the Finger Flatiron. It is a steep potentially dangerous and beautiful climb. It is not a beginner's route, but for those competent at this level, Mere Wall provides an exhilarating experience. This route attracts a lot of sunshine and sometimes when other routes are cold and snowy, you can spot climbers taking advantage of this fact. The route starts in the alcove between the final summit tower of Shark's Fin and Finger Flatiron. Approach by following the Shark's Fin approach to the base of the wall.

The route follows an incipient ramp angling west (left) across the face. You follow this weakness in the steep face from the ground to the summit, and the diagonal nature of this route makes it dangerous for the second as well as the leader. The climb starts 10 feet east of a 12-foot chockstone wedged between the summit tower of Shark's Fin and the Mere Wall. This point is 10 feet above the top of the gully between Shark's Fin and Finger Flatiron.

Climb 20 feet straight up the wall (5.0–5.2), then angle west on the incipient ramp. The climbing is steep and beautiful 5.3–5.4 on sharp holds. Seventy feet up is a small 5.5 bulge, which is the crux of the first pitch. More clean 5.3–5.4 climbing leads to an exposed but secure belay stance in a vague hollow. This stance is at the intersection of the incipient ramp and the highest transverse crack that angles east toward the edge of the east face. The first pitch is 110 feet long, and the protection is good.

The second crux pitch continues angling west along the incipient ramp. The "ramp," which has been vague from the beginning, now disappears into a vertical 10-foot bulge 20 feet beyond the belay, and this is the route's 5.8 crux. Make a few delicate 5.5–5.6 moves to reach the bottom of the bulge, climb it (5.8) and continue 20 feet up the reappearing ramp (5.7). Read the rock carefully. Near the top, climb some sharp holds on the low side of the ramp (5.5–5.6). You will reach the broken summit area on its south side. The second pitch is 90 feet long, and the protection is fair.

Variations

8172V1 You can start the climb on the west side of the chockstone wedged between Shark's Fin and the Mere Wall. Angle east (right) up a transverse crack to reach the incipient ramp (5.5–5.6).

8172V2 Near the top of the second pitch, take a slightly higher line and finish with some 5.8 smearing across shallow scoops.

818 THE BOX

This rock is 100 yards north of Finger Flatiron and west of Red Devil. It has a ferocious clean overhang near the bottom of its east face. This overhang blocks simple passage up the east face, but there is an easy route. Approach from the amphitheater below Mallory Cave by continuing 100 yards north beyond the bottom of Finger Flatiron.

8181 South Ramp Class 4

This is a scruffy route up a ramp on the awesome south face of the Box. Hike up from the bottom of the rock under the south face and work up onto the ramp west of and above the ferocious east overhang. Follow the ramp for 100 feet into the huge crack between the two summits (Class 4). Worm up through this crack and a hole to the saddle (Class 4), and walk east onto the lower east-

818 The Box
8181 South Ramp
        Class 4

ern summit. Reach the higher western summit by scrambling 50 feet near the south edge of its upper east face (Class 3) or by climbing a 5.0–5.2 crack near the center of the face.

Descent

8181D Return to the saddle between the two summits, follow a ledge northwest and descend 10 feet to the ground (Class 3).

Extra Credit

8181EC A third summit lies below the higher western summit. For those possessed with a desire to bag every bump, its tiny east face is a Class 3 scramble when you approach it from the north.

819 BACKPORCH

This is the northernmost rock in the second tier of rocks on the east face of Dinosaur Mountain. It is 200 yards north of the Box. Unlike most rocks on Dinosaur Mountain, the summit of the Backporch is northeast of the summit of Dinosaur Mountain. The Backporch is considerably more defiant looking than the other rocks huddled around Mallory Cave, and it has a distinctive V-shaped overhang on its east face. This east face is considerably steeper than the average Flatiron slab and the climbing is correspondingly harder. The best approach to the Backporch is to follow the Porch Alley Route past the Frontporch and the Lost Porch until the Backporch comes into view.

Descents

This is a dangerous rock to be on top of without a rope.

819D1 Rappel 150 feet west from the summit to the ground. One hundred and fifty-foot ropes just make it. This spectacular rappel is mostly free.

819D2 Do two 75-foot rappels down the west face. You can use a precarious ledge halfway down for the second rappel.

819D3 Do two or more rappels down the east face.

8191 East Face 5.6 *Classic – Top Ten*

This is the finest 5.6 climb on Dinosaur Mountain and a recommended climb in any domain. You can climb the standard route up the face in two 150-foot pitches or break it into three or four shorter pitches. From the low point of the

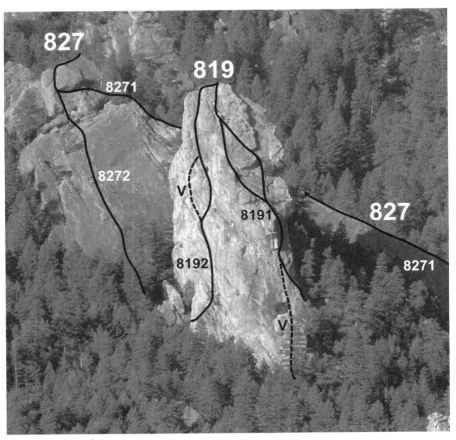

819 Backporch
8191 East Face 5.6
8192 Southern Exposure 5.7

827 The Rainbow
8271 Primal Rib 5.3–5.4 S
8272 East Face 5.0–5.2

rock, scramble 100 feet along the north side of the rock to a steep scruffy area. The start of the climb is below a 2-foot arch.

Traverse south and climb onto the east face. Climb up the slab, passing a nice 5.3–5.4 stretch, to a point below the big V-shaped overhang. You can use this stance for a belay if you desire shorter leads. The V-shaped overhang has an obvious fault on its north side. To reach it, climb north a few feet and head up a 5.5–5.6 slab north of the V-shaped overhang. At the top of this slab, climb south over the 5.6 crux. Pass a small tree and continue up to a larger tree that is 150 feet from the start of the climb.

You can do the remaining 150-foot pitch to the summit in one of two ways. The original way is near the north side of the east face, passes the final step at an appropriate place, and ascends easier rock to the summit. A harder cleaner pitch is near the south side of the east face. From the tree at the top of the first pitch, angle south (left) and climb over a 5-foot overhang in or near a fist sized crack (5.5–5.6). Above this obstacle, climb a classic 5.0–5.2 slab to easier rock near the top. Although you can avoid it, a sharp 10-foot finger crack makes a nice 5.5–5.6 finish to this climb. To find this finger crack, stay near the center of the rock near the top.

Variation

8191V You can start at the low point of the east face, and after overcoming a 5.7 overhang, join the East Face Route below the V-shaped overhang.

8192 Southern Exposure 5.7

This scary route ascends the south face of the Backporch. The route is best done in three pitches. Start behind a large freestanding flake, and scramble east to reach a tree at the bottom of the south face. Climb diagonally west (left) up a ramp for a pitch to a big square flake (5.7). On the second pitch, climb straight up the wall to a prominent belay flake. On the third pitch, climb straight up above the belay flake, then angle west (left) on easier ramps.

Variation

8192V From the belay flake at the top of the second pitch, climb straight west (left) until it is obvious to head straight up (5.7).

820 ACHEAN PRONOUNCEMENT
Closed 2/1 – 7/31

This is the easternmost of three long rock ribs on the south side of Skunk Canyon. It is south of Satan's Slab at the northern end of the second tier of rocks on Dinosaur Mountain. The Achean Pronouncement is more of a Flatiron than a rib. It has an east face that is several hundred feet high and a short steep west face. A ferocious overhanging summit block waits for you, and there are no easy routes to the summit of the Achean Pronouncement. Satan's Slab and the Achean Pronouncement form a statuesque gateway in Skunk Canyon. When approaching up Skunk Canyon, you will see a long crack with a tree near its top on the north end of the east face. This is the route.

820 Achean
     Pronouncement
8201 East Face 5.7
827 The Rarinbow
8271 Primal Rib
     5.3–5.4 S
828 North Ridge of
     Dinosaur Mountain

8201 East Face 5.7 *Classic*   *Closed 2/1 – 7/31*

Just getting off the ground onto this rock is exciting. The northern end of
the Achean Pronouncement, which drops into Skunk Canyon, is well defended
by a vertical wall. Hike to the low, northern end of the east face and you
will discover that a small overhang guards entrance onto the east face. This
barrier continues south for a long distance along the base of the east face. A
break in this overhang is 60 feet south of the low point, and this is the start of
the route.

Climb a short smooth 5.7 slab south of a big bush and reach some large
trees below the long crack visible from Skunk Canyon. From the large trees at
the bottom of the crack, climb 165 feet up the fun, fist sized crack to another
large tree (5.0–5.2). Watch out for a patch of poison ivy in this crack. A good
intermediate belay stance is 120 feet up the crack.

From the large tree at the top of the crack, continue 90 feet straight up to a spectacular stance at the northern end of the Achean Pronouncement's long summit ridge (5.0–5.2). From this stance, climb onto the east face and ascend it for 35 feet to the airy crest of the long north ridge (5.0–5.2). Climb south along the Class 4 ridge and reach a belay stance 120 feet from the spectacular stance at the northern end of the ridge.

Continue south along the now quite easy ridge, and after another 120 feet of Class 4, reach the northeast corner of the summit block. Traverse south under the east face of the summit block and move around under its south face (Class 4). The final 40-foot pitch ascends the vertical south face of the summit block and is the hardest pitch of the route. Start the pitch near the center of the face, pull over a 5.6 overhang, angle west (left) on nervous undercut flakes (5.7) and shoot up to the top.

Variations

8201V1 You can escape the fist sized crack above the initial 5.7 slab. After ascending the fist sized crack for 100 feet, climb south onto the main east face, climb up a 5.3–5.4 slab, then follow a 5.0–5.2 weakness up to a nice ledge 10 feet south of the large tree that is 165 feet up the fist sized crack. It is also easy to climb south from this tree to reach this ledge. From this ledge, move south into another crack system, and climb this crack to join the regular route near the northern end of the summit ridge (5.3–5.4).

8201V2 From the bottom of the final crack system of Variation 1, traverse south across the barren unprotected 5.5–5.6 slab, get into another dihedral system and ascend it to the summit ridge.

Descent

8201D *This is a dangerous rock to be on top of without a rope.* Rappel 50 feet down the south face of the summit block. The best hiking descent from here is to traverse south, cross over to south-facing slopes, and descend the broad gully between the Frontporch and the Lost Porch. Pick up the Porch Alley trail and follow it down to the Mesa Trail.

822 FEE

This is the lowest and southernmost of the four rocks Fee, Fi, Fo and Fum. These four rocks form the third tier on Dinosaur Mountain. Fee does not have the characteristic shape of the others, but provides a longer, and except for a couple of moves, easier climb. You may approach Fee by using the approach for Fi, which uses the Der Freischutz–Hand saddle. Approach Fee's south ridge by hiking up from Bear Canyon.

Descents

822D1 Downclimb the sharp 20-foot north ridge of Fee (Class 4).

822D2 Sling the summit block, rappel 45 feet east to a large ledge and walk north. The gully between Fee and Fi is hikeable.

8221 South Ridge 5.3–5.4

The shortest approach to the base of this climb is to leave the Bear Canyon Trail just after the trail crosses the creek after traversing high above the creek on the south side of Bear Canyon. The base of the climb is 250 feet north of Bear Creek, and if you are not familiar with the area, it may be difficult to identify Fee. The angle of Fee's 550-foot long south ridge is lower than other climbs on Fi, Fo or Fum, and the climbing is correspondingly easier.

The first 450 feet is solid Class 4. You will cross an escape notch, and find a beautiful unbroken slab, which, if it were higher angle, would provide ferocious climbing. Reach a second escape notch, a deep chimney, and climb the steep slab on the other side, which is the route's crux. You can do this by moving diagonally east (right) with a few 5.3–5.4 moves. Above the crux, either follow the steeper 5.0–5.2 ridge, or traverse north on a large ledge on the east face and climb a nice 5.0–5.2 hand crack to regain the ridge near the summit.

Extra Credit

8221EC There is another summit between Fee and Fi that is slightly higher than Fee. Its east side provides a short weird 5.0–5.2 climb that reaches the summit from the north. Some loose killer blocks are near here.

8222 East Face 5.5

Start west of the west face of Der Freischutz. Climb a break in a low overhang, and climb straight up a clean red slab to the highest false summit on the south ridge. Cross the crux notch of the South Ridge Route, and continue on that route to the summit.

823 FI

Counting from the south, this is the second rock in the third tier of Dinosaur Mountain. It is well hidden from most Boulder locations, and you cannot see

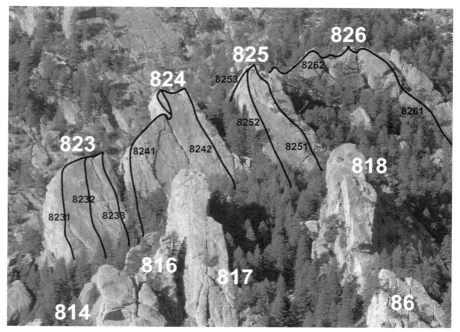

814 The Hand
816 Shark's Fin
817 Finger Flatiron
818 The Box
86 Red Devil
823 Fi
8231 Fi Fun 5.1
8232 Extraterrestrial 5.6

8233 East Face North Side
  5.0–5.2
824 Fo
8241 Quadratic Equation
  5.6
8242 East Face 5.6
825 Fum
8251 East Face North Side
  5.0–5.2

8252 East Face South Side
  5.5–5.6 S
8253 South Face 5.5–5.6
826 Dum
8261 East Face 5.0–5.2
8262 South Ridge 5.3–5.4

it from the Mallory Cave Trail. It is visible from the summits of Der Freischutz, the Hand and Finger Flatiron. The summit of Fi is west of Shark's Fin and Finger Flatiron. Fi and its partners Fo and Fum, provide some of the best climbing on Dinosaur Mountain. The high-angle east faces lead to spectacular summit ridges with superb open views in all directions. Fi has a champion summit ridge.

Approach Fi by following the Mallory Cave Trail between Dinosaur Rock and Der Zerkle. Leave the trail where it turns north toward the west side of Der Zerkle, hike west into the hiking gully between Der Freischutz and the Hand and follow this gully west to the Der Freischutz–Hand saddle. The rock west of here is Fee. Hike west into the broad north-south gully east of Fee, and hike 100 feet north to the bottom of Fi.

Descent

823D *This is a dangerous rock to be on top of without a rope.* Rappel 40 feet down the east face, swing north and drop another 20 feet to a large boulder in the Fi–Fo saddle. The most innovative and secure anchor, and one that leaves the summit clean, is to put your climbing rope around the entire summit block. It will pull down ok.

The Fi–Fo gully to the east is not hikeable. For a hiking descent, scramble north up the Fumbledeedum trough just west of Fo. This trough is full of giant boulders with fun little routes between and under them. The Fo–Fum gully, although it looks promising, is also not hikeable. From the Fo–Fum saddle, continue north up Fumbledeedum, staying west of Fum, and walk through a large hole. From a point north of Fum, you can hike down to the east or continue west and north to the top of Dinosaur Mountain.

8231 Fi Fun 5.1 *Classic*

This is the classiest 5.1 climb on Dinosaur Mountain. It ascends the southern side of Fi's east face and follows a sensational summit ridge north to the high point. This east face looks imposing when you see it from the east, but it has good holds on it. This 360-foot climb breaks into three nice pitches.

Start at the low point of the east face. On the first pitch, climb 130 feet of charming Class 4 to a ledge with a tiny tree. On the second pitch, continue 150 feet straight up steep 5.1 rock near the southern (left) edge of the east face to a perch that looks like it is only 10 feet from the top. On the third pitch, climb these 10 feet and continue 70 magnificent feet north to the summit. Enjoy.

8232 Extraterrestrial 5.6

For a delicate small holds climb, start below the center of Fi's small east face and climb straight up the center of the face to the summit.

8233 East Face North Side 5.0–5.2

The northern edge of the east face provides a shorter, less spectacular route to the summit. Start near a large boulder under the northern edge of the east face and climb up 200 feet of enjoyable Class 4–5.2 rock to the summit.

824 FO

Counting from the south, this is the third rock in the quadruple of rocks Fee, Fi, Fo and Fum. Like the others, Fo provides higher angle Flatiron rock and excellent climbing. Fo has a backwards L-shaped summit ridge that is often prominent on Dinosaur Mountain's skyline. Approach Fo by following the Mallory Cave Trail to the bottom of Finger Flatiron. Continue north, then hike west up the broad gully between Finger Flatiron and the Box. Continue west and get into the large north-south gully east of Fee, Fi, Fo and Fum. Descend 100 feet south to the bottom of Fo. Also, when using the little Class 3 gully and notch south of Finger Flatiron, you will emerge east of Fo.

Descent

824D From the highest point, downclimb 40 feet west (Class 4), then turn north and climb 20 feet east down a Class 4 ramp into the Fo–Fum saddle. The gully east of this point is not hikeable since a drop off is lower down. For a hiking descent, scramble north on the west side of Fum's summit and walk through a large hole. This is the top of the Fumbledeedum Route. From the saddle north of Fum, it is easy to hike east or turn west and continue to the summit of Dinosaur Mountain.

8241 Quadratic Equation 5.6 *Classic*

This recommended 400-foot, three-pitch climb on Fo's solid east face starts at the rock's lowest point at the southern edge of the east face. Climb up and angle slightly north (right) across a tricky 5.6 slab to easier rock above. Continue straight up over some 5.3–5.4 rock, and work out a belay on the face. On the second pitch, continue up steep 5.0–5.2 rock to the low southern end of the backwards L summit ridge. The first part of this ridge is easy, spectacular and fun. Follow it to its northern end, and contemplate your future.

A deep chimney separates the steep summit block from the rest of the summit ridge, and the whole business may look a little improbable at first. On the final pitch, get into the chimney and climb 15 feet down to the east until you can climb out onto the east face of the summit block. To minimize excitement, diagonal 20 feet north (right) across a 5.5–5.6 slab to easier rock. To maximize excitement, head 40 feet straight up a 5.6 slab to the top. The highest point is 40 feet north (Class 3).

8242 East Face 5.6

Start near the north side of the east face and climb directly to the summit.

825 FUM

This is the highest northernmost summit of Fee, Fi, Fo and Fum. Not quite as spectacular as Fi or Fo, Fum still has excellent rock. To approach Fum, follow the Mallory Cave Trail past Finger Flatiron, hike north then west to the saddle west of the Box. The bottom of Fum is directly west of the Box. You can climb Fum's 300-foot east face in two or three pitches.

Descent

825D Scramble off the top by either of two different routes and get into a large crack system that descends northwest to the ground. The scramble down this crack is Class 3 except for a few 5.0–5.2 moves near the ground. It is 50 feet from the summit to the ground.

8251 East Face North Side 5.0–5.2

After a midsummer ascent, I suggested the name ants in the pants for this route, since one section was festooned with the beauties (ants not pants). Start at the lowest point of the rock, which is at its southeast corner. Angle north (right), follow a zone of weakness, reach the broken north side of the east face and follow it to the summit, passing several trees and ledges en route.

Variation

8251V Two hundred feet up, a large ledge runs diagonally across the face from lower right to upper left. Follow this ledge to the south side of the face (Class 3), and climb the last pitch of the East Face South Side Route via a few 5.5–5.6 moves above the ledge, 15 feet of 5.3–5.4 slab, then easier rock to the top.

8252 East Face South Side 5.5–5.6 S

The south side of the east face is a beautiful, clean ant-less slab of pure Fum fun. The slab is a bit too clean, since there is a 200-foot pitch with minimal protection possibilities and no good belay stance. Start at the rock's low point and climb 300 feet straight up to the summit. For the first 40 feet follow a crack, which soon poops out into a beautiful 5.3–5.4 face. After 140 feet, the climbing eases to 5.0–5.2. After 200 feet, reach a large Class 3 ledge angling across the face. Make a few 5.5–5.6 moves near the south edge of the face to get above the ledge, and climb 15 feet up another 5.3–5.4 slab. The climbing eases to 5.0–5.2 and the summit is not far beyond.

8253 South Face 5.5–5.6

Fum has a short, steep south face that provides a fun 90-foot pitch. Start directly below the summit, and climb up to a peculiar flake in the center of the face. Climb east (right) of the flake (5.5–5.6) and continue up easier rock to the broad summit area.

826 DUM

This rock is in a neglected spot, high on the east face of Dinosaur Mountain. It is southwest of and above both the Backporch and the summit of the Rainbow. Dum is in the third tier and is north of and higher than Fum. The east face of Dum has a somewhat northern exposure and this face does not have the pristine qualities of its southern neighbors. Dum's summit is a flat slab 20 feet in diameter perched on two would-be summits. This tabletop is 250 feet east of and only slightly lower than the top of Dinosaur Mountain. It is a wonderful place to perch. I describe two routes that provide a rocky way to continue on to the top of Dinosaur Mountain after completing other climbs nearby. The routes have different approaches.

Descent

826D Scramble down off the tabletop summit into the broad hiking saddle to the west, which is the top of the Bowling Alley.

8261 East Face 5.0–5.2

Reach this climb by following the approach for the Backporch and hiking west, staying south of both the Backporch and the Rainbow. The bottom of this face is 100 feet south from the bottom of the neat alleyway on the descent from the top of the Rainbow, and this climb makes a logical extension to an ascent of the Rainbow. By combining the Primal Rib and Dum's East Face Route you can come very close to climbing all the way from Skunk Canyon to the top of Dinosaur Mountain on rock.

When viewed from the bottom, Dum's 450-foot east face sweeps up in pretty waves, but trees and lichen detract from the climbing. Start at the low point and climb 280 feet, angling south (left) to stay on the face. The climbing is solid 5.0–5.2 near the bottom, easing to Class 4 higher up. You can escape off the north side of the face after 200 feet. Higher, climb south into a large crack that splits the upper part of the face (5.0–5.2). Hike and scramble 100 feet up this crack, wind up through some dark holes and emerge into the sunlight on the rock's west side. Climb 50 feet south to Dum's tabletop summit (Class 4).

8262 South Ridge 5.3–5.4

This 200-foot route is useful for people heading toward the top of Dinosaur Mountain who would rather climb on rock than hike. Although short, this route is nicely positioned high on the slopes of Dinosaur Mountain and has a spot of difficulty to keep you in climb mode. The route starts in the scruffy Fum–Dum saddle north of Fum, which is often reached after ascents of Fi, Fo and Fum. The Fum–Dum col is also the top of the Fumbledeedum Route.

Start in the Fum–Dum col and climb 60 feet north up a clean ridge to a false summit (5.0–5.2). Climb down onto this summit's short east face, and zoom up to a second summit (Class 4) from which you can clearly see Dum's tabletop summit 100 feet north. The crux of this route is descending north from this second summit. To do this, climb a few feet down along the north edge of the east face, then climb down and across a short pebble-strewn north face (5.3–5.4). With this difficulty safely behind you, move stately north and step proudly onto Dum's magnificent tabletop summit (Class 4).

Extra Credit

8262EC The top of Dinosaur Mountain is 100 feet west of Dum's tabletop summit and is hard to ignore. You can reach it by heading straight west, climbing a 50-foot Class 4 slab, crossing a narrow hiking gully and climbing a 20-foot Class 3 slab to the exposed summit. You can avoid the 50-foot Class 4 slab by moving a few feet north or 50 feet south and climbing west up 15-foot Class 3 cracks into the narrow hiking gully that takes you easily to the 20-foot summit slab.

827 THE RAINBOW   *Closed 2/1 – 7/31*

This is a large angular Flatiron rising from the depths of Skunk Canyon that sweeps up in a graceful rainbow-like arc and culminates southwest of the Backporch. The Rainbow is the middle of three ribs on the south side of Skunk Canyon, and is just west of the Achean Pronouncement. I describe two routes with different approaches.

Descent

827D From the summit, descend 50 feet east to the alcove. Scramble south through a large hole formed by the two summit blocks. Wind down to the west and south through a neat alleyway between large boulders to hiking territory on the south side of the Rainbow. Descend along the south sides of the Backporch and Frontporch via Porch Alley.

8271 Primal Rib 5.3–5.4 S *Classic*   *Closed 2/1 – 7/31*

This route ascends the Rainbow's accented edge along its graceful arc. Your position is spectacular for several hundred feet. You can cover this 1,000-foot long tour in six long pitches. Since you are never far from the ground, it is easy to escape from this route. Approach by hiking up Skunk Canyon to a point west of the portal formed by the Achean Pronouncement to the south and Satan's Slab to the north. The bottom of the Rainbow extends almost to the floor of Skunk Canyon, but the first few hundred feet are scruffy and not worth climbing. Hike south above Skunk Canyon in the gully east of the Rainbow until the rock becomes well formed.

The first pitch contains the only 5.3–5.4 climbing on the route. Climb onto the rib, and ascend Class 4 rock to some difficulties marked by an east-facing dihedral capped by a large bush. Climb a nice fist size crack in the dihedral to the bush (5.3–5.4). Overcome the dihedral wall below the bush (5.3–5.4) and cruise up easier rock above. On the second long pitch, climb casual Class 4 rock near the edge of the rib to a large ledge system below the primal part of the rib. It is easy to escape east on this ledge.

Climb 200 beautiful sweeping feet from the ledge to a small tree near the edge of the rib. The best climbing is within 20 feet of the edge lower down and very close to the edge higher up. The difficulty in this stretch is consistent 5.0–5.2, and belay stances and protection are difficult. Climb another 200 feet from the small tree to a notch where the primal part of the rib joins the rest of the rock to the south. This pitch is mostly Class 4, and since the ridge is lower angle here, it is easy and spectacular to move right along the ridge. Beyond the notch, follow broken rock 250 feet southwest to a small alcove below two summit blocks (Class 4). The western block is the highest and easy to ascend. From the top you can peer back down along the Primal Rib, but it looks quite different from this vantage point. The west face of the Backporch dominates your eastern view.

8272 East Face 5.0–5.2   *Closed 2/1 – 7/31*

This route ascends the 350-foot southern edge of the Rainbow. This route is far removed from the Primal Rib. Use Porch Alley to approach this climb by hiking up under the south face of the Backporch. The bottom of this climb is hiding in the trees 200 feet south of and below the notch on the west side of the Backporch.

Climb the slab, angling north (right) for two 150-foot pitches to a large ledge with big trees on it. The first pitch contains appealing and consistent 5.0–5.2 climbing, and the second pitch eases to Class 4. The large ledge is east of and below the lower of the two summit blocks that form the top of the Rainbow. Hike around to the north side of the lower summit block, reach the alcove on the Primal Rib Route, and continue to the western summit block. For a cleaner, more direct way to finish this climb, ascend the southern edge of the lower summit block to a large ledge, climb south (left), dodge two overhangs, step around an exposed 5.0–5.2 corner and cruise up to the top of the lower block. Scramble west to the true summit.

828 NORTH RIDGE OF DINOSAUR MOUNTAIN   *Closed 2/1 – 7/31*

This is the third and westernmost rib of rock rising from Skunk Canyon on the north side of Dinosaur Mountain. This north-facing rib is shaded during winter and holds more snow than other rocks nearby, hence a lot of lichen is on the rock, and in places the rock is friable. The redeeming feature of the rib is that it provides a continuous remote ascent on rock from the floor of Skunk Canyon to the summit of Dinosaur Mountain. The upper part of the rib is easy, and if you are looking for more of a mountaineering challenge than a pure rock climb, this rib will be satisfying. To approach the rib, hike up Skunk Canyon past the Achean Pronouncement and the Rainbow. Find the bottom of this rib, which is only a few feet south of the floor of the canyon.

8281 North Ridge of Dinosaur Mountain 5.0–5.2   *Closed 2/1 – 7/31*

If climbed roped all the way, this climb will require eight pitches. Start climbing near the lowest point of the rock at the bottom of the east face. Climb 200 feet up clean, consistent and memorable 5.0–5.2 rock to the top of the first tower. Near the top of this first tower, the 5.0–5.2 route traverses south (left), but an elegant and worthwhile variation is to stay right on the ridge, finishing in a 15-foot V-shaped crack (5.3–5.4).

Beyond the first tower, the character of the climb changes abruptly if you follow the path of least resistance. Two hundred feet of Class 4 is followed by 100 feet of 5.0–5.2, after which the difficulty should never be greater than Class 4. On its upper reaches, you can easily escape east off the rib, but if you stay on the rock, you will be rewarded with a classy approach to the top of Dinosaur Mountain.

829 SOUTH GREEN MOUNTAIN

Closed 2/1 – 7/31

South Green Mountain is the 8,073-foot rock summit a half-mile south of Green Mountain's summit. This magnificent mountain is the highest Flatiron summit on Green Mountain, and is the culmination of a continuous rock rib that starts in Bear Canyon. There is a large drop to the west, and the view from this summit is unobstructed in all directions. This summit, more than any other Flatiron summit, evokes a feeling of being in the high mountains. If you have never been there, make it your next outing.

Descent

829D Downclimb the North Sneak Route (5.0–5.2). Finding this obtuse route while downclimbing can be difficult.

829 South Green
   Mountain

8292 East Face 5.0–5.2

G Green Mountain

EG East Green
   Mountain

BC Bear Canyon

8291 North Sneak 5.0–5.2   *Closed 2/1 – 7/31*

This is the shortest and easiest way to reach the summit of South Green Mountain. The route starts on the west side of the south ridge of Green Mountain, and the easiest way to reach this point is to hike a half-mile south from the summit of Green Mountain, staying west of Green's rocky south ridge. It is easy to identify the summit tower.

Start northwest of the summit, scramble up a steep broken area and climb a short Class 4 gully to a notch north of the clean, vertical north face of the summit tower. It looks hopeless from here, but there is a way. A few feet east of the notch climb an improbable 15-foot pitch up to the east across the vertical north face, and reach the east face of the summit tower (5.0–5.2). Finding and climbing this weakness in the north face is the route's crux. Once on the east face, climb 100 feet southwest up the face's exposed north edge to the summit (Class 4).

8292 East Face 5.0–5.2   *Closed 2/1 – 7/31*

An ascent of this route and descent of the North Sneak Route makes a wonderful traverse of South Green Mountain. One of the best mountaineering tours above Boulder is to ascend all four summits of Green Mountain, and this traverse of South Green Mountain is the key to that tour. A favored version of this tour starts by hiking beyond Mallory Cave to the summit of Dinosaur Mountain, descending to the Dinosaur–South Green saddle, traversing South Green Mountain, hiking north to the summit of Green Mountain and catching Green's eastern summit on the way down. If you have read this far, this tour should catch your interest.

For the East Face of South Green Mountain, start at the Dinosaur–South Green saddle. You can reach this saddle by traversing Dinosaur Mountain or hiking up the Southwest Slopes Route on Dinosaur Mountain and continuing into the saddle. From the saddle, hike west up the broad ridge until you bump into a scruffy Flatironette east of the main east face of South Green Mountain. Stay south of this Flatironette and get into the south-facing gully between the Flatironette and South Green's main east face. From here, there are two choices.

For the easiest route, climb the broken part of the east face south of the summit. Many ledges, trees and gullies are in this section of the face. A direct ascent to the ridge leaves you in a series of nasty notches, so move north before it's too late, climb onto the smooth upper part of the east face, angle north across this part of the face, pass two 5.0–5.2 steps and reach the spectacular summit ridge south of the summit. Follow the ridge north, climb a small south-facing 5.0–5.2 wall to reach an east-facing slab and climb it to the summit.

For a cleaner route involving more 5.0–5.2 climbing, climb to the notch between the eastern Flatironette and the smooth part of the east face. From here, climb directly up the face, reach the summit ridge south of the summit, follow the ridge north, climb a small south-facing 5.0–5.2 wall to reach an east-facing slab and climb it to the summit. The large ubiquitous summit area is a rock paradise high over Boulder. Enjoy.

First Pinnacle of Gregory Amphitheater

NINE

The Nebel Horn

The Nebel Horn is the 7,580-foot summit a half-mile northeast of Bear Peak between Bear and Fern Canyons, and the top of Fern Canyon is the Nebel Horn–Bear Peak saddle. You can easily approach climbs on the Nebel Horn on the Bear Canyon, Mesa or Fern Canyon Trails. Nebel Horn means Fog Horn in German, and it is pronounced Nay–bael Horn.

91 OVERHANG ROCK

This is the provocative rock fin low on the north face of the Nebel Horn, a short distance above Bear Canyon. The fin runs north-south and has steep east and west faces with pronounced overhangs. The rock's long north ridge culmi-

BC Bear Canyon	93 Hamon's Flatironette	98 Goose Eggs
FC Fern Canyon	94 Seal Rock	FA Fern Canyon
913 Nebel Horn	96 The Penguin	Amphitheater
91 Overhang Rock	97 The Goose	99 Fern Canyon Slabs

91 Overhang Rock
911 East Face 5.6
911EC 5.4
92 South Pinnacle

93 Harmon's Flatironette
932 East Face South Side Class 4
933 East Face North Side Class 4

nates in the main summit near the south end of the rock. A smaller astonishing pinnacle is south of the main summit, and a pronounced notch separates the two summits. These steep climbs are obtuse, and Overhang Rock is more difficult to climb then most Flatirons. Approach by hiking a short distance into Bear Canyon on the Bear Canyon Trail, then hiking south to the low point of the rock.

Descents

This is a dangerous rock to be on top of without a rope.

91D1 From the main summit, rappel 130 feet southeast to the ground.

91D2 From the main summit, rappel 60 feet south into the notch, downclimb 10 feet east to a tree and rappel 60 feet east to the ground.

91D3 From the southern pinnacle, either downclimb (5.4) or rappel north into the notch, and rappel 60 feet east to the ground.

911 East Face 5.6

This two-pitch climb is the easiest way to reach the summit of Overhang Rock. From the rock's low point, hike up under the east face. The start of the route is 50 feet north of a point directly below the notch between the main summit and the southern pinnacle. Climb a south-angling crack system for 30 feet (5.0–5.2), then continue south (left) across some 5.3–5.4 slabs into a large shallow bowl below the notch. Climb a nondescript 5.0–5.2 wall on the bowl's north side, and finish the pitch by angling south (left) on a small Class 4 ramp to reach the notch. From the notch, climb 30 feet up the steep south wall of the main summit (5.3–5.4). Do a sneaky exposed 5.6 traverse east around a corner, get into a bomb-bay groove and climb it to the summit.

Variations

911V1 Start the climb on the east side of the rock at a point directly below the notch between the main summit and the southern pinnacle. Overcome the initial overhang via an awkward 5.7 layback on a flake and continue up easier rock to join the first pitch in the bowl.

911V2 You can reach the notch from the west via a grungy 5.4 pitch.

Extra Credit

911EC From the notch, climb the spectacular pinnacle south of the main summit via a short 5.4 pitch.

912 Junior Achievement 5.6

This is a steep exposed route up the main west face of Overhang Rock. During the hot season it is a good route to be on in the morning, since the sun does not hit this face until afternoon. Conversely, in colder months you can enjoy this route when it is basking in the late afternoon sun. Start on the rock's west side, north of a point below the notch between the main summit and the southern pinnacle, below the northernmost of two nondescript crack systems. Scramble north up to the start of the climb.

On the first 50-foot pitch, reach the northernmost of two prominent cracks on the upper part of the face. En route, climb over two exciting, slightly overhanging 5.6 bulges. Several hidden buckets are along the way, but they always seem to be out of reach. To make your position more exciting, this is one of those pitches that has instant exposure, since the rock drops steeply northwest. Fifteen feet beyond the bulges, reach a comfortable belay on a large ramp below a south-facing inside corner.

On the second 150-foot pitch, angle 75 feet south (right) across a 5.0–5.2

ramp to reach the upper part of the southern crack. Climb another tricky 5.4 bulge to reach the main part of this crack system, then climb the steep upper part of this crack system to reach the summit ridge north of the summit (5.0–5.2). A lot of loose rock is on the upper part of this pitch. Scramble joyously 80 feet south to the summit (Class 3).

Variation

912V On the second pitch, continue straight up and climb an overhanging 5.8 crack in the south-facing inside corner. Above the inside corner, angle south (right) on broken rock to reach the summit ridge.

913 South Ridge of Southern Pinnacle 5.7

Climb a dangerous 50-foot route on the south side of the southern pinnacle over a series of small bulges. This is an extraordinary summit.

92 SOUTH PINNACLE

More of a curiosity than a climb, this rock is still worth mentioning. Sometimes called Devil's Pinkie, the pinnacle is halfway up the north face of the Nebel Horn west of Overhang Rock. You can see it on the skyline from the east and from Bear Canyon. From some vantages, it even looks exquisite. To approach, leave the Bear Canyon Trail just before it crosses to the north side of the creek, and bushwhack south up to the rock. Climb 20 feet up the rock's sloping southeast side (Class 4). From the exposed summit, you can peer down at hikers on the Bear Canyon Trail and pretend that you are on top of the world.

93 HARMON'S FLATIRONETTE   *Closed 4/1 – 10/1*

This delightful Flatironette is between Overhang and Seal Rocks, and from its summit there are good views of these mighty neighbors. Harmon's Cave is in the base of this Flatironette. To approach, leave the Mesa Trail (a road at this point) 100 feet south of its junction with the Bear Canyon Trail. Hike 200 yards west to the bottom of the rock. The cave is closed, but there are some short climbs in this charming area. Many variations exist.

931 Harmon's East Class 3   *Closed 4/1 – 10/1*

Forty feet east of the cave is a small Flatironette. Reach the rock's southeast ridge from its west side, 30 feet uphill from the low point of the rock, and scramble up 100 feet of low angle Class 3 rock to a nice summit.

Variation

931V Start at the rock's low point, and make a 5.0–5.2 move over a bulge.

Descent

931D Downclimb the route.

932 East Face South Side Class 4   *Closed 4/1 – 10/1*

This 200-foot climb ascends the main section of the east face of Harmon's Flatironette. Start 50 feet south of the cave and head up. If you follow the easiest line, the climbing will be Class 4, but it is easy to stray onto 5.0–5.2 rock on this route.

933 East Face North Side Class 4   *Closed 4/1 – 10/1*

Start this 250-foot climb east of and below the cave at the low point of Harmon's Flatironette. Climb over the cave, pass a tree and climb over a small arch above the cave. Continue up easier rock to the summit.

Extra Credit

933EC Climb the spectacular little summit above the arch with an exposed summit move on jug handholds (Class 4).

Descent

933D From the top of Harmon's Flatironette, scramble 40 feet southwest (Class 3).

94 SEAL ROCK

This well-named Flatiron is on the east-facing slopes of the Nebel Horn south of Bear Canyon. It has a pronounced elbow in its northeast ridge, and when you view the rock from the east, it is this elbow that gives the rock its seal-like shape. The climbs on Seal Rock are refreshing. The large rock provides a Flatiron playground far from the crowded routes on the major Flatirons. To approach, leave the Mesa Trail (a road at this point) 100 feet south of its junction with the Bear

B   Bear Peak
913 Nebel Horn
91 Overhang Rock
93 Harmon's Flatironette
94 Seal Rock
941 East Face North Side
    Class 4

942 East Face South Side
    5.4
95 The Pup
951 North Ridge 5.0–5.2
96 The Penguin
97 The Goose
971 East Face Class 4

971V1 5.3–5.4
971V2 5.3–5.4
FA Fern Canyon
    Amphitheater
98 Goose Eggs

Canyon Trail. Hike 200 yards west to the vicinity of Harmon's Cave, then angle south to the bottom of Seal Rock nestled in the trees.

Descents

94D1 Scramble 50 feet east from the summit to an anchor, and rappel 165 down Seal Rock's amazing north face to reach the ground.

94D2 Downclimb or rappel the top two pitches of the standard East Face Route (Class 4) near the north edge of the east face to the prominent elbow on the north ridge. Scramble 75 feet down the ridge (Class 3), and climb west down an improbable 10-foot overhang to the ground (Class 4).

94D3 You can rappel down the south face. From the summit, rappel or downclimb 40 feet west into a notch (5.0–5.2) and climb 90 feet east down a ramp on the south face (Class 4). Rappel 135 feet south to the ground.

941 East Face North Side Class 4

This 800-foot route along the north edge of the east face is the longest, easiest route on Seal Rock. You can climb it in five pitches with a 165-foot rope, but it is more convenient to break the climb into six pitches. This route is not as clean as the East Face South Side Route, but the climbing is easier, the protection good and you can escape the route at the large elbow in the northeast ridge. Start at the low point of the rock at its northeast corner. Don't confuse the low point of Seal Rock with the low point of the Pup, a much smaller Flatironette 100 feet east of Seal Rock. A Class 3 start is 20 feet south of the low point, but if you climb straight up from the lowest point, a 20-foot smooth 5.6 slab will surprise you.

Climb up within 50 feet of the north edge of the face. In the first 400 feet there are plenty of trees for anchors and protection. After 500 feet, you will

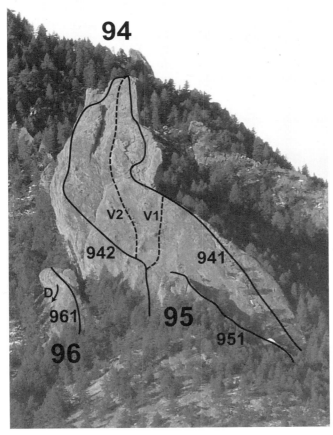

94 Seal Rock
941 East Face North Side Class 4
942 East Face South Side 5.4
942V1 5.0–5.2
942V2 5.0–5.2
95 The Pup
951 North Ridge 5.0–5.2
96 The Penguin
961 East Face 5.3–5.4

arrive at the great elbow in the ridge that gives Seal Rock its distinctive shape. You can escape the rock 75 feet below the elbow by climbing west down an improbable 10-foot overhang to the ground (Class 4). Steeper rock rises above the elbow. Climb two more pitches near the north edge of the east face. If you follow the easiest route, the climbing is never harder than Class 4, but the devious easiest line will test your rock reading skills, so be prepared for harder climbing. The bumpy summit area is substantial, and you can sometimes observe various forms of marine life in large pools. Looking north, you can see an array of rocks that helps you understand how much rock is above Boulder.

942 East Face South Side 5.4 *Classic*

This 650-foot five-pitch climb up the south side of Seal Rock is a Flatiron masterpiece. The sustained nature of the first pitch plus the exposed nature of the pitches above the steep south face set this climb apart from other east face romps. When approaching Seal Rock, stay east of the Pup, the Flatironette nestled under Seal Rock's east face. The start of the route is a few feet west of the Pup's southeast corner, where Seal Rock's east face and the small south face of the Pup come together.

The first 150-foot 5.4 pitch is the most sustained and hardest of the climb. Follow the crack between the Pup and Seal Rock's east face for 25 feet, then engage the east face of Seal. Climb straight up to a ledge with a tree. On the second pitch, angle hard south (left) on easier Class 4 rock, cross a shallow gully, and after 150 feet, find a nifty 3-foot chicken head that you can use for an anchor. On the third pitch, climb straight up 130 feet of 5.0–5.2 rock near the south edge of the face to some ledges below a little wall. On the fourth pitch, climb this cruxy 5.3–5.4 wall and continue up steep 5.0–5.2 rock to lower angle rock above. Climb a fifth Class 4 pitch to polish off this delightful route.

Variations

942V1 A hundred feet up the first pitch, traverse north (right) on a 2-foot ledge to a chockstone in the saddle between the Pup and Seal Rock. From here, climb two nice 5.0–5.2 pitches straight up to the elbow on the north edge of the east face and continue on the East Face North Side Route.

942V2 From the tree at the top of the first pitch, continue straight up on engaging 5.0–5.2 rock. Angle slightly north (right) and join the East Face North Side Route at the elbow or stay in the middle of the rock and finish on an independent line.

943 Southwest Face 5.4

This peculiar two or three-pitch climb starts on the Seal Rock's south face and ends on the west side. Hike up under the south face to a weakness in the rock's defense and do a thoughtful ascending traverse east (right) onto the south face (5.4). Traverse into the easternmost ramp system and follow it up to the west (left) into the notch between Seal Rock's summit and the exposed false summit to the west (Class 4). From this notch, climb a short west wall to the summit (5.0–5.2).

Extra Credit

943EC For a look at some big air, climb west from the notch below the main summit to the pinpoint western summit (Class 4).

95 THE PUP

This inquisitive Flatironette at the bottom of Seal Rock's east face is separated from Seal Rock by a brushy, often snow-filled gully that turns into a chimney at its high point. This gully is not a hiking route from one side of Seal Rock to the other. The Pup's summit provides an expansive view of Seal's east face.

951 North Ridge 5.0–5.2

Start at the bottom of the north ridge and scramble onto the slab from the east. For a harder start, scramble onto a boulder and climb across a gap using a hand jam (5.5–5.6). Climb 150 feet along the ridge over some decent 5.0–5.2 climbing and scramble up to a boulder-filled notch (Class 3). Climb west (right) out of this notch, engage the upper summit ridge and reach the summit via a short steep climb on indented chin-up bar handholds. These holds plus the view of Seal Rock make this climb worth doing once.

Descent

951D Downclimb the chin-up bars and return to the boulder-filled notch. You can hike either east or west from here.

96 THE PENGUIN

This dapper Flatironette is south of Seal Rock. Approach by hiking to the vicinity of Harmon's Cave, then hike south, staying east of the low points of

Seal Rock and the Pup. Continue 100 feet south past the south edge of Seal Rock to the Penguin. Continue south downhill to the lowest point of the rock.

961 East Face 5.3–5.4

This amusing, 250-foot two-pitch climb starts hard and gets easier near the top. Start at the low point of the rock, climb 30 feet of 5.0–5.2 rock, angle south (left) to avoid a small overhang and tiptoe up a clean 5.3–5.4 slab near the south edge of the east face. Continue up 5.0–5.2 rock that tapers to Class 4 near the top. This summit provides a nice view of the Goose and a neck-bending view of Seal Rock's south face.

Descent

961D Climb 50 feet down the east face (Class 4), scramble south and downclimb an interesting quilt of low-angle, southeast-facing groves (Class 4).

97 THE GOOSE   *Closed 2/1 – 7/31*

This is the large Flatiron south of Seal Rock. The Goose is higher than Seal Rock and has two summits, the northern being the higher. The bottom of the east face has a huge overhang on its south side, and this overhang is the largest east-facing overhang on any of the Flatirons. It typifies the broken inconsistent climbing on the Goose. Seal Rock and the Fern Canyon Slabs provide more equable climbing. Approach the East Face Route by leaving the Fern Canyon Trail at an appropriate point and hiking up to the north side of the face. To approach the South Face Route, follow the Fern Canyon Trail well past the Southern Goose Egg, which is the prominent rock near the trail that forms the entrance to Fern Canyon, then hike steeply north until you reach the south side of the Goose.

971 East Face Class 4   *Closed 2/1 – 7/31*

This 320-foot route is more of a mountaineering experience than a rock climb. It is the easiest and shortest route up the east face. To make it longer and more difficult, add one or more of the variations. Hike up along the north side of the rock and find a place where it is easy to walk south and observe the bottom of the overhangs. An overhang near the north edge of the east face prevents easy access to the face at this point. The start is 200 feet farther west. The hiking along the north edge of the east face in this area is steep, slab-ridden and rude. Take care to find the area where you can do a short traverse across

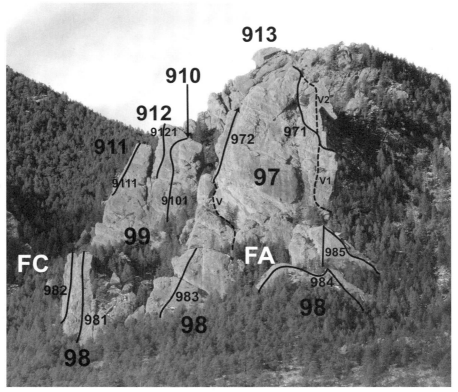

913 Nebel Horn
97 The Goose
971 East Face Class 4
971V1 5.3–5.4
971V2 5.3–5.4
972 South Face 5.4
972V 5.4
98 Goose Eggs
981 Southern Egg East
   Face 5.0–5.2

982 Southern Egg South
   Ramp 5.0–5.2
983 Broken Egg East Face
   5.0–5.2
984 Smallest Egg East Face
   5.0–5.2
985 Northern Egg East
   Face 5.0–5.4
FA Fern Canyon
   Amphitheater

FC Fern Canyon
99 Fern Canyon Slabs
910 Fiddlehead
9101 East Face 5.4
911 Pellaea
9111 East Face 5.5
912 Onoclea
9121 East Face 5.3

awkward slabs and get onto the east face at a large ledge. If you follow
the easiest line higher up, this traverse will provide the hardest moves of
the climb.

Once on the large ledge, climb the slab directly above it. This classic slab is
deeply scoured with improbable grooves, and you may have difficulty deciding
which handhold to use. After 100 feet, reach another ledge, traverse south on
this ledge and climb easy rock to some large trees not far below the saddle

between the two summits. Climb the gully above the trees, then angle north (right) on easy rock below the summit tower. A deep chimney capped by several large blocks splits the summit tower. Find a nice platform north of the summit blocks and reach the highest point from the north. This summit will give you goose bumps.

Variations

971V1 Starting at the lower point, where it is easy to walk to the edge of the face, makes the climb more than 200 feet longer and 5.3–5.4. A small overhang above this starting point prevents easy access to the north (right) edge of the face. Work out a devious start on the slabs south (left) of the overhang and climb up a small rubble-filled gully. This start and gully provide 210 feet of diverting 5.3–5.4 climbing to the large ledge at the beginning of the East Face Route.

971V2 In addition to the classic, deeply grooved slab above the large ledge at the beginning of the East Face Route, you can climb two more similar but harder slabs near the north edge of the face and reach the large bench just north of the summit. Each of these slabs provides 5.3–5.4 climbing and this variation avoids the grubby gullies farther south.

971V3 Several large blocks leaning against each other form the summit of the Goose. Do a Class 3 scramble through the tunnel underneath the summit block, move 10 feet north and reach the highest point from the north.

971V4 Climb the east-facing slab immediately south of the tunnel of Variation 3, and climb a south-facing wall near a bomb-bay groove above the tunnel (5.5–5.6). For a direct finish from the east, climb an exciting 5.8 overhang a few feet south of the top of the tunnel.

971V5 Climb the elegant 5.3–5.4 slab 20 feet south of the tunnel and reach the highest point from the south.

Descent

971D In spite of the spectacular nature of this summit, there is a Class 3 route down. From the highest point, downclimb to the bench north of the summit (steep Class 3). Scramble south on the west side of the summit block and get into the large crack splitting the summit area. This crack is a continuation of the tunnel under the summit blocks. Scramble west down this crack to a steep broken area. Avoid the temptation to scramble south and continue scrambling west. Scramble a few feet south of a 25-foot summit spire, get into a deep crack, go under a chockstone, sneak behind a 10-foot flake and scramble a few feet west to hiking territory.

972 South Face 5.4   *Closed 2/1 – 7/31*

There is a surprising 400-foot three-pitch route up the south face of the south summit of the Goose. This face looks steep and imposing when you first view it from below, but on closer inspection you can see that the upper part of the face lays back and has a long ramp under the southern edge of the east face. The rock is solid, which makes this a more enjoyable climb than the East Face Route. The South Face Route is somewhat difficult to protect, but it provides a moderate tour up a steep face for those experienced at the 5.4 level.

Climb 90 feet up a blocky southwest-facing dihedral on the eastern end of the south face to a small notch (5.0–5.2). From this notch you can look down into the Fern Canyon Amphitheater. Climb 15 feet above the notch up a shallow east-facing scoop to reach easier rock above (5.4). Climb 30 feet west, angle north across the strata and reach a platform below the long ramp below the southern edge of the east face (Class 4). Make a few steep 5.4 moves west onto the ramp. Some good cracks for an anchor are 50 feet up the Class 4 ramp. Climb another 150 feet up the genial ramp, passing two 5.0–5.2 spots. From the top of the ramp, climb a 10-foot south-facing wall to reach the exposed southern summit (Class 4).

Variation

972V You can reach the notch at the top of the initial dihedral by doing a devious ascent from the Fern Canyon Amphitheater. Climb up the slabs below the giant overhang and traverse south (left) on the large ledge below the overhang. Climb a 5.4 crack with a dead tree in it and reach the notch at the top of the dihedral 50 feet beyond the tree. Continue on the upper part of the South Face Route.

Descent

972D From the south summit, scramble north along the narrow summit ridge into the saddle between the two summits (Class 4). From here, scramble and/or rappel west down the gully between the two summits, or climb to the higher northern summit and follow the Class 3 descent from there. The most direct way to reach the main summit from the notch is to follow Variation 5 of the East Face Route (5.3–5.4).

98 GOOSE EGGS and
FERN CANYON AMPHITHEATER *Closed 2/1 – 7/31*

These four Flatironettes are east of and below the bottom of the Goose. The west faces of the central eggs and the lower slabs of the Goose form the Fern

Canyon Amphitheater. The southern egg is the most impressive as it looms north of the Fern Canyon Trail where the trail enters Fern Canyon. The routes on the southern egg are gracious, the next egg north is broken into two distinct pieces and the third egg is much smaller and lower. The two central eggs provide short climbs of varying difficulty while the northernmost egg is less appetizing. The Fern Canyon Amphitheater is a tiny wonderland tucked away from Boulder that sees far fewer visitors than the Gregory Amphitheater. The Fern Canyon Amphitheater does not provide the variety of climbs that the Gregory Amphitheater does, but it is a good place to practice rappelling and jumaring.

Approach the amphitheater and the Goose Eggs by leaving the Fern Canyon Trail before it enters Fern Canyon and hiking west to the base of the two central eggs. The bottom of the southern egg is 100 feet north of the Fern Canyon Trail just after it swings west into Fern Canyon. The gullies on either side of the smallest egg are hikeable. To reach the amphitheater, hike up the gully north of the smallest egg, continue beyond the egg to a small notch overlooking the amphitheater and downclimb a Class 4 move into the amphitheater. You may also reach the amphitheater by leaving the Fern Canyon Trail west of the southern egg, scrambling up through a broken wall, then descending to the north. This approach is much longer than the east side approach.

981 Southern Egg East Face 5.0–5.2   *Closed 2/1 – 7/31*

This east face is slightly lower angle than most other Flatirons. Start at the low point of the rock and climb 450 feet up to a gentle summit. The climbing is mostly Class 4, punctuated by a few little 5.0–5.2 cruxes.

Descent

981D From the summit, move south and downclimb a 15-foot vertical wall (5.0–5.2). From the base of the summit block, scramble west into a large hiking gully.

982 Southern Egg South Ramp 5.0–5.2   *Closed 2/1 – 7/31*

Climb a 30-foot wide east-facing ramp south of the main east face that is separated from the main east face by a vertical south-facing wall. This ramp provides a lively 400-foot climb to a separate slightly higher summit than that of the East Face Route. The view of the Goose is impressive from these summits.

Descent

982D Walk west off this summit.

983 Broken Egg East Face 5.0–5.2   *Closed 2/1 – 7/31*

The east face of this egg is broken into two distinct pieces. The lower face is a straightforward, 250-foot 5.0–5.2 climb that starts at the low point of the rock at its northeast corner. Climb straight up, angle south (left) up the easier ramp and reach a small summit on the south edge of the rock. Climb a steep difficult step onto the upper face, then climb directly up the easier slab to a broken summit with a tree.

Descents

983D From the summit of the lower face, scramble 150 feet northeast down the ramp separating the two pieces (Class 4). From the summit of the upper face, scramble west toward the Fern Canyon Amphitheater (Class 3).

984 Smallest Egg East Face 5.0–5.2   *Closed 2/1 – 7/31*

This egg is also in two pieces. Start at the low point of the lower piece, climb its 80-foot east face, scramble off its summit and engage the larger upper piece. Overcome a tricky stretch near the bottom and continue 100 feet up to the top.

Descent

984D Scramble west (Class 3) to the gully between the first and second piece.

985 Northern Egg East Face 5.0–5.4   *Closed 2/1 – 7/31*

The low point of the Northern Egg is nestled in the trees on the south side of the gully between Seal Rock and the Goose. Starting at the low point, the north side of this face provides 300 feet of climbing. There is one 5.3–5.4 move 30 feet off the ground, but the rest of the climb is easier. Although the first 150 feet are grubby, the last 150 feet are quite enjoyable.

If you start near the south edge of the east face, you can do a 200-foot 5.0–5.2 climb that avoids the grubby rock on the north edge of the face. Overcome a 1-foot overhang 25 feet off the ground, angle north (right) and join the north side route on the clean upper slabs.

The broken summit area is in hiking territory. You can extend your ascent by continuing up the Goose. To do it, hike west from the summit of the Northern Egg into a small amphitheater under the large gully system in the center of the east face of the Goose. From here, climb the right side of the amphitheater and join Variation 1 of the East Face Route on the Goose.

99 FERN CANYON SLABS   *Closed 2/1 – 7/31*

These soaring slabs on the south side of the Nebel Horn above Fern Canyon are home to five excellent routes. Often unseen, the Goose hides these slabs from northern eyes. There are two main layers of slabs. The eastern layer has two distinct summits and the western layer holds three summits. A deep gash that you can see from the southeast separates the remarkable two lower sum-

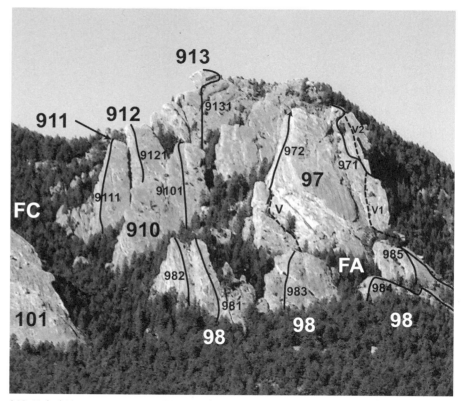

913 Nebel Horn	982 Southern Egg South Ramp 5.0–5.2	9111 East Face 5.5
97 The Goose		912 Oncolea
971 East Face Class 4	983 Broken Egg East Face 5.0–5.2	9121 East Face 5.3
971V1 5.3–5.4	984 Smallest Egg East Face 5.0–5.2	9131 The Nebel Via 5.0–5.2
971V2 5.3–5.4		101 The Slab
972 South Face 5.4	985 Northern Egg East Face 5.0–5.4	FC Fern Canyon
972V 5.4	910 Fiddlehead	FA Fern Canyon Amphitheater
98 Goose Eggs	9101 East Face 5.4	
981 Southern Egg East Face 5.0–5.2	911 Pellaea	

mits on the western layer. The highest summit on the western layer is the summit of the Nebel Horn. To approach, hike up the Fern Canyon Trail past the Southern Goose Egg that guards the entrance to the canyon, and hike north to the base of the rocks.

910 FIDDLEHEAD   *Closed 2/1 – 7/31*

This is the lower southern tower on the eastern layer of the Fern Canyon Slabs. Fiddlehead has an overhanging southwest face and what appears to be a raised block forms the summit. The rock's low point is within 100 feet of the Fern Canyon Trail, but the lower 200 feet are not inviting and do not connect coherently with the main face higher up. Hike east of these initial rocks and find the low point of the main part of the east face.

9101 East Face 5.4 *Classic*   *Closed 2/1 – 7/31*

Fiddlehead's east face hosts a fine 600-foot four- or five-pitch climb. The 5.4 rating is a result of a 20-foot section on the last pitch, but if you follow the easiest line the rest of the climb is no harder than Class 4.

Climb directly up the face and cross two ledge systems (Class 4). Between 200 and 250 feet up, there are several trees. The face above these trees is smooth and the easiest line follows a deep 4-inch wide crack angling north from the northernmost tree. Cross to the north side of a developing gully and climb to a large tree on the southeast ridge at the 420-foot level. Thirty feet north of this stance, climb the wall above to another tree (Class 4). From this ledge, climb a 140-foot pitch up the face south of the imposing raised summit block. Some 5.4 climbing is halfway up this

910 Fiddlehead – West Face

pitch. It is not necessary to get on top of the raised summit block, since you can reach the highest point by staying on the face south of it. The view from the summit is exciting and so is the drop-off to the southwest.

Descent

9101D *This is a dangerous rock to be on top of without a rope.* Thread a large hole between the two summit blocks with a nine-foot sling, and rappel 50 feet northwest to a large ledge on the exposed northwest face. Don't confuse this northwest face with the larger overhanging southwest face. Scramble down 40 feet north on this ledge, rig another sling and rappel 60 feet north into the large gully north of Fiddlehead. You can hike east or west from the primal boulders near the top of this gully.

911 PELLAEA   *Closed 2/1 – 7/31*

This lowest southernmost tower on the western layer of slabs is separated from its higher northern neighbor Onoclea by a deep gash. You can see this gash from the southeast but not from the Fern Canyon Trail. Both Pellaea and Onoclea are exclusive summits that provide Flatiron climbing at its best. A short distance after it climbs under a bodacious boulder, the Fern Canyon Trail passes within 10 feet of the bottom of Pellaea

9111 East Face 5.5 *Classic – Top Ten*   *Closed 2/1 – 7/31*

This beautiful 470-foot, four-pitch climb reaches a rare summit. The 5.5 rating comes from a small crux on the first pitch; a second 5.4 crux is on the last pitch, and the rest of the climb is comfortable 5.0–5.2. A leader fall from either crux could leave the leader dangling on the steep southwest face. From the rock's low point, hike 50 feet up under the east face to where it is easy to get onto the face.

Climb past a tree 25 feet up and angle up to Pellaea's well-defined southeast ridge below a bulge running completely across the face. The easiest passage over this crux bulge is near its southwest (left) end near the ridgeline. Climb a steepening wall to a tiny tree (5.5). Above this first crux, climb 260 feet of varied 5.0–5.2 rock on the east face below the ridge to the second crux wall that also runs across the now much narrower face. It has a commodious ledge below it. Climb this bulge on its southwest (left) end via a smooth wall with a curious 18-inch hollow in it. The move out of the hollow is 5.4. Above this wall, climb a 20-foot face to the summit. This wall is 5.0–5.2 on its northeast (right) end, but climbing up the center provides an exciting 5.5 finish. Many deep potholes grace the summit and Onoclea towers overhead to the north.

Variations

9111V1 You can avoid the initial crux wall by starting the climb farther north.

9111V2 You can do a direct start from the low point of the rock. This start provides an additional pitch and 5.5–5.6 crux wall that is also climbed on its southwest (left) end.

9111V3 Climb directly up the southeast ridge all the way to the summit. This adds two more 5.5–5.6 cruxes and a lot of excitement.

Descent

9111D *This is a dangerous rock to be on top of without a rope.* On the northeast end of the 30-foot long summit is a thread deep in a crack. Sling this hole with a 9-foot sling and rappel 60 feet north into the deep gash between Pellaea from Onoclea. This special gash is fern heaven. From the west end of the gash, climb south and west to hiking territory (Class 4).

912 ONOCLEA   *Closed 2/1 – 7/31*

This is the second tower on the western layer of the Fern Canyon Slabs. It is just as beautiful as its lower southern neighbor Pellaea. These two summits are separated from each other by a deep gash. Leave the Fern Canyon Trail where it comes within 10 feet of the bottom of Pellaea and hike up under Pellaea's east face. Look sharp for the deep gash above. At the bottom of the face the gash is reduced to a small crack that is easily missed. Thirty feet north of the crack it is reasonable to get onto Onoclea's east face.

Descent

912D *This is a dangerous rock to be on top of without a rope.* Scramble 70 feet northeast down to a tree (Class 3) and rappel 25 feet north to the ground. For a hiking descent from here, hike east into the approach gully.

9121 East Face 5.3 *Classic*   *Closed 2/1 – 7/31*

This adorable 450-foot, three- or four-pitch route is not as difficult as it appears from a distance. There is only a little 5.3 climbing, the rest being 5.0–5.2 or easier. You can climb to the alluring call of the canyon wren.

Climb 80 grubby feet to a tree near the now better-formed southeast ridge of Onoclea. The deep gash above will be evident, and you should be on the north side of it. Climb the face to a higher tree, also near the southeast ridge. Above this tree, climb a pretty, 30-foot 5.3 section on the broad ridge to yet another tree on a ledge below a steep bulge. This ledge is 200 feet from the start of the climb. The bulge above this ledge looks imposing at first, but traverse left a few feet toward the deep gash and climb some surprising chin-up bar buckets (5.0–5.2). Pass another tree, climb the 5.3 wall above, and reach a large ledge even with the top of the deep gash. Twenty feet above this ledge is another ledge with better anchors. You can now begin to peer down on the summit of Pellaea. Climb the short steep wall above (Class 4) and romp easily up to the summit. From the broad summit you can spy on hikers in the saddle on the

9121 Enroute on Onoclea's East Face

Fern Canyon Trail. The summit of the Nebel Horn looks impressive from here.

Variation

9121V From the Pellaea–Onoclea notch, scramble east down the deep gash, move north onto Onoclea's east face, join the East Face Route and follow it for two pitches to the top. This connection allows you to climb Pellaea and Onoclea together.

Extra Credit

9121EC Lark Ascending

A transcendent Class 4 route goes from the bottom of the 25-foot rappel off Onoclea to the summit of the Nebel Horn. From the open area below Onoclea's small north face, climb west to a small notch 30 feet north of the main notch immediately north of Onoclea (Class 4). Descend a few feet west and cross a 5-foot Class 4 wall to a flat-topped chockstone jammed above a large drop. Overcoming this awkward maneuver is your entrance fee to the secret.

Foil the drop by walking north across the chockstone into a large gully. Scramble west (left) around another larger chockstone (Class 3) and hike up the gully beyond. From a point almost directly below the overhung beak-like

9121EC The transcendent route to the Nebel Horn

summit of the Nebel Horn, climb a charming, 40-foot easy Class 4 west face that leads to the ridge south of the summit. This is the picnic area on the Nebel Via Route. Scramble north up a large ledge and reach the summit of the Nebel Horn from the east (Class 3). You can climb on rock from the Fern Canyon Trail to the summit of the Nebel Horn by combining Pellaea, Onoclea and this Extra Credit.

9122 West Face 5.7   *Closed 2/1 – 7/31*

Start this short sweet route in the Pellaea–Onoclea notch. Climb northwest up a ramp, go around a corner to reach Onoclea's west face and climb it on small sharp holds to the summit.

913 NEBEL HORN   *Closed 2/1 – 7/31*

This proud summit is both the summit of a Flatiron and the summit of a peak. You can see the summit's spectacular overhang from south Boulder. You can reach the summit from the saddle between Bear Peak and the Nebel Horn with a little Class 3 scrambling. This saddle is at the top of the Fern Canyon Trail. From the saddle, hike northeast, stay north of some small spires, hike east and do a Class 3 scramble to the second notch north of the Nebel Horn's summit. A steeper, harder Class 4 climb leads into the first notch north of the summit. From either notch, scramble south and reach the summit from the east (Class 3).

For an easier route to the summit, leave the Fern Canyon Trail some distance below the Nebel Horn–Bear Peak saddle and hike north up the broad gully between the eastern and western layers of the Fern Canyon Slabs. Near the top of this gully, angle back southwest. If you find the easiest route, it is Class 2, but it is easy to stray onto harder ground near here. Join the other route below the Class 3 scramble on the east side of the summit.

9131 The Nebel Via 5.0–5.2   *Closed 2/1 – 7/31*

This 450-foot route winds its way up the third and highest slab of the western layer of the Fern Canyon Slabs. The route ends on the summit of the Nebel Horn, and this is a good route for an evening's tour. If you time it right, you can enjoy the late sun and a great view of the high peaks from the summit. Leave the Fern Canyon Trail where it comes within 10 feet of the bottom of the western layer of the Fern Canyon Slabs and hike up along the base of the east faces of Pellaea and Onoclea. Find the bottom of the main piece of the third slab, which is 100 feet above and north of the level of the large notch between the two slabs of the eastern layer.

After a short 5.0–5.2 start, the climbing eases to Class 4. Wander up the face above, moving north (right) where it is easy to do so. The upper part of this face is crisscrossed with a series of large ledges and gullies. Follow the path of least resistance and reach the southeast ridge below the Nebel Horn's large overhung summit block, which is a good place for a view-picnic. From here, follow a broad ledge north under the east face of the summit block, and from the north end of this ledge, do a Class 3 scramble to the summit of the Nebel Horn. Enjoy.

Descents

9131D1 Downclimb the Class 3 summit pitch, scramble north to the second notch and scramble west to hiking territory. Hike 150-yards west to the Nebel Horn–Bear Peak saddle and the Fern Canyon Trail.

9131D2 From a point east of the summit block, hike northeast down to the approach gully between the eastern and western layers of the Fern Canyon Slabs. Hike south down this gully to the Fern Canyon Trail.

9131D1 Master Jim Foley descending the Nebel Horn

TEN

Boulder Mountain

With the exception of the Matron, the climbs in this chapter are on the east face of 8,461-foot Bear Peak, which is the main summit south of Bear Canyon. When you view it from central Boulder, Bear Peak appears to have a pointed summit, but when you view it from the east or south you can see that the summit is at the northern end of a long south ridge. The distinctive Devil's Thumb rises above this ridge. The Matron is on the east side of the long south ridge of 8,549-foot South Boulder Peak. The massif of Bear and South Boulder Peaks is called Boulder Mountain. The climbs on Bear Peak are varied, and amazing classics soar near broken-down Flatirons. Many of Bear Peak's rocks have numerous overhangs with rotten red undersides. The longer approaches to Bear Peak's secrets will reward you with solitude.

101 THE SLAB

The Slab, the largest Flatiron on Bear Peak, is south of Fern Canyon and shaped like a parallelogram with the high point on the upper left and the low point on the lower right. The rock's north edge looks impressive from the Fern Canyon Trail, and it looks like the Slab would provide dozens of routes, but there are only seven natural lines. This is because two south-facing dihedral systems segment this huge face into thirds. These dihedrals are difficult to cross and the routes are confined to smaller sections of the face. You cannot see these dihedral systems from Boulder and the face appears to be more continuous than it is. Also, much of the lower east face is very steep or overhanging, which prevents easy starts.

The approach to the Slab is simple since two different trails come very close to the rock. Follow the Fern Canyon Trail to the entrance of Fern Canyon and cross the canyon to reach the northeast corner of the rock. Or, 50 yards south of the point where the Mesa Trail crosses Fern Canyon, the Northern Shanahan Trail crosses the Mesa Trail and goes directly up to the bottom of the Slab. Open meadows are near the base of the east face. I describe the routes from north to south across the face. The routes all reach the summit ridge at some point, and the upper part of the summit ridge is common to all routes. I describe the complete summit ridge and the escapes from it with the Diagonal Route.

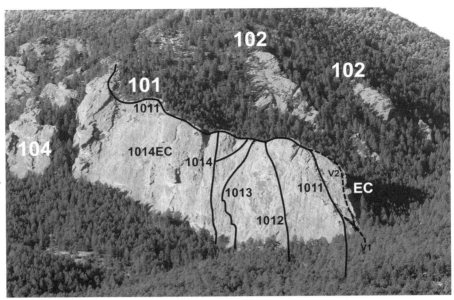

101 The Slab
1011 Diagonal 5.3
1012 Bulges 5.0–5.2 S
1013 Left 'n Up 5.0–5.2

1014 Syzygy 5.0–5.2
1014EC 5 more routes
102 The Advisors
104 Northern Shanahan Crag

Descent

101D Downclimb the summit block's 15-foot west face to reach hiking territory (Class 4).

1011 Diagonal 5.3 *Classic*

This is the longest route on the Slab, since it climbs from the low point at the northeast corner to the high point at the southwest corner. If measured with a rope, this route is 15 pitches long and is the longest rock tour near Boulder. Most of the summit ridge is very easy, however, so the length of the climb is not as impressive as it might seem at first. You can escape from the summit ridge to make the climb shorter.

Start at the lowest point of the rock, which is a few feet south of Fern Canyon, and climb the east face, angling slightly south (left) for five pitches to the north end of the summit ridge. The 5.3 climbing on this route is confined to the first 250 feet, where belays and protection are sparse. The natural line stays within 100 feet of the northern edge of the rock. As you approach the summit ridge, the difficulty drops to Class 4, and once you are on the summit ridge, the difficulty drops to Class 3 and even Class 1. The northern end of the summit ridge is a wonderful place to spend some time. The west side of the ridge is overhung, and this rock park perched high over Boulder is accessible only to climbers and scramblers. The view of the Goose and the Fern Canyon Slabs from here is arresting.

Continue scrambling south along the ridge, passing some Class 4 notches on the way. There is a small notch from which you can reach the ground with a 60-foot rappel down the west face. Farther south along the ridge, you can hike sedately west. If the summit is important, continue scrambling south and find the narrow upper section of east face below the summit. Traverse on a gully-like ledge, climb over a nifty Class 4 bulge, and climb directly up the summit block's east face (5.0–5.2). While this summit is not one of Boulder's best, you should feel good that you have persevered for so long.

Variations

1011V1 To avoid the difficulties of the initial slab, hike 100 feet uphill from the low point of the rock along the rock's northern edge, climb 100 feet south up a convenient Class 4 ramp onto the east face, traverse south (left) and join the Diagonal Route 200 feet above the low point of the rock.

1011V2 After climbing 100 feet up the convenient ramp described above, continue straight up near the east face's north edge, climb a steep Class 4 bulge, and reach another south-angling ramp. Either follow this ramp south or continue up the edge of the face over a cruxy 5.0–5.2 bulge, climb 100 feet to a sensational 20-foot fin overhanging the north face and climb above the fin near the edge of the face on engaging Class 4–5.2 rock.

1011V3 Keyhole 5.8

This peculiar two-pitch variation starts 80 feet west of the convenient ramp of Variation 1. Climb a ramp system on the north face, overcome a roof, climb under the sensational 20-foot fin overhanging the face, wiggle through the keyhole west of the fin and join Variation 2 above the fin.

Extra Credit

1011EC The Key

When passing by, take the time to scramble north onto the sensational 20-foot overhanging fin appropriately called the Key (exposed Class 3). This is an eclectic place to perch; the view from the Key can help unlock your imagination.

1012 Bulges 5.0–5.2 S

This route ascends the northern section of the east face 100 feet south of the Diagonal Route. An imposing bulge 250 feet off the ground is between this route and the Diagonal Route, and Bulges is north (right) of the left-angling dihedral system separating the northern and central portions of the face. The Northern Shanahan Trail reaches the Slab near a meadow below the northern part of the east face. Start Bulges near the small high point between this meadow and Fern Canyon. Climb directly up the smooth 600-foot face for five pitches to the summit ridge. In the first 350 feet, protection and belay stances are sparse but possible. The difficulty is largely Class 4 if you do careful route finding through the numerous bulges on this section of the face.

1013 Left 'n Up 5.0–5.2

This 700-foot route ascends the central portion of the east face south of the dihedral system separating the central and northern portions of the face. You can see a prominent tree on the summit ridge from the meadow at the bottom of the central portion of the east face. Start a few feet north of the low point of this meadow. Climb 120 feet, then make a judicious traverse south (left) to avoid the dihedral system hovering overhead. Do a few more traverses south, then climb directly to the summit ridge in the vicinity of the lone tree, which you can see overhead during your climb.

1014 Syzygy 5.0–5.2

After an improbable start, this 700-foot route ascends a sanguine section of the east face 150 feet south of the northern/central dihedral system. This route ascends the geometric center of the east face, and you can climb in syzygy with the meadow at the beginning of the route and the lone tree on the summit ridge. Start 100 feet south of the meadow's low point, climb to a sloping ledge 40 feet off the ground, climb a 5.0–5.2 bulge 15 feet south of a small water-polished gully and reach the easier face above. Above this crux bulge, the difficulty drops to Class 4 and you can roam upward at will to reach the summit ridge near the lone tree.

Extra Credit

1014EC At least five more routes are on the Slab. CLIMB!

102 THE ADVISORS

Three small broken Flatironettes are west of the Slab. These rocks may not look like much, but they are responsible for choreographing the shapes of the great Flatirons. In particular, they decide where the overhangs should be. Approach by hiking into Fern Canyon past the Slab and angle south to the base of the rocks. Climbing on these small rocks is a matter of choice, but treat the Advisors with respect.

103 EASTERN SHANAHAN CRAG

This curious little rock is the first you come to when hiking up Shanahan Canyon. The crag is north of Shanahan Canyon, well south of the Slab. It consists mostly of a 100-foot-high south face. An east ridge offers 300 feet of racy Class 4 climbing and there are two short routes on the south face. Start the eastern south face route at a 10-foot block leaning against the base of the face, climb 90 feet directly up the moderately steep portion of the face on lovely holds and join the east ridge below the summit (Class 4). For the 100-foot western south face route, climb a steep wall on surprising holds, angle west (left) and climb a final wall to the summit (5.4). You can hike north. This rock makes a nice scrambling addition to Mesa Trail hikes or runs.

104 NORTHERN SHANAHAN CRAG

The Northern Shanahan Crag is the first rock south of the Slab. A small cave is in the bottom of the northern crag's south face.

101 The Slab
104 Northern Shanahan Crag
1041 East Face 5.0–5.2

105 Central Shanahan Crag
1051 Southeast Ridge of Southern Summit Class 4

1052 Southeast Ridge of Northern Summit Class 4

1041 East Face 5.0–5.2

Climb two nice 5.0–5.2 pitches to a big ledge below a barrier overhang. Zigzag through the overhang near the south side of the rock (Class 4) and scramble to the crag's twin summits.

105 CENTRAL SHANAHAN CRAG

This crag provides high quality easy climbing on sound rock. Approach by hiking up Shanahan Canyon 100 yards beyond the south face of the Eastern Shanahan Crag.

Descent from the southern summit

105D1 Scramble 100 feet north to hiking territory (Class 3). Hike north, then east down the gully between the central and northern crags.

Descent from the northern summits

105D2 Scramble and hike into the gully north of Central Shanahan Crag.

1051 Southeast Ridge of Southern Summit Class 4 *Classic*

This 600-foot, five-pitch route has an elegant position, consistent simplicity and sunny disposition. Start at the low point and climb the obvious crest and small east face. After 400 feet surmount some small overhangs near the center of the east face and prance up to the satisfying summit.

1052 Southeast Ridge of Northern Summit Class 4

This 450-foot route parallels its southern counterpart and leads to the lower northern summit. It lacks the clean beauty of the longer route on the higher summit, but it still provides a nice climb. Start at the rock's low point and hike uphill along the base of the east face to the bottom of the central gully. Climb up and right to gain the crest of the ridge, then follow it upwards. After 260 feet, the ridge bumps into the vertical wall of a summit block. Move south (left) and climb easy slabs under the summit block's south face. After 400 feet, reach hiking territory in the saddle between the higher southern summit and the northern summit. There are actually three northern summits, all of which are easy scrambles from this point.

1053 South Face 5.4 *Classic*

This clean beautiful 140-foot pitch on the steep south face of the southern summit is easy to protect. If a road were nearby, this climb would be very popular. From the rock's low point, hike 300 feet west under the crag's south face. The start of the route is 50 feet east of the smooth red vertical portion of the south face. Climb 50 feet up a nearly vertical crack on chin-up bar holds, overcome a short 5.4 crux after 60 feet and continue up easier lower angle rock. Reach the ridge after 140 feet where a secure belay stance is a few feet east. This point is on the Southeast Ridge Route. Follow the Southeast Ridge Route over its small upper overhangs to the higher southern summit (Class 4).

106 THE WINGS

Soaring high on the slopes of Bear Peak are two large Flatirons that look like great wings. These rocks start at a higher elevation than the tops of most other Flatirons and have the highest Flatiron summits above Boulder. The South Wing is the higher and larger of the two wings and it forms part of Bear Peak's south ridge. This Flatiron provides acres of superb smooth slabs. The South Wing is slightly lower angle than other Flatirons and generally provides cheer-

| 106N North Wing | 107 The Keel | 109 Pegasus |
| 106S South Wing | 108 The Sphinx | |

ful easy climbing. The North Wing is broken into two pieces with the east face having a slightly more northern exposure.

Sweeping up from Shanahan Canyon to the bottom of the North Wing is a graceful curve of rock known as the Keel. You can hike between the Keel and the North Wing. Directly below the wings are two Flatirons known as Pegasus and the Sphinx. Pegasus is broken but still powerful. The Sphinx is a stately rock guarded by ferocious overhangs near the base of its east face. Below Pegasus and the Sphinx are some small Flatironettes.

The approaches to these rocks are longer than other Flatirons, but you will be rewarded with solitude. You can use the Wings to make a nice mountaineering ascent of Bear Peak by climbing either Wing, continuing on to the top of Bear Peak and descending another way. The approaches to these rocks are up either Shanahan Canyon or Shanahan Draw. Shanahan Canyon is 100 yards north of the Mesa Trail–Southern Shanahan Trail junction and Shanahan Draw is 100 yards south of this trail junction.

107 THE KEEL

This narrow Flatiron curves gracefully up and almost touches the North Wing. Its ascent will never be a classic, but you will be rewarded with privacy. In the spring, the gentle sounds of Shanahan Creek may serenade you as you climb the lower part of the rock. The rock offers 1,000 feet of easy scrambling and can add some mountaineering interest to a hike up Bear Peak. Approach the Keel by hiking up Shanahan Canyon and staying south of the Eastern and Central Shanahan Crags. The low point of the Keel is 100 yards south of the Central Shanahan Crag's south face.

1071 Northeast Ridge Class 3–4

Start at the low point of the rock and climb scruffy slabs to gain the northeast ridge, then follow this low angle ridge to the summit. You can hike north off the ridge at a number of points. The 1,000-foot-long Class 3 ridge may seem like a hike that happens to take place on rock instead of a trail. Halfway up, you can cross a small double arch. The steeper summit block provides a solid 20-foot Class 4 challenge. From the summit you will have a nice view of the North Wing, and by combining the Keel with the North Wing, you can extend your mountaineering adventure.

Descents

1071D1 If you are desperate, you can climb down a large tree that comes close to the top of the overhang west of the summit (T2).

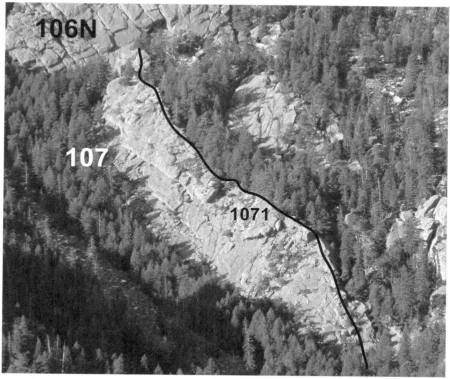

107 The Keel   1071 Northeast Ridge   106N North Wing
                                Class 3–4

1071D2 If you prefer rock to trees, then either climb (Class 4) or rappel 50 feet east down the summit block to easier rock. Scramble 50 feet down to the ground on the south side of the rock (Class 3).

108 THE SPHINX

According to Greek mythology the sphinx is a winged monster having the head of a woman and the body of a lion that destroyed all who could not answer its riddle. The riddle of the sphinx is: What animal walks on four legs in the morning, two legs in the afternoon, and three legs in the evening? Remember that the lower half of the Sphinx lay buried for a long time.

This rock indeed provides some enigmatic climbs, but they are easy to see. The Sphinx is the breathtaking tower that resides centrally below the Wings. The lower east face is festooned with overhangs and the south face is a forbid-

108 The Sphinx
1081 Upper East Face Class 4
1082 Lower East Face 5.7 S

1083 The Tiller 5.0–5.2
109 Pegasus
106S South Wing

ding wall with a sharp overhang in its base. The upper part of the rock has a steep north face and a rather incoherent west ridge. Below the northeast side of the rock is a small addendum rock along the small ridge between Shanahan Canyon and Shanahan Draw that provides a tiller for the Sphinx. To approach the low point of the Sphinx or its south face, hike up Shanahan Draw, which is 100 yards south of the Mesa Trail–Southern Shanahan Trail junction. This draw stays south of the Tiller and reaches the low point of the Sphinx. To approach the Upper East Face Route or the north side of the Sphinx, hike up Shanahan Canyon, which is 100 yards north of the Mesa Trail–Southern Shanahan Trail junction.

Descent

108D Downclimb (Class 4) or rappel the Upper East Face Route.

1081 Upper East Face Class 4

This 350-foot route is the easiest way to reach the summit of the Sphinx. It only ascends the upper half of the rock and avoids the riddles of the overhangs on the lower east face. The route starts on a big ledge above these overhangs, and you can easily walk onto this ledge from the north. Climb 110 feet up an obvious gully to a small notch in the northeast ridge, then climb south (left) up the remainder of the east face to the broad summit area. If climbed roped, this route breaks naturally into three moderate length pitches. You will not find the key to the riddle by only climbing the upper part of the face.

1082 Lower East Face 5.7 S

The answer to the riddle of this Sphinx lies in climbing from the low point to the high point. At first it may seem that it is not reasonable to overcome the overhangs of the lower east face, but there is a way. This is one of the more enigmatic routes on the Flatirons. Start at the lowest point of the rock, climb a 90-foot Class 3 slab to a ledge, climb the bulge above the ledge near its north end (5.0–5.2) and climb 90 more feet to a broad hiking ledge that traverses completely across the lower east face. Hike 100 yards south along this ledge to the southern edge of the rock. Climb 120 feet up a deep chimney (5.3–5.4) to a large isolated tree on the lower portion of the south face. The crux of this route is the steep, exposed, hard to protect 60-foot 5.7 wall above this tree. Aim for a smaller tree at the southern end of a higher ledge. Scramble north along this ledge (Class 3) to the bottom of the Upper East Face Route.

Escapes

1082E You can hike away from this route on any of the three main ledge systems on the lower part of the face.

1083 The Tiller 5.0–5.2

This rock is on the small ridge below the north side of the Sphinx. Approach by hiking directly up the slope from the Mesa Trail–Southern Shanahan Trail junction and follow the ridge above until you reach the bottom of the rock. The Tiller consists of three pieces of rock separated by notches. From east to west the three pieces provide 75 feet of Class 4, 90 feet of Class 4, and 100 feet of 5.0–5.2. On each piece the hardest moves are near the bottom. The descents into the notches and off the summit are Class 3 scrambles, and you can hike north but not south from the notches. A curious cave is tucked under the south side of the notch between the second and third pieces, near the low point of the Sphinx.

109 PEGASUS

This is the misshaped overhang-ridden Flatiron south of the Sphinx, below the southern Wing. In Greek mythology, Pegasus was a winged horse that was the son of Poseidon—the god of the sea and horses. It's complicated, but springing from a higher birth, Pegasus had special powers, however those who rode the flying steed did not fare well. Like lore, this Flatiron is complicated, and you should approach it with caution. Multiple overhangs impede simple progress, but there are passages through the barriers. Similar to the Sphinx, the climbing on Pegasus is either too hard or too easy. There are several riddles and routes on this overlooked Flatiron, and I leave the solutions for adventure seekers. From the scruffy summit of Pegasus you can easily continue up the South Wing.

1010 THE APOSTLE

This is the lowest rock below Devil's Thumb and it provides comfortable climbing on good rock. The rock has two areas of east face separated by a small scruffy south wall. The northern piece is more coherent and prominent. This rock provides nice scrambling extensions to Mesa Trail hikes and runs.

1010 The Apostle
10101 Southeast Ridge
    Class 4
1011 Devil's Advocate
10111 Northeast Ridge
    5.6
1012 Tiny Tower
10121 East Face 5.6
1013 Flying Flatiron
10131 East Face 5.6
10131EC Flying Arch 5.7
1014 Devil's Thumb
10141 East Face 5.7
10141V Toponas 5.8+

For the easiest approach, leave the Mesa Trail where it crosses the drainage a few hundred yards south of the Southern Shanahan Trail junction. This drainage is 150 yards north of a water trough on the Mesa Trail. A curious stone structure is situated under a large boulder 200 yards west of the Mesa Trail, and the low points of both sections of east face are 200 yards above this structure.

10101 Southeast Ridge Class 4

This simple 550-foot route has a nice position. Start at the low point of the northern section of east face. Climb along a small ridge crest that is well defined in its middle section, where you can peer over the small scruffy south wall to the southern section of the rock's east face. Most of the difficulty is Class 3 with only an occasional spot of Class 4. You will find the easiest climbing close to the ridge crest, but the exposure is greater here. If you are climbing roped, you will need four 140-foot pitches. There are good trees for all the belay anchors. The broken summit area provides nice views of the Devil's Advocate, Tiny Tower and the Flying Flatiron.

Descent

10101D From the summit area, scramble 30 feet west to hiking territory (Class 3).

1011 DEVIL'S ADVOCATE

This rock is below and north of Devil's Thumb, directly below the Flying Flatiron and north of the Apostle. The rock has a savage south face and an impressive overhang guards the bottom of the east face. Approach by leaving the Mesa Trail 200 yards south of the Mesa Trail–Southern Shanahan Trail junction and angling southwest to the bottom of the rock. If you are hiking north on the Mesa Trail, leave the Mesa Trail 200 yards north of the water trough and head straight west up the hill.

10111 Northeast Ridge 5.6

On a first inspection, this rock does not seem to offer any reasonable routes, but a devious 450-foot route bypasses the ferocious overhangs and gains the easier rock above. Start at the low point of the rock, climb 50 feet up a low angle slab and climb north (right) to some big trees on the north side of the rock (Class 4). The next deceptive pitch is the crux of the route. It sneaks around onto the rock's north face to avoid the overhang at the base of the east face. From the big trees, climb west up a small ramp, get onto the north face and climb 40 feet straight up the wall to reach the east face above the overhang (5.6). You will find a good belay ledge 30 feet farther up the east face. For the rest of the climb, scramble 250 feet up the northeast ridge to the summit (Class 3).

Descent

10111D This descent requires a little route finding. From the summit, scramble north then west through a hole to a broken area west of the summit (Class 3). South and west of this ledge is a deep crack running down to the west. Scramble into the bottom of the crack and wiggle west (Class 3). Climb down a 10-foot overhang with the aid of two dead trees leaning up against the rock (T1).

1012 TINY TOWER

This rock is 100 yards north of the Devil's Advocate. It is connected to the northern low point of the Flying Flatiron, but is quite distinctive by itself. Small overhangs on the narrow east face plus a small steep south face give this rock character, and Tiny Tower provides several short excellent routes. The approach is the same as for the Devil's Advocate.

Descent

1012D From the top of the tower, climb 15 feet down the east face, move north a few feet and scramble 30 feet west down a deep crack to the ground (Class 4).

10121 East Face 5.6 *Classic*

This 250-foot route solves the complexities of the east face, and offers some tiny surprises along the way. Two-thirds of the distance up the east face is a small stimulating fin that forms the low end of a right-facing dihedral system. The first 155-foot pitch is 5.0–5.2. Start at the low point of the rock, climb 50 feet and move a few feet south (left). Approach the stimulating fin after 125 feet, move back north (right) and get into the right-facing dihedral. Climb 30 feet up the dihedral to some bushes and a dead stump that provide a cozy belay.

The second pitch is shorter but contains the crux of the route. From the belay, move south (left) and make an awkward 5.4 move to overcome the short

wall of the dihedral system. This will leave you perched just abo
thrilling fin and below a smooth steep slab. Climb this slab with *now*
and reach easier rock above. Overcome the upper overhang by clin-*moves*
2-foot wide crack that splits it (Class 4). The tiny summit is just be)

10122 West Ridge 5.0–5.2

Climb Tiny Tower's ornate 50-foot west ridge directly to the summit.

1013 FLYING FLATIRON

This large Flatiron is above the Devil's Advocate, north of and below Devil's
Thumb. This summit is spectacular when seen from the Mesa Trail, and you
can see the Flying Arch in the summit from the north or south. The east face is
quite broad at the bottom but tapers to a knife-edge ridge a few feet below the
summit. The bottom of the east face has two rocket-fin prongs. The northern
prong connects to Tiny Tower, and this section of the face is not very coherent.
The southern prong is the lowest point of the rock and is the start of the
climb. Follow the approach for the Apostle and continue uphill, staying south
of the Apostle. The low point of the southern prong is 100 yards south of and
a little below the west side of the Devil's Advocate.

10131 East Face 5.6

You can do this 1,000-foot climb in seven long pitches. Except for the first and
last pitches, and a spot or two in between, the climbing is much easier than
5.6. The southern portion of the east face contains many overhangs, and the
route ascends the center portion of the face, avoiding most of the worst overhangs. The rock's low point is below a 30-foot overhang, so start the climb a
few feet south, and make a 5.6 move over a 3-foot overhang onto the steep face
above. Avoid getting too far south (left) into a gully system that leads to large
overhangs above. After the initial 5.6 move, climb the steep 5.0–5.2 wall above
and angle 120 feet slightly right to a large tree. Numerous easier starts are
north of the overhang above the low point.

After the first pitch, the climbing becomes much easier and will seldom be
harder than Class 4 if you follow the easiest route. Climb five more 160-foot
pitches to the base of the summit ridge. Some steep spots on the third and
sixth pitches provide 5.3–5.4 climbing. On the sixth pitch, climb the broad face
as it rapidly narrows to a slender ridge. On the seventh pitch, overcome a steep
5.5–5.6 headwall at the base of the summit ridge and climb 100 feet on the

ı side into the Flying Arch.

rch, which appears quite large from a distance, has an opening only
rid' diameter. Several loose blocks are under the arch. You can peer
n the arch at Devil's Thumb and the Maiden, and the South Wing sails
.ssively to the north. You can consider this point the top of the climb.

escent

10131D With a 20-foot sling, you can sling the eastern supporting column of
the arch for an anchor. Rappel 50 feet north to the ground.

Extra Credit

10131EC Flying Arch 5.7

To continue from the inside of the arch to the top of the arch, move through
to the south side of the arch, and climb west up an exposed ramp to a tiny
overhung notch halfway up the west face of the arch. Climb the upper west
face of the arch (5.7), and balance carefully to the highest point.

1014 DEVIL'S THUMB

You can easily see this overwhelming pinnacle soaring on the skyline of Bear
Peak's south ridge. People sometimes mistake it for the lower but more famous
Maiden a quarter mile south. Devil's Thumb does not provide the excellent
climbing that the Maiden offers, but its ascent is still a worthwhile adventure.
This outstanding landmark's original Indian name "Toponas" has been largely
lost. Approach Devil's Thumb from the Mesa Trail; it's a long hike.

10141 East Face 5.7

The east face of Devil's Thumb is, in general, lower angle than most Flatirons,
but a 15-foot overhang halfway up the face foils an easy ascent. Start near the
south edge of the east face and climb easy slabs to the overhang. There are two
cracks that you can climb to get past the overhang. The southern (left) crack is
the easiest and is 5.7. Climb the Class 4 slabs above the overhang, and enjoy
the low-angle face leading to this large airy summit.

Variation

10141V Toponas 5.8+

Climb the right crack through the crux overhang.

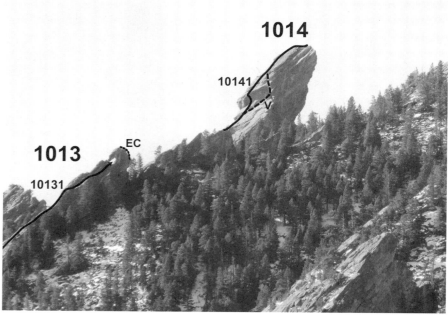

1013 Flying Flatiron
10131 Upper East Face 5.6
10131EC Flying Arch 5.7

1014 Devil's Thumb
10141 East Face 5.7
10141V Toponas 5.8+

Descent

10141D *This is a dangerous rock to be on top of without a rope.* Scramble and climb down to the top of the 15-foot overhang and do a short rappel to the slabs below. Downclimb or rappel to the ground. Rappelling off the north or west sides of Devil's Thumb requires very long ropes. Climbers who have mistaken Devil's Thumb for the Maiden have rappelled west only to discover that they still have 60 feet of air to deal with after reaching the end of their rope.

1015 ICARUS

This two-summited Flatiron is south of and below the Flying Flatiron and just north of the Fatiron. Its twin summits resemble folded resting wings. If the rock does take flight, hopefully it will learn from its higher neighbors. Climbing on Icarus is largely a matter of choice. You can do a moderate two- or three-pitch climb on the north side of the east face to reach the lower

1015 Icarus
1016 The Fatiron
10161 East Face 5.4

1017 The Maiden
1018 The Crackiron
10181 East Face 5.6

northern summit. It is a short scramble south and west from the northern summit to the ground. You can do a longer harder climb to the higher southern summit. From this singular summit, you will have to downclimb your top pitch or do a rappel to reach the ground.

1016 THE FATIRON

This is the thick Flatiron north of the Maiden. The rock has two contiguous pieces separated by an overhang. The lower, larger fat piece connects to a lower-angled upper face. The east face of the fat piece looks steep and smooth from a distance. There is also a broken Fatironette below the Fatiron that provides some easy scrambling. The Fatiron provides a climb that is as worthwhile as the classics on the major Flatirons, and in addition to compelling climbing, provides excellent views of the north side of the Maiden. Leave the Mesa Trail just north of the open water trough below the Maiden and hike west up the gully north of the Fatiron. The beginning of the climb is north of the east face where the Fatironette connects to the main east face. If you hike up the gully south of the Fatiron, you will be cut off from the beginning of the climb.

1014 Devil's Thumb
1015 Icarus

1016 The Fatiron
10161 East Face 5.4

10161 East Face 5.4 *Classic – Top Ten*

This unique 1,000-foot route provides a variety of challenges. Climb to the broken saddle area between the Fatironette and the east face of the fat piece and continue to some trees at the 140-foot level (Class 4). The smooth part of the face begins 20 feet above these trees and the climb becomes more difficult. The easiest climbing is on the face north (right) of a long largely incipient crack that splits the steeper face above. On the second 140-foot 5.4 pitch, climb

20 to 30 feet north of the crack and traverse south to a healthy 6-inch tree growing out of the incipient part of the crack. Climbing to the tree south (left) of the crack provides an obliging but unprotected 5.5–5.6 alternative. On the third pitch, climb 150 feet of attentive 5.4 rock. The crack is more useful in this stretch, but overcome the steeper rock near the top of the pitch on the face north (right) of the crack. From this point, climb 200 feet of amiable Class 4 rock to the summit of the fat piece. The view of the Maiden is overpowering from here.

Scramble 100 feet west and south and either rappel 20 feet to the slabs of the second piece or climb down an overhanging crack 25 feet south of the rappel (5.4). Once in the notch between the first and second pieces, either continue up the second piece or escape the rock by rappelling down the ramp on the north side. The second piece is much easier than the first, and you can climb its 350 feet of cordial Class 4 rock in three pitches. You will need to do a little route finding to find the easiest line. The attractive highest summit provides a unique view down to the top of the Maiden.

Descents

10161D1 A sturdy tree is a few feet from the highest point. Rappel 40 feet west to the ground.

10161D2 For a climbing descent, climb 150 feet down the east face and move to its north edge (Class 4). Get into a deep 2-foot wide crack near the north edge of the face, do an awkward twisting descent down it (Class 4), then downclimb 30 feet to the ground (Class 4).

1017 THE MAIDEN

With its trademark west-side overhang, the Maiden is the most unusual pinnacle near Boulder. The summit rises above a narrow east-west fin that is wider at the summit than in the middle. This plus the overhang give the Maiden its distinctive character and the most spectacular rappel in the Boulder area, a rappel that has made the Maiden famous. An ascent of the Maiden is always a special occasion, and the airy summit is bound to evoke emotion, especially on a first visit. Approach from the Mesa Trail, and don't confuse the Maiden with Devil's Thumb north of the Maiden. Leave the Mesa Trail at a water trough, hike 200 yards west then southwest on the Shadow Canyon Trail, follow a faint trail west, cross an old quarry road and hike west on a cairned climber's trail to the south side of the Maiden. The view of the Maiden from the ridge west of it is awesome and has often struck terror deep into the hearts of the unprepared.

1017 The Maiden
10171 Beginning of North Face 5.6 S
CN Crow's Nest

10172 South Face 5.8 S
1016 The Fatiron

Descent

1017D *This is the big one, and this is definitely a dangerous rock to be on top of without a rope.* From the west end of the summit, take one step off the edge and rappel 115 feet free to the Crow's Nest, which is a small aerie on the narrow ridge. From here, either rappel 105 feet south to the ground, or climb west up a 5.0–5.2 ridge to a small summit and downclimb 20 feet west to the ground (5.3).

10171 North Face 5.6 S *Classic – Top Ten*

This is the easiest route to the summit of the Maiden. It is an unusual route that consists mostly of downclimbing and traverses across the north face until it reaches the Maiden's easy upper east face. Because of its oblique nature, this climb is normally done in six short pitches. A fall from any of these pitches could leave either the leader or second in a bad position, so consider belaying inexperienced climbers from both sides on this route. In spite of its drawbacks, this is an intriguing route on one of the world's finest pinnacles. The start of the route is on the upper west end of the fin below and west of the Maiden's large west-facing overhang.

The first short pitch climbs a knobby 40-foot west-facing wall to a small summit (5.3). The view of the Maiden from here has made some parties turn back. From the small summit, climb east down narrow 5.0–5.2 slabs forming the crest of the ridge for one long or two short pitches to the Crow's Nest, which is the small notch below the west overhang.

From the Crow's Nest, climb 30 feet east down a ramp on the north side of the ridge. Do a 12-foot ascending traverse east (left) across the wall above the ramp to a large ledge with a tree on it (5.6). This wall is the route's crux. The lowest crossing of this wall is the easiest. You can protect both the leader and the second on this crux by using a fixed piton above and east of the Crow's Nest. This traverse is called the "pendulum pitch" because people used to pendulum across the crux wall. From the ledge east of the crux wall, scramble east past the tree and climb an 8-foot slot to another comfortable ledge.

From this ledge, climb 30 feet down a precarious ramp to the bottom of a vertical crack in a northwest-facing dihedral (5.4). Traverse 6 feet east around a corner and climb southeast up a small ramp to reach a secure stance in a large hollow (5.3). This is an exposed devious pitch. From the large hollow, climb to the small east face above (5.3–5.4), then climb 120 feet up the face to the summit (5.0–5.2). After this airy climb, the summit will seem large and comfortable.

Variations

10171V1 Climb the crux wall 10 feet above the easiest crossing and do a short downclimb to reach the ledge with the tree on it (5.7).

10171V2 The Walton Traverse 5.5

From the comfortable ledge east of the tree, climb up and slightly east (left), then traverse east down a small vanishing ledge to a large ledge (5.5). Traverse east on the ledge to join the regular route in the large hollow. This is a popular variation.

10171V3 From the bottom of the vertical crack below the northwest-facing

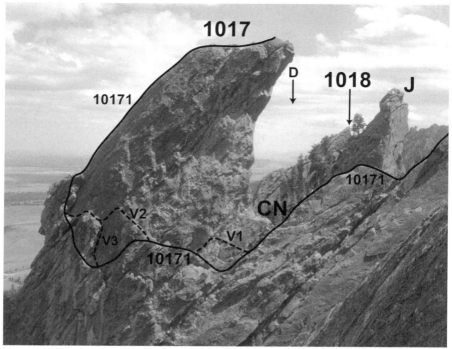

1017 The Maiden
10171 North Face 5.6 S
CN Crow's Nest
10171V1 5.7

10171V2 The Walton Traverse 5.5
10171V3 5.7
1018 Summit of the Crackiron
J Jam Crack Spire

dihedral, climb the dihedral to the large ledge at the end of the Walton Traverse (5.7).

10172 South Face 5.8 S

This is an acute route on the Maiden's steep south face. You can do the climb in five pitches, and the last pitch is the same as the North Face Route. Start 80 feet west of the low point of the rock at a talus block leaning against the base of the south face. Step off the talus block onto the wall, climb up for 10 feet, then do an ascending traverse 130 feet west along the strata to a stance (5.5). Traverse east (right) around a bulge and climb to a stance below a large scooped-out area on the upper face (5.7). Traverse 20 feet east, then climb straight up on elegant small holds to a notch on the east ridge (5.8). Climb the east ridge, skirt an overhang on its north side and reach a secure stance (5.5). Climb 120 feet up the upper east face to the summit (5.0–5.2).

1017 The Maiden
CN Crow's Nest
10172 South Face
   5.8 S
C Note Climbers

1018 THE CRACKIRON

The large Flatiron south of the Maiden waits for aficionados of the recondite. As the name suggests, the Crackiron's east face is broken into multiple ribs by deep cracks that are difficult to cross, and the Crackiron can reopen your route finding canister. The highpoint of the Crackiron is a rounded summit at the top of the main central rib. Jam Crack Spire, which is almost a separate rock, sails above the lower northern rib. To approach the bottom of the east face, leave the Mesa Trail at a water trough, hike 200 yards west then southwest on the Shadow Canyon Trail, follow a faint trail west, cross an old quarry road and hike west on the cairned climber's trail that is destined for the south side of the Maiden. This trail passes within 100 feet of the northeast corner of the Crackiron.

Descent

1018D Downclimb 80 feet east from the summit (5.2), downclimb 10 feet north to a large boulder in the saddle between the north and central summits (Class 4) and downclimb west off the boulder (Class 4). Scramble 80 feet up to the broken saddle area between Jam Crack Spire and the small northern summit, and scramble 200 feet northeast down broken ramps to the ground (Class 3).

10181 Master Jim Long going where youth don't dare on the East Face of the Crackiron

10181 East Face 5.6

This 700-foot route reaches the top of the Crackiron, not the top of Jam Crack Spire. The Crackiron's namesake cracks do not extend all the way to the bottom of the east face, and overhanging rock guards the bottom of the Crackiron. The route's most difficult moves are in the first few feet. Find the bottom of the main rock 100 feet south of the broken northeast corner. Where the barrier overhang is reduced to 1 foot, climb 6 feet up a smooth slab to the barrier overhang (5.6), overcome the overhang (5.6) and reach easier rock above. This opening sequence will ensure that you are in climb mode. Stepping carefully to avoid slick pine needles, climb 60 feet up 5.3 rock and chose your rib. If you angle south (left), you will be on the central rib, and if you angle north (right) you will be on the northern rib.

The central rib provides continuous pockmarked rock to the summit ridge, where you can scramble north to the exposed summit. The northern rib provides more varied terrain, where steeper sections are interspersed with easy surges. From the small northern summit below Jam Crack Spire, downclimb 10 feet west, scramble 80 feet down to the southeast and make an overhung Class 4 move up onto a large boulder in the saddle between the north and central summits. Climb 10 feet up the north wall of the central summit tower (Class 4) and climb 80 feet west to the summit (5.2). The view down the steep west face will ensure that you are alert.

1019 THE MATRON   *Closed 2/1 – 7/31*

This eloquent spire is thicker in the middle than the Maiden, but the routes are still excellent. The Matron is southwest of Shadow Canyon on the slopes below South Boulder Peak's long south ridge. The rock has a narrow Flatiron-like east face and steep south, west and north faces. The Matron dominates the area, and you can easily see it when approaching from the south or west. The Matron is a mile north of Eldorado Springs, and it sees a lot of traffic because of its proximity to that great climbing Mecca. Approach from the South Mesa Trailhead, follow the Mesa Trail, stay left at the junction with the Shadow Canyon Trail and continue west until the Matron pops dramatically into view.

1019 The Matron
10191 East Ridge 5.5
10193 South Face 5.6

When the Shadow Canyon Trail (a road at this point) turns north and crosses the small gully descending from the Matron, leave the road and follow a small trail uphill to the bottom of the rock.

Descent

1019D *This is a dangerous rock to be on top of without a rope.* Rappel 60 feet west from a summit bolt to another bolt. Rappel 100 feet west to the highest notch at the base of the west face and scramble west down to the ground. It is 140 feet from the second bolt to the ground if you continue rappelling down the west face. Hike down under the Matron's north face.

10191 East Ridge 5.5 *Classic*   *Closed 2/1 – 7/31*

This climb's 5.5 rating refers to a few moves in the first 40 feet, above which the climbing is 5.0–5.2 or easier. From the low point of the rock, a nasty overhang blocks easy access onto the east ridge, so start this route 50 feet above the low point on the rock's north side. Climb the wall for 10 feet, overcome an awkward 5.5 bulge, then follow a left angling crack for 20 feet (5.3–5.4) to the edge of the east face. Move south, sneak around an exposed 5.3–5.4 bulge and reach a secure exposed ledge with a tree on it. This position is just above the east ridge's initial overhang. Climb four long pitches from this point to the top of the Matron. After 330 feet of sensual Class 4 reach a slightly lower angle section where both the north and south face routes join the east ridge. Above this, the ridge steepens and the difficulty increases to 5.0–5.2. Pass a tree 100 feet below the top and move south (left) to avoid the final headwall. You can climb this headwall directly to enjoy a more difficult finish to a fine climb.

10192 North Face 5.5 *Classic – Top Ten*   *Closed 2/1 – 7/31*

This is a splendid popular route on excellent steep rock. Hike 300 feet up under the north face to a massive block. Either climb a 10-foot chimney left of the block or wiggle through a hole on the right to get to the top of the block that forms a comfortable bench at the base of the route. Two crack systems angle left across the face above. Climb 100 feet up consistent beautiful 5.5 rock in the right crack system to a stance below an overhang, climb a classic 5.5 roof to a ledge with a tree and climb a 30-foot 5.4 crack to the east ridge. Follow the East Ridge Route to the summit.

Variations

10192V1 North Face Left 5.6

From the bottom of the climb, step across a gap, climb the left crack (5.6) and

1019 The Matron
10191 East Ridge 5.5
10192 North Face 5.5
10192V1 North Face
    Left 5.6
10192V2 North Face
    Right 5.5

angle right to the stance below the classic roof. Many climbers have felt the sting of 5.6 immediately after committing to the crack.

10192V2 North Face Right 5.5
Climb a large left-facing dihedral 30 west (right) of the standard start (5.5) and traverse east (left) to the tree above the classic roof.

10193 South Face 5.6   *Closed 2/1 – 7/31*

This obtuse three- or four-pitch route traverses across the steep south face from the base of the west face to the midpoint of the east ridge. The exposure and excitement increase as you approach the east ridge, and the crux traverse across a friction slab is in an amazing position. Hike up under the north face to the west side of the rock. From the highest notch on the west side, hike 40 feet south down along the base of the west face, then scramble 20 feet east to a large tree. Start the climb by descending a large trough across the south face. From the wide shelf at the base of the trough, continue 20 feet east to a cozy belay beyond a large boulder. On the second pitch, continue east and follow the path of least resistance by climbing up then down. Start the crux pitch from a tiny exposed hollow, from which the exposed traverse to the east ridge will be evident. Descend slightly, then traverse over big air to the east ridge (5.6). Once on the ridge, climb 30 feet up to a belay. Angle north and follow the upper part of the East Ridge Route to the summit.

10194 West Face 5.8 S   *Closed 2/1 – 7/31*

This difficult route ascends the beautiful imposing slab forming the Matron's west face. Since this route is near the rappel route, you can top-rope it after an ascent of another route. Start near the highest notch on the west side. Climb 20 feet straight up the slab, then traverse north (left) above a large overhang on small holds and imbedded pebbles (5.8). Climb the slab's north edge to reach the rappel bolt 100 feet above the notch (5.6). Continue to the summit via an 80-foot right-facing dihedral (5.6).

Have you solved the riddle of the Sphinx yet?

Solving a secet somewhere in the Flatirons.

About the Author

GERRY ROACH is a world class mountaineer. After climbing Mount Everest in 1983, he went on to become the second person to climb the highest peak on each of the seven continents in 1985. In more than 50 years of mountaineering, Gerry has climbed in all 50 states and dozens of countries. He has been on nineteen Alaskan expeditions, ten Andean expeditions and seven Himalayan expeditions, including first ascents in the kingdom of Bhutan. He summited Gasherbrum II in the Karakorum in 1997 and became the first person to climb every major peak over 16,000 feet in North America in 2003. He is a member of the American Alpine Club.

Closer to home, Gerry has climbed more than 1,500 named peaks in Colorado, including all the Fourteeners which he completed in 1975. He finished climbing every named peak in the Indian Peaks Wilderness and Rocky Mountain National Park in 1978. He has also climbed every named peak in the Colorado counties of Boulder, Gilpin, Clear Creek and Jefferson.

Gerry is also an accomplished rock climber. His first book, *Flatiron Classics*, is a guide to the trails and easier rock climbs in the Flatirons above Boulder. His second book, *Rocky Mountain National Park*, is a guide to the classic climbs in the park. His guide *Colorado's Indian Peaks*, now in its second edition, remains the definitive mountaineering guide to that special area. Gerry's guide *Colorado's Fourteeners* has remained the most popular guide to Colorado's highest peaks for more than a decade.

In the second edition of *Flatiron Classics* Gerry continues to convey his intimate knowledge of and love for the rock garden where he started climbing in 1955. He continues to climb there actively today to hone his skills. Rock climbing and mountaineering in this rugged and beautiful state forms the foundation for his successful expeditions to earth's great peaks. Gerry lives in Boulder, Colorado with his wife and climbing partner, Jennifer Roach.

Index